INTERPRETING THE SCRIPTURES

A. Robert — A. Feuillet

INTERPRETING
THE SCRIPTURES

translated from the French by

Msgr. Patrick W. Skehan — Lasalle P. Caron
Juniper Cummings, o.f.m. Conv.
Peter Nickels, o.f.m. Conv. — Patrick Stevens

with an Appendix on

THE DOGMATIC CONSTITUTION ON DIVINE REVELATION
by Wilfrid Harrington, o.p. and Liam Walsh, o.p.

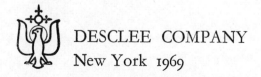

DESCLEE COMPANY
New York 1969

Except for the Appendix, the original French of *Interpreting the Scriptures* was published as a General Introduction to the Bible in *Introduction à la Bible*, Vol. I (Paris-Tournai; Desclée, 1959 ff.) The present English translation has updated the the bibliography and adapted the French text for the English-speaking reader.

The English translation of the Constitution *Verbum Dei* was taken with permission from *Vatican II on Revelation* (Dublin : Scepter Publishers Ltd., 1967).

Nihil obstat : Roderick MacKenzie, S.J., Censor deputatus, Rome, November 10, 1968.

Imprimatur : Hector Cunial, Vicar General, Rome, November 18, 1968.

Library of Congress Catalog Card Number : 69-20372

Printed in Belgium

TABLE OF CONTENTS

Section I. The Inspired Books
> by A. BARUCQ, Professor at the Catholic Faculties of Lyon, and
> H. CAZELLES, Professor at the Catholic Institute of Paris

Chapter I. Faith in the Inspired Books

Chapter II. Inspiration

Chapter III. The Canon of the Inspired Books

Section III. The Catholic Interpretation of Sacred Scripture
by P. GRELOT, Professor at the Catholic Institute of Paris

Chapter I. The Foundations of Christian Exegesis

Chapter II. The Practice of Christian Exegesis

Chapter III. Present State of the Problem

Appendix : The Dogmatic Constitution on Divine Revelation *(Dei Verbum)*,
by Wilfrid HARRINGTON, O.P. and Liam WALSH, O.P.

CONTRIBUTORS

André BARUCQ, *S.D.B.*, Professor at the Catholic Faculties of Lyon

Henri CAZELLES, *P.S.S.*, Professor at the Catholic Institute of Paris

André FEUILLET, *P.S.S.*, Professor at the Catholic Institute of Paris

Pierre GRELOT, Professor at the Catholic Institute of Paris

Wilfrid HARRINGTON, *O.P.*, Dublin, Ireland

Liam WALSH, *O.P.*, Dublin, Ireland

LIST OF ABBREVIATIONS

1) Books of the Bible :

Abd	Abdias	Lam	Lamentations
Acts	Acts of the Apostles	Lk	Gospel of St. Luke
Ag	Aggeus	Lv	Leviticus
Am	Amos		
Ap	Apocalypse	Mal	Malachias
		1 Mc	1st Book of Machabees
Bar	Baruch	2 Mc	2nd Book of Machabees
		Mi	Micheas
Col	Epistle to the Colossians	Mk	Gospel of St. Mark
1 Cor	1st Epistle to the Corinthians	Mt	Gospel of St. Matthew
2 Cor	2nd Epistle to the Corinthians		
Ct	Canticle of Canticles	Na	Nahum
		Neh	Nehemias
Dn	Daniel	Nm	Numbers
Dt	Deuteronomy		
		Os	Osee
Eccl	Ecclesiastes		
Eph	Epistle to the Ephesians	1 Par	1st Book of Paralipomenon
Esd	Esdras	2 Par	2nd Book of Paralipomenon
Est	Esther	Phil	Epistle to the Philippians
Ex	Exodus	Phlm	Epistle to Philemon
Ez	Ezechiel	Prv	Proverbs
		Ps	Psalms
Gal	Epistle to the Galatians	1 Pt	1st Epistle of St. Peter
Gn	Genesis	2 Pt	2nd Epistle of St. Peter
Hb	Habacuc	Rom	Epistle to the Romans
Heb	Epistle to the Hebrews	Ru	Ruth
Is	Isaias	Sir	Ecclesiasticus
		1 Sm	1st Book of Samuel
Jas	Epistle of James	2 Sm	2nd Book of Samuel
Jb	Job	So	Sophonias
Jdt	Judith		
Jer	Jeremias	Tb	Tobias
Jgs	Judges	1 Thes	1st Epistle to the Thessalonians
Jl	Joel		
Jn	Gospel of St. John	2 Thes	2nd Epistle to the Thessalonians
1 Jn	1st Epistle of St. John		
2 Jn	2nd Epistle of St. John	Ti	Epistle to Titus
Jon	Jonas	1 Tm	1st Epistle to Timothy
Jos	Josue	2 Tm	2nd Epistle to Timothy
Jude	Jude		
		Wis	Wisdom
3 Kgs	1st Book of Kings		
4 Kgs	2nd Book of Kings	Za	Zacharias

MT means Massoretic Text, LXX indicates the Greek translation of the Old Testament called the Septuagint.

2) Dictionaries, collections and reviews :

AAS   *Acta Apostolicae Sedis* (Vatican City).

AASOR *Annual of American Schools of Oriental Research.*

ANEP   *The Ancient Near East in Pictures relating to the Old Testament* (PRITCHARD) Princeton Univ., 1954).

ANET   *Ancien Near Eastern Texts relating to the Old Testament* ² (PRITCHARD) (Princeton Univ., 1955).

AOAT   *Altorientalische Texte und Bilder zum Alten Testament²*, 2 Vols. (H. GRESSMANN) (Berlin-Leipzig, 1927).

APOT   R. H. CHARLES, *Apocrypha and Pseudepigrapha of the Old Testament* (Oxford, 1913).

BA   *Biblical Archaeologist* (Baltimore).

BASOR *Bulletin of the American School of Oriental Research* (New Haven).

Bi   *Biblica** (Rome).

BiTod   *The Bible Today* (Collegeville, Minn.)

BJRL   *Bulletin of John Ryland's Library* (Manchester).

BO   *Bibliotheca Orientalis* (Leyden).

BZ   *Biblische Zeitschrift** (Freibourg im Breisgau).

CBQ   *Catholic Biblical Quarterly** (Washington).

CSEL   *Corpus Scriptorum Ecclesiasticorum Latinorum* (Vienna, 1866 ff.).

DAFC   *Dictionnaire Apologétique de la Foi Catholique** (Paris, 1911-1922).

DBV   *Dictionnaire de la Bible** (F. VIGOUROUX) (Paris, 1895-1912).

Denzinger or DB   *Enchiridion symbolorum** (Freiburg im Breisgau : Herder).

DTC   *Dictionnaire de Théologie Catholique** (Paris).

EB   *Enchiridion Biblicum** (Rome, 1955).

ERE   *Encyclopaedia of Religion and Ethics* (J. HASTINGS) (Edinburgh).

EsBi   *Estudios Biblicos** (Madrid).

ETL   *Ephemerides Theologicae Lovanienses** (Louvain).

HE   *Histoire Ecclésiastique d'Eusèbe de Césarée.*

IB   *Interpreter's Bible* (New York, 1952 ff.).

IDB   *Interpreter's Dictionnary of the Bible* (New York, 1962).

JBL   *Journal of Biblical Literature* (Philadelphia).

JBR   *Journal of Bible and Religion.*

JNES   *Journal of Near Eastern Studies* (Chicago).

JTS   *Journal of Theological Studies* (London-Oxford).

NRT   *Nouvelle Revue Théologique** (Louvain).

NT   *Novum Testamentum* (Leyden).

NTS   *New Testament Studies* (Cambridge).

OGIS   *Orientis Graeci Inscriptiones Selectae* (DITTENBERGER) (Leipzig, 1903-1905).

OTMS   *Old Testament and Modern Study*, ed. H. Rowley (Oxford, 1951).

PG   *Patrologia Graeca* (J. B. MIGNE) (Paris).

PL   *Patrologia Latina* (J. B. MIGNE) (Paris).

PO   *Patrologia Orientalis* (R. GRAFFIN) (Paris).

RB   *Revue Biblique** (Paris).

REJ   *Revue des Études Juives* (Paris).

REP   *Real-Encyclopädie der klassischen Altertumswissenschaft* (PAULY-WISSOWA) (Stuttgart).

RGG   *Die Religion in Geschichte und Gegenwart*[2] (Tübingen, 1927-1932).

RHE   *Revue d'Histoire Ecclésiastique** (Louvain).

RHPR   *Revue d'Histoire et de Philosophie Religieuse* (Strasbourg).

RHR   *Revue de l'Histoire des Religions* (Paris).

RSPT   *Revue des Sciences Philosophiques et Théologiques** (Le Saulchoir).

RSR   *Recherches de Sciences Religieuses** (Paris).

RTP   *Revue de Théologie et de Philosophie* (Lausanne).

Scr   *Scripture** (Edinburgh).

SDB   *Supplément au Dictionnaire de la Bible** (L. PIROT, A. ROBERT, H. CAZELLES) (Paris, 1928 ff.).

STh   *Summa Theologica of Saint Thomas Aquinas.*

TD   *Theology Digest* (St. Marys, Kansas).

TLZ   *Theologische Literaturzeitung* (Berlin).

TS   *Theological Studies** (Woodstock, Md.).

TWNT   *Theologische Worterbuch zum Neuen Testament* (G. KITTEL) (Stuttgart).

TZ   *Theologische Zeitschrift* (Basel).

VC   *Verbum Caro* (Lausanne).

VD   *Verbum Domini** (Rome).

VT   *Vetus Testamentum* (Leyden).

ZAW   *Zeitschrift für die Alttestamentliche Wissenschaft* (Giessen-Berlin).

ZKT   *Zeitschrift für Katholische Theologie** (Innsbruck).

ZNW   *Zeitschrift für die Neutestamentliche Wissenschaft* (Giessen-Berlin).

ZTK   *Zeitschrift für Theologie und Kirche* (Tübingen).

GENERAL BIBLIOGRAPHY

SIMÓN-PRADO, *Praelectiones biblicae*[4]* (Turin, 1946).

J. RENIÉ, *Manuel d'Écriture Sainte*[6]*, I (Paris-Lyon, 1949).

A. MERK, A. VACCARI, A. BEA, *Institutiones biblicae*[6]* (Rome, 1951).

D. G. M. PERELLA, *Introduzione generale alla Sacra Biblia*[2]* (Turin, 1952).

*A Catholic Commentary on Holy Scripture** (London, 1953).

A. ROBERT and A. TRICOT, *Initiation biblique*[3]* (Paris-Tournai, 1954); Eng. trans. M. R. P. McGUIRE and E. P. ARBEZ, *Guide to the Bible* 2 Vols. (Tournai-New York, 1951 ff.).

C. RINALDI, (ed.), *Secoli sul Mondo** (Turin, 1955).

C. CHARLIER, *The Christian Approach to the Bible** (Westminster : Newman, 1958).

H. HÖPFL and L. LELOIR, *Introductio generalis in sacram scripturam** (Rome, 1958).

J. LEVIE, *La Bible, parole humaine et message de Dieu** (Paris-Louvain. 1958), pp. 229-336; Eng. trans. ROGER CAPEL, *Word of God in Words of Men* (New York : Kenedy, 1962).

J. GIBLET, (ed.), *The God of Israel, the God of Christians** (New York : Desclée, 1961); paperback edition (Glen Rock : Paulist Press, 1966).

G. AUZOU, *The Formation of the Bible** (St. Louis : B. Herder, 1963).

THE INSPIRED BOOKS

by A. Barucq and H. Cazelles

BIBLIOGRAPHY

M. J. LAGRANGE, " L'inspiration des Livres saints, " *RB* (1896), pp. 199-220.

E. MANGENOT, " Inspiration de l'Écriture, " *DTC*, VII (1923), cols. 2068-2266.

H. LUSSEAU, *Essai sur la nature de l'inspiration scripturaire* (Paris, 1930).

A. BEA, *De Scripturae sacrae Inspiratione quaestiones historicae et dogmaticae; De Inspiratione et inerrantia sacrae Scripturae** (Rome, 1947).

P. SYNAVE and P. BENOIT, " La Prophétie, "* in ST. THOMAS AQUINAS; *Somme théologique*, Rev. des Jeunes edition (Paris, 1947), pp. 293-376, Eng. trans. A. R. DULLES and T. L. SHERIDAN, *Prophecy and Inspiration* (New York, 1961).

G. COURTADE, " Inspiration et Inerrance, " *SDB*, IV (1949), cols. 482-559,

Dom C. CHARLIER, *La lecture chrétienne de la Bible** (Maredsous, 1950), pp. 105-135 and 232-249; Eng. trans. *Christian Approach to the Bible* (Westminster, Md., 1958).

C. H. DODD, *The Authority of the Bible* (New York : Harper, 1958).

P. BENOIT, " Inspiration, " *Guide to the Bible*, I² (New York, 1960).

K. RAHNER, *Inspiration in the Bible** (New York : Herder and Herder, 1962).

J. L. MCKENZIE, " The Social Character of Inspiration, " *CBQ*, 24 (1962), 115-124.

D. J. MCCARTHY, " Personality, Society and Inspiration, " *TS*, 24 (1963), pp. 553-576.

L. TOPEL, " Rahner and McKenzie on the Social Theory of Inspiration,"* *Scripture*, 16 (1964), pp. 33-44.

P. BENOIT, *Aspects of Biblical Inspiration* (Chicago : Priory, 1965).

L. ALONSO SCHÖKEL, *The Inspired Word** (New York : Herder and Herder, 1965).

Many religions have their *sacred books*. This universal phenomenon is an integral part of the history of civilizations. How could it have been otherwise that men desired to set down in writing, and thus preserve, this facet of their life and thought closest to their hearts, namely, their relationship with God? They revere these texts as a sacred deposit as they handle them with faith and hope to find in them an answer to the questions of their souls, a light to direct their lives.

Divine revelation, as preserved in the Jewish religion, and therefore Christian, also has its *Sacred Scripture*, its *holy books*, as the first book of Machabees already mentioned (1 Mc 12, 9). Before we go ahead and study their contents, we must tell what is the source of this *holiness* which sets them apart from all others. For believers who have discovered the true religion among all the variety of religions that run where man's religious feeling wanders, these books are in a class by themselves. They can read the sacred books of non-Christian religions with an understanding and sympathy that tries to find in them a trace of man's efforts in seeking God. But the Bible is something unique for them. In it, man not only calls upon God and seeks to understand His response, but God speaks to man of His own accord. The Bible is actually His very Word. At times, the text can offer only a rather limited human interest, as in the somewhat tedious genealogical lists, or in the anecdotical history about persons more or less edifying. It makes no difference, for God communicates His message through all of this. The thoughts of the human authors to whom we owe these works, their philosophy of life, their mentality, and their culture are not the main element in the works which they have written. All their human genius is put to the service of something greater. They wrote under the influence of the Spirit of God, the Spirit *(ruaḥ)* who gave a superhuman power to the liberators of Israel (Jgs 13, 25), the Spirit who animated the prophets (Os 9, 7), the Spirit who is now poured forth in the Church of Christ and gives it life. According to the word of the Second Epistle to Timothy, Scripture is holy because it is divinely inspired *(theopneustos : 2 Tm 3, 16)*. What then is inspiration?

We are not discussing ordinary inspiration, such as that of a poet or an artist. Nor do we mean the ecstatic inspiration of the Pythian priestess at Delphi, who made herself lose her control of both senses and reason. Nor is it the religious inspiration which we find even in certain non-Christian works, for that does not go beyond the level of simple human genius.(Biblical inspiration is a supernatural act of God, restrained and profound, fully respecting the human personality of the authors—for God does not do away with men He has created; he lifts them above themselves—for God is capable of doing this. Just for this reason, the books resulting from the activity of these authors are not human thought, but the thought of God. Still they remain rooted in human nature : everything in them is fully from God; everything in them is fully from man. Just as the apostles, upon hearing Christ, received a divine message expressed in a human way, so the reader of the Bible finds the divine Word announced in a human way. This is a basic fact which we must never overlook when studying the holy books.)

Just knowing that the Word of God is announced in human language does not guarantee that there will be no surprises. We have no doubt about the extent to which our own manners of expression are formed from the world in which we live, as well as from our habits and thought patterns. We take little relish in imagining that God might have used other means of expression. It takes a strong culture and a good philosophy to admit that the divine simplicity of God could have been refracted through the endless complexity of creation, whence language draws its terms and its images. [1] A book coming from God and being addressed to all humanity had to take shape through a rich variety in the means of expression, whereas each group is only familiar with a few of them. [2] The apparent paradox of a creating God who is simple and transcendent but makes Himself known through the rules of a created language is the mystery which makes up Scripture. We must become aware of this before any attempt to discover His message.

---

[1] " Since some like to object that the sacred authors... related some things rather inaccurately, we assert that this only involves the manner of expression and narration customary to the ancients, the common ways of expressing themselves in their everyday life " (enc. *Div. Affl. Sp.*, *EB*, 560). " It was necessary to study more closely the literary process, the psychology, and the manner of expression among the people of the ancient Near East... " (Letter of the Bib. Comm. to Card. Suhard, *EB*, p. 581).

[2] " Nobody should be surprised to find among the sacred writers, as among the ancients, certain modes of description and narration, certain idioms proper to Semitic languages. " (*EB*, p. 559).

This process of becoming aware can only be done in the light of the testimony of the sacred authors themselves, who have set down their message in Scripture, to which must be added the testimony of the Fathers. It requires the study of *faith in the Holy Books* as expressed among the Chosen People and in the Church of Christ. This study is followed by that of the notion of *inspiration*, as it has developed through the centuries, thanks to the work of theologians, especially St. Thomas Aquinas, [3] sanctioned in part by the Church. The study is concluded by a treatment of the two essential consequences of inspiration : the formation of a definitive *Canon* of the inspired books and of the *inerrancy* of Sacred Scripture.

---

[3] " De Prophetia, " *Summa Theologica*, II^a-II^æ, q. 171-178.

CHAPTER I

FAITH IN THE INSPIRED BOOKS

§ 1. The Church Speaks

I. THE SOLEMN DEFINITIONS

The Church has been nourished by Scripture for many centuries before being led to define solemnly her faith in the inspiration of the holy books. Both Orthodox and Protestants share this faith, aside from the disagreement over the interpretation of the word that expresses it, *theopneustos* (2 Tm 3, 16). The Church has made her belief more precise on two occasions. At the Council of Trent, April 8, 1546, she affirmed that God is the author *(auctor)* of the Old and New Testaments alike, and gave a list of the books she considered " sacred. " [1] She was struggling at that time not to safeguard the principle of inspiration but to maintain it in all its implications, for the sacred character of some books was under attack (those called deuterocanonical [2]).

At the First Vatican Council, the very principle of inspiration was at stake, for some were denying all supernatural intervention on the part of God. [3] On April 24, 1870, the Council formulated the following principle : " If anyone does not accept as sacred and canonical the complete books of Sacred Scripture with all their parts, according to the enumeration of them by the Council of Trent, or *if anyone denies that these books are divinely inspired*, let him be anathema. " [4]

II. THE LIST OF THE HOLY BOOKS

Therefore the Church believes in the inspiration of a certain number of books which she has fixed precisely in a list in order to curtail all discussion. The order and classification of these books has varied, and the Church makes no imposition in this regard. Here is one of the possible classifi-

---

[1] *DB*, 784.

[2] Cf. below p. 37.

[3] *EB*, 77 : " *Eos vero Ecclesia pro sacris et canonicis habet, non ideo quod sola humana industria concinnati, sua deinde auctoritate sint approbati ; nec ideo dumtaxat, quod revelationem sine errore contineant ; sed propterea quod Spiritu Sancto inspirante conscripti Deum auctorem habent, atque ut tales ipsi Ecclesiae traditi sunt. *"

[4] *DB*, 1809.

cations which, for the OT, respects the order of the Hebrew Bible while adding to it books preserved only in the Greek Bible :

Old Testament

The five books ascribed to Moses, or the Pentateuch : Genesis, Exodus, Leviticus, Numbers, Deuteronomy. These are the books of the Law, or *Torah*.

Josue, Judges, 1 and 2 Samuel, 3 and 4 Kings. These books are called the Former Prophets by the Jews *(Prophetæ priores)*.

Isaias, Jeremias, Ezechiel, and the 12 minor prophets : Osee, Joel, Amos, Abdias, Jonas, Micheas, Nahum, Habacuc, Sophonias, Aggeus, Zacharias, Malachy. These are called the Latter Prophets *(Prophetæ posteriores)*.

Psalms, Proverbs, Job, Canticle of Canticles, Ruth, Lamentations, Ecclesiastes (or *Qoheleth*), Esther, Daniel, Esdras, Nehemias, 1 and 2 Paralipomenon (or Chronicles). These are the Hagiographa or *Ketubim*.

Baruch, Tobias, Judith, 1 and 2 Machabees, Wisdom, Ecclesiasticus (or Sirach). These books have come into the Church through the Greek Bible.

New Testament

The four Gospels, according to Matthew, Mark, Luke, John.

The Acts of the Apostles.

The fourteen Epistles preserved under the name of Paul : Epistles to the Romans, Corinthians (2 Epistles), Galatians, Ephesians, Philippians, Colossians, Thessalonians (2 Epistles), Timothy (2 Epistles), Titus, Philemon, Hebrews.

The " catholic " Epistles : two of Peter, three of John, one of James, one of Jude.

The Apocalypse of John.

Such is the actual belief of the Church. In the books we have just named, she recognizes the presence of divine inspiration. But where does this faith come from? How did the dogma here involved come to be gradually affirmed before being neatly defined?

§ 2. Sacred Scripture according to the Old Testament

In the OT, books evolve, establishing ancestral_traditions, organizing them according to the needs of a catechesis and a cultual parenesis, glossing them according to the religious orientation which finds its great spiritual fountainhead in the prophets. Similarly, some of them arise through the annals and chronicles of the period when Israel was a monarchy. All these memories are put down in writing because they have a relationship to the sacred. Thus the patriarchal traditions concern those who store the divine promises, who have been blessed with theophanies. Their deeds and their words have been transmitted near the sanctuaries, the privileged places for divine communications, where we still go to honor their memory. At times a book comes into being to collect and to make universally accessible the accounts of these first appearances and revelations of God to the Fathers.

Some writings will also include the memories which the nation has preserved concerning the leaders given by God to His people. Men like Moses, Josue and David received His Spirit and were invested with His authority. When the age of annalists began, the latter were preoccupied in setting down in live context or from memory the words and deeds of these men of God. Then there appeared the nucleus of a royal history (sacred history because it was of the " house of David "), and of a national history, which is that of the Chosen People. Alongside these, books were formed to preserve the oracles of the prophets, the great seers. The prophets utter the Word of God; they themselves, or their followers, compile this word. Collections form around their names and their writings, with the addition of often heterogeneous elements. The Pentateuch is built around the name of Moses. The name of Isaias dominates a prophetic collection encompassing pronouncements of widely differing dates. The Psalter is built around the name of David, and the writings of Wisdom are grouped around that of Solomon.

Thus these books are marked with a religious character. No text before the Exile attributes its redaction to God Himself, but sometimes the setting down in writing of an oral account or of a series of oracles which are to give birth to the book is attributed to His will. Isaias and Jeremias have told us of the order they received from God to preserve such of their oracles in a book (Is 30, 8; Jer 36, 2. 28. 32), without anything else being said about the supernatural character of its composition. It is also reported that Moses " wrote the words of Yahweh " (Ex 24, 4) or " upon the order of Jahweh " (Nm 33, 2; cf. Ex 17, 14). There is some question about the " book of the law (of Yahweh) " in the books redacted during and after the Exile (4 Kgs 22, 11; 2 Par 17, 9; 34, 14; Neh 8, 8. 18), but this expression is not equivalent to " a book of God, " absent in the OT. Thus Neh 8, 1 specifies that we are dealing with the " book of the law of Moses which Yahweh has prescribed to Israel. "

Yet (at that time it seems that the belief in the sacred character of certain books is specified by the very veneration that surrounds them.)

Such is the case with this " book of the law of God, " comprising what
Esdras holds and reads solemnly to the people.   Such is the case with the
books which form a collection known as Nehemias, with those which Judas
Machabee took pains to collect after their dispersion at the time of the
persecution of Antiochus Epiphanes (2 Mc 2, 13-15 and 1 Mec 1, 59 ff.).
For the first time in biblical literature we find the expression " the Holy
Books " to designate the Scriptures (1 Mc, 12, 9) which were a consolation
in the time of persecution (cf. 2 Mc 8, 23).

A good witness to the Jewish belief in the sacred character of Scripture
is the letter of pseudo-Aristeas. [5]   It bears witness to one *fact* : the
preoccupation of the Jews of the Diaspora in having in their own language
the Pentateuch and the other books read in Jerusalem (cf. also 2 Mc 2, 15
and the prologue of the Book of Ecclesiasticus), and of a *belief* : that of a
divine intervention in the gift of the holy books.   When the author
of 4 Esd (14, 23-47) pictures God dictating to Esdras for forty days
204 books, of which only 66 will be published, he bears witness to the same
idea.   In saying that these books " soil the hands, " the later Jews
merely expressed the same belief in terms of an interdict : as to their
origin, these books have a sacred character.

§ 3.   Sacred Scripture according to the New Testament

Our Lord, coming to fulfill the Law and the Prophets, does not do away
with the religious attitudes of His contemporaries.   Like them, He
discourses while referring to the Scriptures, emphasizing His statements
with the phrase in current use in the schools : " as it is written " (cf. Mt 4,
4-10; 21, 13; Lk 19, 46...), a formula which the apostles take up on their
own (Mt 2, 5; Acts 7, 42; Rom 1, 17; 3, 4; 1 Pt 1, 16 etc...).   By this
they mean to commit the authority of Scripture, the only divine authority,
alone capable of guaranteeing the outcome of future events.

St. Paul clearly testifies to the credit given to Scripture in Jewish
and Christian circles when he writes to Timothy : " Since childhood you
have known the Scriptures which can give you the wisdom that through
faith in Christ Jesus leads to salvation.   All Scripture is divinely inspired,
and useful in teaching, in reproof, in correcting faults, and in training
in uprightness, so that the man of God will be adequate, and equipped for
any good work " (2 Tm 3, 15 ff.).   2 Peter expresses the same teaching :
" So we have the message of the prophets more fully guaranteed.   Please

---

[5] See pp. 28 and 86.

pay attention to that message, as a lamp shining in a dark place, until the day dawns and the morning star rises in your hearts. You must understand this in the first place, that no prophecy in Scripture can be understood through one's own powers, for no prophecy ever originated in the human will, but under the influence of the Holy Spirit men spoke for God " (2 Pt 1, 19-21).

From these two texts we derive more than a simple affirmation of the authority of Scripture. They furnish its justification in already formulating the essential of the doctrine of inspiration. Sacred Letters are an object of teaching and of tradition, like other religious truths (cf. 2 Tm 3, 14). What is more, they are a source of wisdom, of salvation, and are the basis of Christian teaching and formation. More precisely, they are " inspired by God " [6] *(theopneustoi, divinitus inspiratae)*. This means that the Holy Spirit is their origin. This same assertion is found in 2 Peter : they owe nothing to the will of man, but are the work of the Holy Spirit acting in the hagiographers. Thus the Scriptures, concludes the author, are the work of men moved by the Spirit, and are in no way subject to individual interpretation, neither by the author nor the reader. Since they come from on high, only a man fully animated by the Spirit from on high can understand them.

With the study of these texts two expressions enter into the realm of theological language : that of *inspired writer*, a term used by Latin writers to translate the Greek expression of 2 Peter, and that of *inspired book* according to the term found in 2 Timothy. Thus we will see them habitually used by the Fathers and the theologians to express both the special character of the biblical books and that of their authors.

§ 4. The Fathers and Scripture

Little by little, Christian terminology spelled out this mysterious concept of an inspired book and an inspired writer. This gave rise to the term *inspiration*, attributed to both book and author (St. Gregory of Nyssa). The Fathers seek above all to put into concrete terms their idea of the inspiring action of God. They say it consists in *pronouncing* (Gr. *legein*), *suggesting* (Gr. *upagoreuein*), *dictating* (Lat. *dictare*) what the hagiogra-

---

[6] The text of 2 Peter cited above tends to give a passive sense to the word *theopneustos*. Inspiration by an active, " inspiring God, " though philologically possible, only appears with Origen (*PG* 13, 356) who does not distinguish it from the other sense. Among the moderns, only Cramer maintains it for 2 Tm 3, 16, to the exclusion of the passive sense; Moulton himself rejects it.

phers must have handed down to us. Thus they wish to emphasize the primacy of divine action rather than materializing its intervention. It often happens that with these very anthropomorphic representations several distortions take place. The theology of inspiration will not always be free from a mechanistic representation of divine action, which can lead to an astonishing literalism in the interpretation of the text.

By way of the African councils of the 4th and 5th centuries and of the anti-Manichean professions of faith which they imposed on the bishops, another expression will enter into the language of theology : that of " *God, the Author of Scripture.* " [7] This phrase is formed in reaction to the Manichean theory : neither is there double authorship in the economy of the world, nor are there two authors in the history of salvation, although there were two covenants. If the professions of faith contained in the *Statuta Ecclesiae antiquae* [8] are aimed first of all at the dualist error, it seems that the terms chosen to indicate the double phase of the Covenant of which God is proclaimed the unique " Author, " namely " the Law, the Prophets and the Apostles, " are well applied to the books containing the history of both OT and NT. This is expressly stated in the texts of the later councils which resume the formula (Second Council of Lyons, Council of Florence in the Decree for the Jacobites, Councils of Trent and Vatican I).

With regard to the statement that God was really Author of the holy books, tradition has always maintained that the *hagiographers* were also the *authors* of the books written by them. To say that the Bible was the " word of God " was equivalent to attributing to God the principal authorship, while emphasizing at the same time the imprints left by the originality of each author on his work. This is seen in the style, the thought, and the organization of the material. Thus St. Cyril of Alexandria remarks that St. Paul constructs his phrases well, and that John the Apostle renders the discourses well. One finds similar remarks in St. John Chrysostom and St. Augustine. But the same St. Augustine specifies that these literary qualities are also a gift of God to the writer. He was concerned with emphasizing their dependence for everything on the divine Author.

Certain images help convey this dependence. According to the Fathers these writers are the *instruments* of God, his pen and his lyre (*Cohortatio ad Graecos*, Hippolytus, St. Gregory of Nyssa). Through

---

[7] A. BEA, " *Deus auctor sacrae Scripturae* : Herkunft und Bedeutung der Formel, "* *Angelicum*, XX (1943), pp. 16-31.

[8] *EB*, p. 30.

these images the thought seeks its way and risks being cumbersome.   The intention was to point out the hierarchy of causes in the birth of a sacred book, and to safeguard the primacy of divine causality; there seems to be a danger of reducing the role of man to one of a mechanical instrument.

If we add to this the frequent and varied affirmations on the absolute inerrancy of the Bible, we will have summed up the main elements of the doctrine of inspiration during the patristic era.   It will be the work of following generations to start with this data and to attempt a more rational and more profound theological synthesis.

CHAPTER II

INSPIRATION

BIBLIOGRAPHY

G. M. PERRELLA, " *La nozione dell' inspirazione scritturale secondo i primitivi documenti cristiani,* "* *Angelicum,* XX (1943), pp. 32-52.

R. A. F. McKENZIE, " Some Problems in the Field of Inspiration, " *CBQ* (1958), pp. 1-8.

A. JONES, " Biblical Inspiration : A Christian Rendez-Vous, "* *Scr.* (1958) pp. 97-110.

The study of a theological doctrine begins with the scriptural, patristic and ecclesiastical texts. The theologian finds in them the expression of Faith, and discovers the continuity of this Faith. It is for this reason that he searches the scriptural texts in order to understand the doctrine of inspiration. It might seem to be a vicious circle to demand from them proof of their own inspiration; no one is a witness in his own case. But the unbeliever himself can recognize in these texts a witness to the Faith of Israel, or what is more, to the Faith which was lived by a certain number of Israelites, among whom Our Lord Himself and His apostles are included. Thus it seems to be established that an ever greater attention is given to all the concrete facts which specify the origin of the books and determine the exact importance of their historical testimony.

§ 1. History of a Doctrine

I. THE MIDDLE AGES

The first theological reflections on the mode of inspiration in the holy books are full of confusion in thought and terminology. *Hugh of St. Victor* (d. 1141) attempts a distinction between prophets and hagiographers; already this was very helpful. *St. Thomas* takes up this distinction without introducing it into the study of inspiration, a study which he never did. With him and *Henry of Ghent,* theology begins to reflect on the respective roles of God and man when one effect results from their mutual cooperation : this is the case of prophecy. St. Thomas, occasionally talking about the sacred books, applies a similar theory to them by saying : " the *principal author* of Sacred Scripture is the Holy Spirit... man was the *instrumental author* of it " (*Quodlib.* VII, art. 14, ad 5).

After him theologians like *Peter of Ailly* try to distinguish the action of God and the action of man by referring to the different senses of the word " author " (composer, editor, compiler, voucher). Others, like *Cano*, attempt a distinction between what is *revelation* and what is *motion* performed with help. But their thought remains uncertain.

II. FROM THE 16TH CENTURY TO THE FIRST VATICAN COUNCIL

Banez maintains the distinction between revelation and an impulse given to the hagiographer. Yet it is surprising to find in his writings an assertion which does nothing less than make God *dictate* the very words of the book in order to avoid any misunderstanding of the ideas which He inspires. It is not strange to see unbridled opposition arising against such a demand. This is formulated by *Lessius*, a Jesuit of Louvain : " If it happened that some book (perhaps 2 Mc) was written by human efforts alone without the assistance of the Holy Spirit, and then the Holy Spirit attested that no error was found therein, it would become by this very fact Sacred Scripture. " One of his colleagues, *Bonfrère*, was to take up the same idea to describe *subsequent inspiration*, so named after him. Struck by the differences in depth of thought, intensity of religious feeling, and style among the various books, these theologians sought for an explanation in the diversity of the modes of inspiration. Thus there is direct revelation for books judged to be superior, inspiration without dictation, or simple direction aimed at preventing the writers from error in books judged to be less sublime, and simple approbation after composition for those which were found to be too human.

Actually, Lessius was to disavow the above statement in trying to explain it. Such a book, he concedes, would enjoy divine authority independently of its quality as Sacred Scripture. There is no more mention of this attempt to explain inspiration after Bonfrère until 1850, when *Haneberg*, a theologian of Munich, revived it by replacing the subsequent approval of the Holy Spirit, claimed by Lessius and Bonfrère, by that of the Church. Thus the Fathers of the *First Vatican Council*, in their session of April 24, 1870, thought they should specify in the chapter on revelation that the faith of the Church in the inspiration of the sacred books does not rest at all on the fact that " these books composed by the work of men alone, were then approved by the authority of the Church. "[1]

---

[1] *EB*, p. 77.

Doubtless these theories of suggestion and dictation meant to underline the reality of authorship attributed to God. That of subsequent approval fully safeguarded man's authorship while weakening the traditional idea of God as author, which was adopted in the terminology of the teaching magisterium. That is why other theologians attempted an explanation that would reconcile the two demands. Absence of error in the Bible had been constantly affirmed by all tradition. Wasn't this the distinguishing mark of the inspiring action of God? Some seemed to think so. For them, the whole of the inspiring action consisted in a divine help given to the human author " so that he might not err. " Bonfrère had begun by proposing an explanation of inspiration, together with the one we have cited, according to which " God would not act as one inspiring (actually he understands some kind of revelation by this word) or dictating, but would direct the writer so that he might not err.... If he were going to err, the Holy Spirit would aid him with his inspiration. " Bonfrère had only made one of several possible suppositions. *Chrisman* (1792) made it more precise; " This inspiration by which the Holy Spirit directs the sacred authors while they write, so as to prevent them from error, can be considered sufficient. " And *Jahn* (1816) : " Inspiration means that divine assistance which prevents error. "

No doubt these theologians gave credit to the place of divine action in the very composition of the work. But was this enough to justify the title of author given to God by the Church? Thus the First Vatican Council joined its disapproval of the theory of Haneberg to that of the theory of Jahn by saying : " It is not only because they contain revelation without error (that the Church accepts them as sacred and canonical), but because they are written under the inspiration of the Holy Spirit and have God as their author, and have been entrusted to the Church as such. " [2] By these words the Council redirected the attention of theologians to the essential facts of tradition : the sacred books were written under the inspiration of the Holy Spirit (the nature of whose action the Council did not define); in virtue of this fact, they have God as their author, and that is why the Church holds them in veneration.

III. AFTER THE FIRST VATICAN COUNCIL

After the First Vatican Council, special attention is going to be given by theologians to the study of the notion of author. Cardinal Franzelin, seeking to reconcile the respective roles of God and the writer, distinguishes two aspects in the book, their common work. The *formal* element is

---

[2] *Ibid.*, p. 77.

what God intends; He reveals it directly or by simple inspiring grace, when the writer already has a notion of what he should write. The *material* element consists in the words which express these ideas. Thus the opinion of Franzelin : God can be called the author of a book when only the formal element comes from Him. It is not necessary that the material element be His doing. It is not that God is disinterested in the expression of the ideas which He wishes to communicate to us; but, in order that they be rendered correctly, a simple assistance is enough and a verbal inspiration is not necessary. The eminent theologian was not wrong in regard to divine authority, but he was wrong from the standpoint of the origin of the text. We must not in this case disregard the psychological point of view by performing an ill-fitting " vivisection " on the author. When he works, can we separate his ideas from the words which express them?

Twenty years after the work of Franzelin, a document of primary importance was to attract the attention of theologians to the problem of the relationship between God inspiring and the inspired writer. In his encyclical on Sacred Scripture (*Providentissimus*, 1893), Leo XIII propounded a doctrine of inspiration in the act of writing, and specified its effects on the psychology of the writers. He tells us that the Holy Spirit " prompted and moved them to write by a supernatural force, and even assisted them while they were writing so that they conceived exactly *(recte mente conciperent)*, desired to report faithfully, and wrote so as to safeguard the infallible truth of everything that the Spirit ordered them to write, and only what he ordered them to write. Otherwise He would not be the Author of all Sacred Scripture. " [3]

This doctrine avoids the dangers which hindered previous attempts. It gives up speculation on the different senses of the word " author " or the different procedures of literary authors. God does not appear as doing on His side all the actions proper to the author, then causing them in the writer. All God's action is effected in man during the work itself.

There is no more distinction between the formal part of the book which would be the special domain of God, and the material part, more directly the domain of man. Moreover, the encyclical does not present inspiration so much as a quality of the book, but as an action of God united to that of man.

In this mutual collaboration where man furnishes a means of expression to God communicating His message to us, the primacy and the initiative are clearly attributed to God. But man does not appear to be a purely passive instrument, for his intelligence conceives the ideas, his

---

[3] *Ibid.*, p. 125.

will desires to write them accurately, and all his faculties as a writer
are at work to make up an authentic expression of divine thought. In
all of this, man is placed under the impulse, the movement, and the
assistance of God, who commands and determines the content of His
written communication.

We might further remark that this presentation of the doctrine of
inspiration, behind which one senses the thought of St. Thomas on the
question of prophecy (II^a, II^{ae}, q. 171-174), still avoids scholastic terminology. There is no question of principal and instrumental cause,
nor, for an even stronger reason, of physical and moral determination.
This is because the encyclical only wishes to present the divine action
linked with that of man, without detracting in any way from the fundamental fact of God's authorship, and without adding to or detracting
from the sense of this authorship.

Since, even after the encyclical, the treatise on inspiration by
Franzelin continued to form the basis of the majority of textbooks and of
many studies, Père *Lagrange*, theologian and exegete, thought he should
oppose a method which took as its point of departure something that,
according to all the ecclesiastical documents, was only a consequence
of inspiration, namely, the notion of God as author. [4] " It clearly follows
from this *processus* that inspiration need not be explained by the formula
' God is the author of the sacred books, ' but, on the contrary that the
formula ' God is the author of the sacred books ' rests on the truth of
another formula : The canonical books were written under the inspiration
of the Holy Spirit. The notion of inspiration would then have to be
examined in itself, but it would have to be conceived in such a way
as to affirm this conclusion : God is the Author of these books. " [5]

Père Lagrange did not believe either that it was possible to obtain
an exact and complete notion of inspiration through the sole study of the
origin, of the literary form, and of the content of the sacred books.
The critical study of the Bible is far from perfect and definitive, and we
may not derive from it the principles of a faith that did not wait for this
study to express itself. Père Lagrange had no disrespect for the light
which criticism can throw on the study of inspiration. But, as he thought,
a theological fact was involved, and theology itself must be able to render
an account of that which constitutes it essentially. In order to sketch

---

[4] On this question of method, which has caused some uneasiness in its day,
cf. H. Lusseau, " A propos d'un essai sur la nature de l'inspiration scripturaire, "*
Bi, XII (1932), pp. 24-48.

[5] *RB** (1896), p. 206.

an outline of the study of inspiration, he would therefore have recourse to the principles set down by St. Thomas in his study of prophecy.

§ 2.   Inspiration and the Psychology of the Sacred Writers

The preceding pages have allowed us to eliminate the theories which attribute too little either to God or to man.   On the one hand, inspiration is more than an order or even a directive given by God to the writer. We must not forget that the primary cause, even in the natural order, is everywhere present, however subtly.   A fortiori God will leave nothing to chance in the supernatural order, when it is a matter of giving to men a book which will lift them to the knowledge of who He is and what He has done.   On the other hand, the sacred writer is neither an automaton nor a secretary.   He thinks what he is writing and he acts freely.   The best image to describe the inspiring action is that of an instrument. The worker and his instrument intimately cooperate in the same work; the one does not act without the other.   But just as a saw remains a saw when the carpenter prepares the boards, man remains man when God uses him to compose a book in which God will express Himself, and he would not be a man if his activity during composition were not intelligent and free.

Theologians have undertaken the task of defining the relationship between human and divine activity in this cooperation of a special nature. The best way to describe it is to resume and to explain the terms used in the Encyclical *Providentissimus*.

I.   THE ACTION OF GOD ON THE INTELLIGENCE OF SACRED WRITERS

The supernatural action of God on the sacred writers, says the encyclical, " caused them to conceive rightly " what they had to write; *ita ut recte mente conciperent*.   The understanding of a child is enlightened by the explanations of an older person who knows how to choose his images and his expressions so as to communicate his ideas.   In a similar way, the understanding of man can be illuminated by the action of God; God opens to him horizons surpassing his natural limitations, and initiates him into the mysteries of His innermost life shared with men.   Yet there is an essential difference : the teacher acts upon the child from the outside, while God can reach the human understanding at its deepest interior.

From this point of view, the action of God on the inspired writer is similar to His action on the prophet.   To clarify this, we may refer to the very close study of the latter made by St. Thomas. Prophecy, he says, belongs " to the order of knowledge " (II^a II^{ae}, q. 171, art. 1). " God Himself is the principle of the supernatural truths manifested in prophecy, and God cannot be known in His essence by the prophets.... It remains then that the prophetic light exists as a passing impression in the soul of the prophet " (*id.*, art. 2). " By the gift of prophecy the human spirit is lifted above its natural faculties...; first of all, with respect to judgment, by the influx of an intellectual light; then with respect to the representation of the realities through images or ideas " (*id.*, q. 173, art. 2). St. Thomas then specifies that prophetic knowledge is not limited to the announcement of future events, but extends " to all reality, divine and human, spiritual and corporeal " (q. 171, art. 3). This last point is obvious in the case of scriptural inspiration. Thus a close kinship appears between prophet and sacred writer. It is not surprising therefore that the prophets were also called upon at times to compose the books in which their prophecies were set down.

Nevertheless, these two charisms are not identical. " In the case of the prophet who receives from God a message to deliver, the *speculative judgment* occupies the foreground and directly receives the illumination. For knowledge is here the prime consideration. " [6] In other words the prophet is defined as one who receives a *revelation* transcending human possibility, some view about God and His action. Certainly the sacred writer also will write in virtue of such a supernatural view : God would not inspire a writer only to make him transmit truths which the natural power of man would suffice to discover and communicate! But in his case, the *setting down and transmission by writing* occupy the foreground. A series of *practical judgments* ensue, which have their " share in the inspiring influx " : judgment on the choice of words, on the choice of teachings which will guide the thought of the reader to the truth, on the literary genre adapted to the order in which the truth to be transmitted is set. Once enlightened, the prophet speaks to his contemporaries and makes himself understood by his living presence, provided the listener is receptive. As for the sacred writer, under the divine action he must achieve a literary work which speaks and will speak after he is gone; this implies a more diverse action of God, who not only has to raise him up to an awareness of supernatural truths, but to sustain his thought in the whole series of judgments that he must make.

The inspired writer differs further from the prophet in that he is not necessarily the first to receive communication of the divine message which

---

[6] P. SYNAVE and P. BENOIT, *Prophecy and Inspiration,** p. 107. See also "Note complémentaire sur l'inspiration, "* *RB* (1956), pp. 416-422.

he must set down in writing. Inspiration is not revelation. A writer
can be inspired to set down the message *revealed* to another, as Baruch
was inspired to put in writing the revelations made to Jeremias. There
is no less need for supernatural action of God on his mind, otherwise he
might not be able to fully grasp the message which he must set down;
and if he were content with the passive role of a secretary, he would
not be acting as a real *author*, in the fullest sense of the word, in the
redaction of the sacred book.

From this we must conclude that the activity of a prophet and that
of an inspired writer can appear quite different from one another. In
prophecy, the onrush of light from on high and the divine imperative
are often manifested quite bruskly; the oncoming of the Spirit takes
place almost violently. In the redaction of the sacred books, on the
contrary, the author sometimes makes us well aware of his labors and of
his spadework. Thus the redactors of the Books of Kings cite their
sources; the wise men tell us they have labored much to acquire wisdom
and have gone far to acquire it; the redactor of 2 Mc goes so far as to
excuse himself for not having succeeded very well in the composition
of his work; he has weighed all the difficulties of it. Actually, the writer
has only " the prophetic instinct, " in the words of St. Thomas. What
he receives from God is uniquely the supernatural light which allows
him to judge, with divine certitude itself, everything which relates to the
composition of his book.

Does he at least have an awareness of acting as an inspired writer?
Not necessarily. As for the prophet, he often has an awareness of divine
enlightenment : " Oracle of Yahweh! " he cries. But when the biblical
writers speak to us about their works, they seem to be more concerned
with their activity as men, than with divine activity present in them.
The same is true for the action of grace in the life of a Christian. [7] Only
the mystic, by a special charism, receives a living awareness of the
action of grace at the heart of his understanding and his freedom. Even
in the case of prophecy, St. Thomas thinks " that it sometimes happens
that the prophet cannot fully discern whether his words and thoughts are
the result of divine inspiration or of his own mind " (q. 171, art. 5). He
would have admitted this a fortiori for inspiration. But we must not
forget the " fully " of St. Thomas. The sacred author would not have
been a truly human instrument with intelligence and freedom, if he
had had no cognizance of the religious end to which his activity as author
was tending. Would his action have been truly human if it had been

---

[7] Cf. Dom CHARLIER, *La Lecture chrétienne de la Bible,** p. 239.

unconsciously ordained to the supernatural designs of God? An inspired text can appear stripped of any reference to the life of faith, hope, and charity. But actually the study of these texts always uncovers a deeper intention : the author who gathers these documents and composes his work is aware of serving a God who elevates and saves man.

II. THE ACTION OF GOD UPON THE WILL OF THE SACRED WRITERS

In this way we can understand, however imperfectly, the manner in which God was acting upon the will of the writer. Leo XIII affirms such action : God, he writes, stirred up and moved the sacred authors to write *quae ipse juberet*. Thus he has ordered them to write certain things and prompted them to this activity.

The study of the inpouring of grace into the free will of man has always been a problem for religious thought. It is not surprising then that the theologians have also had some difficulty in stating precisely how the will of God and the will of man encounter one another so as to come up with an inspired book. Still, it is certain that God, who has made man free, does not suppress this freedom when He is acting in the accomplishment of a work so exalted as the written expression of divine thought for all time.

This liberty, often exercised in the natural order for such things as the material interest of an individual, the peace of a family, or the prosperity of a state, is also exercised here, but in the supernatural order. In the first case, the human will is urged on by a natural good; in the case of a sacred book, it is prompted in view of a supernatural good : the deliverance of man and the establishment of the kingdom of God. In both cases, man could abstain. If he produces the book which God expects of him, he does so not merely under the impulse of God as the regulator of nature; he is acting under another prompting, a gratuitous appeal which confronts him with something surpassing by far the life of a rational animal : a life of a son of God, associated with God Himself in a particular aspect of His redeeming activity. Such is the supernatural vocation in virtue of which the sacred writer decides to begin his work and brings it to a successful conclusion. This vocation does not imply only a *consciousness* of the end to be achieved, but a *concern of the will*, which is an essential aspect of divine inspiration. Even if, at the outset of revelation, the fullest implications of the designs of God are not grasped in all their dimensions, the authors already know that their activity is directed to the life of the people of Yahweh, which is a life with Yahweh and a gift of Yahweh. God moves their will through the desire of promoting this supernatural good, of which a clear awareness increases as revelation progresses. [8]

III. God and the Powers of Execution of the Hagiographer

As a concrete work, the sacred book is only accomplished when its ideas are clothed in their literary expression. There again, a multiform human activity is at work : literary genius, imagination, memory, delicacy of feeling foreseeing and directing the reactions of the readers, and bodily activity.... When biblical books are concerned, all of this activity can also be attributed to the two authors. Does this exercise of the faculties of execution require a special grace of inspiration? No, answered Franzelin, for this exercise has a close psychological dependence on the intelligence and the will. Therefore, the grace of inspiration given for the exercise of these faculties necessarily affects the faculties of execution. It will suffice to have a positive " assistance " of God destined to safeguard the suitability of the expression to render the thought faithfully. It seems that the encyclical *Providentissimus* requires nothing more from the literary work at this point. Other theologians consider a new grace of inspiration necessary for an activity of a new order, such as the work of expression relevant to faculties other than the intellect and will. They do not, however, intend by this to revert to the theory of " dictation " of the words. As previously, the author maintains his identity, with his own style and capabilities, in the work of expressing the ideas. But this work is done under the direct influence of the Holy Spirit, whose aim is not to render more perfect or easier the literary work, but to make it the very work of God. We only recall these discrepancies of interpretation in order to underline the different aspects in which the redaction of the sacred book can be viewed. We easily find in them a fundamental agreement : the very expression of the idea does not escape the influence of the principal author. Père Lagrange spoke of a " total inspiration " since he was eager to do away with the equivocal expression " verbal inspiration. "

Thus, with mysterious and delicate condescension, God effectively accomplishes, by entering into the complete activity of many writers, this " theandric " act of composition of the sacred books. All their books

---

[8] Concerning the modalities of this movement of the will by inspiring grace (a direct movement of God, or a movement under the efficacious influence of the practical judgment, itself moved by God), it may be profitable to read H. Lusseau, *Essai sur la nature de l'inspiration...,** pp. 146-156. Whatever explanation is retained, we must admit, with the author, that the influence upon the will must put the will in direct relationship with God as regards instrumentality.

thus become a literary manifestation of the Word of God. " Thenceforth the Bible can resemble any other human book, as we learn from its actual study, " writes Père Benoit. " At the same time it is also a divine book, in the true sense of the word, unlike any other. For surely God is at the immediate source of every activity of thought of the interpreter whom he inspires. He is as truly the Author of the Book, the entire Book, as in man, but each on his own level, God being the principal Author, and man, His faithful instrument. [9]

§ 3. The Inspiration and Composition of the Holy Books [10]

Through its action on the writer, inspiration results in the composition of a book. The study we have just made would remain incomplete and too theoretical unless we follow it up by examining its application to the book itself. The composition of a book is actually much more complex than the redaction of an oracle. In former times, sacred authors were somewhat considered as solitary thinkers writing a book once and for all, never to be changed, expressing the thought of its predecessors and their milieu. But the fruitful works of criticism have shed light on the whole complexity of the literary work, and the psychology of the authors has revealed all the elements of this. It has become apparent in the Bible that often many authors have contributed to the elaboration of a book. As a tributary of his sources and of his predecessors, each writer has proved to be all the more dependent on his milieu and on his community even in the redaction of his message. Finally, added to the problem of the inspiration of the author is that of the inspiration of his translators. So many questions which have a theological import and which we must struggle to explain as far as possible.

I. ABILITIES PROPER TO EACH AUTHOR

We have already spoken of the action of God on the faculties of execution of the sacred writers. But we must not conceive of this execution as a purely material task. There was a time when one formed far too schematic an idea of the psychology of the inspired. They were imagined like

---

[9] P. SYNAVE and P. BENOIT, *op. cit.*, p. 100. See also Dom CHARLIER, *loc. cit.*, pp. 235-241 and the pages dedicated by P. Benoit to the total and analogous extension of inspiration to the faculties of the writer, to the content and authors of the book, in *Guide to the Bible*, Vol. I (New York : Desclée, 1960), pp. 28-31.

[10] Cf. M. J. LAGRANGE, " L'inspiration et les exigences de la critique, " *RB* (1896), pp. 496-518.

intellectuals at their worktable, encompassed with the divine influx at
the exact moment of the composition of the book, and left to themselves
once their task was accomplished. Now the prologues of St. Luke,
of 2 Mach, and of Eccles 12, 10-12 show us that things did not happen
this way. When a sacred author begins to write, he already has an
acquisition of experiences and ideas. There is no reason to believe that
Providence has been utterly lacking to him, for the redaction of an
inspired book depends upon it. But we are indeed at pains to bring to
light the infinite and subtle play of grace upon the life of this author.

When he commences work, he must often make a choice of sources
and documents : we have seen that the encyclical *Providentissimus*
admits an assistance of the Holy Spirit in these exertions. But there
are many other factors which then enter into play, particularly the providential circumstances which occasion the redaction of the book : they are
by no means excluded from the divine action. For the composition
of the holy books, God uses all the elements which are helpful to him,
especially the personal abilities of the author. He does not choose
an emotional type to write the juridical texts of the Pentateuch, nor a
scrupulous soul to compose the Canticle of Canticles. All the social
conditions, all the cultures, all the temperaments can thus be retained·
they contribute to the variety of a very rich work in which will be
expressed all that which is God, all that which here below is a divine
activity under manifold aspects.

II. THE PLURALITY OF AUTHORS

In line with the rabbinical tradition, one was led, in former times, to
attribute to a small number of authors the whole of the biblical texts.
Moses was the legislator, David was the author of the Psalms, and Solomon
was the wise man. Likewise one attributed to Isaias, to Jeremias, and to
Ezechiel the whole of the books which bore their names. Criticism has
given evidence of other personalities who, with these outstanding authors,
have collaborated in the redaction of the holy books. Thus, without
denying the existence and the grandeur of Isaias, we can perceive in the
book which has come down to us in his name the work of other literary
personalities, strongly pronounced but anonymous. The situation is
likewise evident in the Pentateuch, in which certain laws cannot be recon-
ciled with the time of Moses.

To draw up a holy book, therefore, God could have used several
human instruments, several authors. The role of inspiration thereby
appears complex and full of nuances. None of the authors who have

collaborated in the composition of an inspired book have escaped divine action, neither the great unknown of the Exile who completed the message of Isaias 150 years after his predecessor, nor the anonymous scribes who took a hand in it thereafter, nor the successive legislators who completed the work of Moses so as to adapt his law to new circumstances and to modified social structures. The divine mind was being manifested in each of these partial works, and it is the sum total of them which expressed the fulness of this thought. Isaias and Moses had laid the foundation, but the Holy Spirit did not speak his final word to them.

It sometimes happened that a new author not only added new elements to the work of his predecessor, but also cut out certain passages. Thus God had inspired the first author only in view of a more perfect work. In the syntheses of this genre, certain materials have been reproduced as they were, but they have received the sense which God wished to give them only in a new context. Thus the great history of the succession of David, probably redacted under Solomon, was taken up again, completed, dismembered, and even truncated by the definitive redactor of the Book of Samuel. All the intentional corrections remaining in the book which we have were willed by God. But they must not be confused with the flaws of the scribe or with accidental glosses. God acts intelligently through intelligent beings; when we can prove that a modification of the primitive text results from an unintentional mistake, we must not seek for divine action in it.

Sometimes the activity of a writer is confined to fusing or setting in order some earlier texts. In literary criticism, we avoid speaking of an *author;* rather we speak of a *redactor.* But the redactors of this sort were also submitted to the charism of inspiration. Besides, we must often remember that their redactions were intelligently done, so as to express precise ideas, or to fulfill certain needs of the community of Israel. Thus the redaction was willed by God; it was not mechanical, but served a definite purpose which criticism can detect. Père Lagrange rightly refused to make the existence of inspiration depend on the authenticity of the text, and he considered as *inspired* all passages of the Book of Isaias, even unauthentic ones, provided that they were in the book. But he treated these problems so as to specify concretely what God had intended to accomplish through the intervention of inspired authors. This is actually how we enter fully into the intelligibility of the Bible and of the history of Israel and the Church, of which the Bible is the privileged witness. Inspiration has animated all these texts. Once we have a glimpse of its life, we discover at the same time the life of the people of God.

III. The inspired person in the community

The preceding reflections have shown in several instances that the inspired writers are dependent on the community in which they live, as echoes and witnesses of its preoccupations. This demands some explanation.

Let us first clarify one point. The preoccupations of the community of Israel were not an accident of history. They were willed and directed by God, with a view towards the education of His people. They formed a part of the providential design. Obviously we must not confuse them with revelation; by themselves, they were not the instrument of revelation, for revelation does not spring from the depths of the collective experience. It comes from God alone through the mediation of the men chosen by Him. But it remains true that in order to be enrooted in the life of the Chosen People, revelation was ordinarily expressed in accordance with its problems; God used the very circumstances of history in order to bring to completion the questions to which He wished to evoke a response. Sometimes this can be carried further. More than one book of the OT records the religious reflections of successive generations, elaborating these from the national heritage : ancient patriarchial traditions; annals of the nation marching toward the promised land, waging the wars of Yahweh and organizing the national life; writings and recollections of prophets. We then realize that the religious thought elaborated in the heart of the community under the direction of the spokesmen of God was the point of departure for divine revelation, as well as the occasional cause of the inspired writings. Thus we have a living grasp of one of the aspects which shows the historical development of the economy of revelation.

The sacred writers, setting themselves to work under the special action of the Spirit of God, were not outside this economy. In more than one case, we can establish that the practical needs of the community, even its actual progress, prompted the composition of a book. This is clear in the case of the letters of St. Paul; we need only to think of the questions asked of the Apostle by the Corinthians (1 Cor 7, 1 ff.). The same may be said for all the works which a catechesis underlies, such as gospels or homiletic parts of Deuteronomy, discourses of Acts, or the fixing of patriarchial traditions in the historical fresco of the so-called priestly writer.

Thus the inspired writer must never be separated from his mileu, and this mileu is not a social or religious group of just any sort, but a community which the Holy Spirit has Himself chosen. He directs it and assists it in a manner analogous to that whereby He directs and assists the Church, although with different means since, for example, there is no magisterium in the OT similar to that of the Church. Nevertheless, in this community, the inspired writer fulfills a distinct function : God uses him as an instrument to set down in a book both revelation itself and the concrete circumstances in which God has given it to men. His religious thought does not necessarily conform to that of the milieu in which he writes; if the Book of Nahum reflects the common joy of the people of Juda after the ruin of Ninive, the Book of Jonas is plainly a reaction to the crisis of particularism which was rampant in the resurging and constantly menaced nation. As to the writings of the great prophets, they show them as inflexible nonconformists stirred up by God to rebuke the illusions of a religion which practices cult while overlooking the moral demands.

To underline this dependence of the writer or of the redactor or even of the glossarist, to admit that it is not without a certain pressure forcing a reaction with or against the wind, is to detract nothing from the specific action of inspiring grace. (The definition of *Providentissimus*, moreover, prevents us from thinking of a collective inspiration applicable to the composition of the holy books.) But the Holy Spirit acts in diverse manners; He directs the people of God, makes the prophet an instrument of revelation, uses the hagiographer so as to give this revelation a written form. All these actions of the Spirit are in close relationship. Thus, sometimes it is the personality of the inspired author which is particularly reflected in his book; sometimes it is the religious life of the people of God whose thought and doctrine he transmits, reflects, or corrects under the divine influence. In every case, the author fulfills the function according to which God calls him within the much wider economy of revelation.

IV. THE QUESTION OF THE INSPIRATION OF THE SEPTUAGINT

In Christian antiquity also the problem of the inspiration of the biblical books extended to their translation, at least as far as the Greek translation of the OT is concerned. We have already described how a sacred book, in Israel, was quickly considered as belonging to the public domain, a fact which laid it open to the insertion of glosses, additions, to which we have no reason to deny inspiration. Moved by the same concern of using the Pentateuch, and then the other Hebrew books, in a language which had become the only one accessible to the faithful, the Jewish community of Alexandria set about on the work of translation from the 3rd to the 1st century B.C. An analogous occurrence would take place with regard to the Aramaic Gospel of St. Matthew, according to Papias.

The position of the Fathers, Greek and then Latin, on the inspiration
of the LXX, has been dominated by the greater or lesser credence which
they placed in the so-called letter of Aristeas and to the exaggerations
caused by it.

St. Jerome (*PL* 28, 150 ff.) rises up against the false legend of the
cells where the translators would have been imprisoned; the letters of
Aristeas and Flavius Josephus make no mention of it.   His refusal to
admit the inspiration of a version goes further and deeper theologically :
for if it is admissible with the prophet " who announces future things, "
it has no reason to exist in the translator who transposes what he understands into his own language.

(The fact that the role once played in the Church by the Greek
version had been forgotten encouraged more and more the theologians
(exclusively Latin theologians since the Middle Ages) to reject the
inspiration of the LXX.) The decree of the Council of Trent on the
juridical authenticity and the use of the Latin Vulgate in the West
brought about the same effect. [11]

(Several recent studies have expressed the belief that the problem
should be re-examined. [12]) They have taken pains to point out all of its
aspects, some of which show little favor to an affirmative conclusion.
They underline the liberties taken by the translators with the Hebrew
original.   They also note the imperfections, sometimes quite noticeable,
of the translation, such as excessive literalism in certain passages, or even
a misunderstanding of the Hebrew text, giving rise to a transliteration,
itself unintelligible.

On the other hand, they also emphasize the fact that the Church
accepts as inspired some texts of which the original Hebrew has
disappeared (Sir, Tb, Jdt, parts of Est).   When archeology restores
for us Hebrew fragments of certain parts of these books, some noticeable
differences are revealed between the Greek text and the Latin of the
Vulgate which often follows it.   Now it is the Vulgate which the Church
uses.

Thus we have a new position on the question.   Might we not consider
the Greek translators as performing a rather new task, quite personal,
starting from the inspired Hebrew text?   Père J. Coste, in an article in
Revue Biblique, [13] has presented a study of Is 25, 1-5, which he concludes

---

[11] *Guide to the Bible*, Vol. I, p. 32 ff. (P. Benoit), opens new horizons.

[12] P. BENOIT, " La Septante est-elle inspirée? "* in *Vom Wort des Lebens.
Festschrift fur Max Meinertz*. . . (Münster, 1951), pp. 41-49.—P. AUVRAY, " Comment
se pose le problème de l'inspiration de la Septante, "* RB (1952), pp. 321-336.

[13] J. COSTE, " Le texte grec d'Isaïe XXV, 1-5, " *RB* (1954), pp. 36-66.

as follows : " This little text... appears to us with a new dimension :
it is fundamentally a rereading within the faith of a passage of Isaias in
continuity with the global message of the book " (*lc.* p. 64).   Might we not
also consider cases such as Is 7, 14 where, under the influence of revelation,
the *almah* of the Hebrew becomes the *parthenos* of the Greek?   Père Benoit
further cited in this sense Ps 15, 8-11 and Gn 12, 5.   Now it is from the
text of the LXX that St. Matthew in 1, 23, St. Peter in Acts 2, 23 ff. and
3, 25, St. Paul in Ac 13, 35-37 and Gal 3, 8 f., draw their arguments to
prove the virgin birth of Christ, the announcement of the Resurrection,
or the spiritual fellowship of all people with Abraham.   Père Auvray
finishes his study on the subject [14] by writing : " A close examination of
various witnesses of the ancient tradition, as well as reflections on the
theology of inspiration, lead us to look with favor upon the idea of an
overall inspiration of the LXX. "

It is sufficient for us to have pointed out the problem.   It can only
be resolved through further works, both in the domain of criticism
which must uncover the theological orientations of the translators
throughout their work, and in the domain of theology itself.

---

[14] Especially *RB* (1952), p. 336.

CHAPTER III

THE CANON OF THE INSPIRED BOOKS

A fact as important as the existence of inspired Scriptures bears multiple consequences from both a private and a social point of view. It is because of this inspiration that some souls find in the reading of Scripture the source of their spiritual life; it is because of it that the Jewish groups have their unity and that the divided Christians preserve a common line.

Two consequences are particularly important and require that we spend more time on them : canonicity and inerrancy. Because Scripture is the word of God set down in writings inspired by the Holy Spirit, 1) the holy books are *canonical*, that is to say, they are the rule of Faith of the Church; 2) they cannot deceive nor be in error, because *inerrancy* is the guarantee of the confidence which the faithful place in them.

§ 1. Canon, Canonical, Canonicity

BIBLIOGRAPHY

H. HÖPFL, " Canonicité, " *SDB*, I, cols. 1022-1045.

R. H. PFEIFFER, " Canon of the Old Testament, " *IDB*, I, pp. 498-520.

S. ZEITLIN, *An Historical Study of the Canonization of the Hebrew Scriptures* (Philadelphia, 1933).

M. J. LAGRANGE, *Histoire ancienne du canon du Nouveau Testament** (Paris, 1933).

S. ZARB, *De historia Canonis utriusque Testamenti** (Rome, 1934).

Protestant positions : S. DE DIETRICH, *Le renouveau biblique* (Paris-Neuchâtel, 1949), pp. 18-38.

G. ÖSTBORN, *Cult and Canon. A Study in the Canonization of the Old Testament* (1950).

F. FILSON, *Which Books Belong in the Bible ? A Study of the Canon* (1952).

FLACK, METZER, *et al.*, *The Text, Canon, and Principal Versions of the Bible* "1956".

A. TRICOT in *Guide to the Bible*, Vol. I (New York : Desclée, 1960), pp. 67-128.

The Council of Trent declared at once holy and canonical all the books
of the Bible because, dictated by the Holy Spirit, they have God as their
author and were read in all their parts in the Catholic Church
(*DB* 783-784). Thus, at the side of the Holy Spirit, author of Scripture,
appeared the Church, guardian of the inspired deposit. It is properly
this relationship of Scripture and the Church that the term *canonical*,
applied to the holy books, expresses.

In themselves, the notions of canonicity and inspiration do not seem
to include one another necessarily. Actually they are bound together.
The Church only recognizes as canonical the inspired books; outside the
collection of books in which she has recognized a canonical authority, she
does not admit that there are inspired books. The question has been
posed with regard to the lost letters of St. Paul, the letter to the Laodiceans
(Col 4, 16) and two letters to the Corinthians (1 Cor 5, 9 and 2 Cor 2, 4).
These texts were never entered into the Canon of the Church. [1] Would
the fact that they spring from an inspired author such as St. Paul necessarily make them canonical texts, if they were rediscovered? The question
can be discussed, for if God inspires certain authors, he does so for the
redaction of well-determined books and not just for any writing. No
theologian would be led to admit that anything written by their hand
was *ipso facto* inspired.

What then is canonicity, so closely linked to inspiration?

The first Christian text dealing with it seems to be a text of
St. Athanasius (*ca.* 350) where he says of the *Shepherd* of Hermas that it
does not form part of the Canon. From the beginning of the 4th century
the term appears quite frequently. The 59th Canon of the Council of
Laodicea (360 or 363) speaks of the " private psalms *(idiotikoi)* which
must not be read in the Church any more than the non-canonical books
(akanonista), but only the canonical books of the NT and OT. " [2] The
term becomes current among the Latin writers such as Priscillian and
St. Augustine.

What did it mean at that time? According to the texts pointed out
here, it serves to make a distinction. Certain books can be read in the
Church, others not. The books admitted are called canonical. A text
of St. Athanasius [3] clarifies this notion of canonicity. The books which he

---

[1] We must, however, reserve the possibility of a hypothesis sustained by certain
critics : we may have in 2 Cor 6, 14—7, 1 and 10—13 some detached fragments of
these lost letters.

[2] *PG* of Migne, 25, 436. The Latin translations of Origen employ this term,
but they are later.

[3] *Ep. fest.*, XXXIX.

declares " canonizable " are the books worthy of being transmitted, worthy of faith, in short, divine books. Therefore canonicity does not appear as a quality somehow added to a book, but as an expression, juridically speaking, of a relationship which the book has with the Church because of its quality as a divine book. God has given it to this Church to be the norm of its belief. It is to express the use which she made of the sacred books that the Church finally came to give them the title " canonical. " The Greek word " *kanon* " actually means " rule, measure. " Thus the canonical books are those which serve as a rule of truth, of faith, of a norm of belief and practice.

Before the general use of this word, Christian practice designated the sacred books by the terms " Scripture, the Scriptures. " These words bore witness to the veneration of the Christians and served to set off a body of Scriptures distinct from any secular collection. The use of the term " Testament " to designate the divine economy among the Jewish people and in the Church gave rise to the term " *Old and New Testament* " for the books which preserved its memory and contained its message. Under this aspect, the most fundamental one, the books considered to be products or witnesses of this economy were called " *endiathekoi* " and the fact of their juridical recognition caused them to be called " *endiathetoi,* " " placed within (the Covenant), " that is to say, in the catalogue or in Church usage. One also spoke of " endorsed books, " accepted by competent authority, that of the local churches before the Roman decisions of the 5th century. It is easy to see that the term canonical, which will little by little replace these other words, bears the meaning of all of them. This is all found again in the terms of the Council of Trent defining the canonicity of the Bible, as well as in the preliminary discussions. The canonical Scripture is for the Church the written word of God, therefore holy, which has been transmitted to her as a norm of belief and of life.

Thereby one recognizes in the word canonical a double significance. The first, which theologians choose to call " active, " underlines the regulatory force of the Bible for the Church of God : it is canonical because it is a rule of belief and of conduct. The second is called " passive " : this is the quality which Scripture receives through its official acceptance by the Church, through the listing of its books in the catalogue of inspired Scriptures. By this listing the Church does not pretend to change anything basic to Scripture. She does not make Scripture divine just as she does not add to it a new holiness or new force in itself. It is in its relationship to Christians that Scripture takes on a new force. It is henceforth set up for their veneration and takes on the force of supreme authority by the fact that the Church, through the divine authority given to her by Christ, takes away any doubt likely to hover over its genuine quality or its content.

It is in this sense that we sometimes speak of the juridical authenticity of Scripture as a consequence of its canonicity and, more fundamentally, of its inspiration. (Historically, the use of Scripture for establishing and defending the faith preceded the official declarations of its canonicity; this clearly shows how the Church lived her faith and exploited its riches before thinking about taking inventory of those.) Only circumstances and polemics led her to this.

The term *authenticity* is still full of ambiguity. It evokes for us more the idea of literary authenticity than that of juridical authenticity. This is why it is little used in this last sense. The literary authenticity of a book counts for nothing in its official recognition by the Church. Only its divine origin matters. If, however, in the ecclesiastical catalogues, the books are inscribed with mention of their authors, at least the ones which at a certain epoch were supposed to be, this mention does not thereby receive any official force. Questions of authorship are not thus eliminated, and their examination remains open to the prudent investigation of exegetes and historians. In certain cases, however, this literary authenticity has some influence on the force of proof taken from the holy books, and the ancient apologists have often vindicated this, especially for the apostolic writings. It remains that Scripture derives its fundamental normative force from its divine origin, and from this alone.

At the end of these considerations we could present the biblical Canon as the collection (and secondarily the list) of the books inspired by God, gathered by the Church and considered by her as a rule of truth in virtue of their divine origin. (Canonicity is the property which the inspired books have of being destined for the Church, and then effectively recognized by her.)

§ 2. The Establishment of the Canon

We are not concerned at this point with making a history of the holy books, but of the authority which has been recognized in them. We do not place ourselves therefore within the point of view of God who inspires the Bible and supernaturally prepares the definitive collection, nor within in the point of view of the human authors, each of whom brings his stone or his labor to the edifice, but within the point of view of the

community which receives these books, preserves them, and lives by
them.   This history of the canonical authority of biblical books is delicate
to retrace.   It is closely linked to the development of revelation and of
dogma.   The given facts which make it possible are often insufficient to
yield definitive conclusions.

I.   THE CANON OF THE OLD TESTAMENT

In studying the Canon of the OT we must distinguish the stages of its
formation, namely, the period preceding the inauguration of Christianity
and that which follows it.

During the pre-Christian period

If the writings of the OT have been conserved during long centuries,
it is because they represented for the Israelites a certain value.   But they
could have been attached to them for various reasons : for their national
importance as in the Canticle of Debora; for their ritual value as in
certain traditions relating to the sanctuaries.   In the early epoch, the
decisions and oracles rendered in the sanctuaries carried an unequaled
religious authority.   The Faith was also attached to the great syntheses
of the patriarchial and national traditions of the North and South.
The fusion of the Yahwistic and Elohistic narratives already bears
witness to the religious authority of these texts : they were fused together
instead of sacrificing the one or the other.

Since Church and State were not distinct in Israel, the authority
of a law of the State as in Deuteronomy is the sign of its canonical
authority.   This law is the foundation of the reform of Josias (4 Kgs 23,
1-3).   Some texts in the spirit of Deuteronomy record the authority of
certain laws in the Pentateuch : thus Jos 24, 26, which speaks of a " Book
of the Law of God, " and Jer 8, 8, which mentions " the Law of God. "
Later, the Law of Esdras will also be a law of the State, and will impose
itself on the Jews as well as on the Samaritans with the agreement of the
Persian authorities.

The fall of the monarchy and the Exile were to hasten the recognition
of the properly canonical authority of the Scriptures.   The sacred text
then becomes the framework of the life of the people and the foundation
of priestly authority.   But it is not only in the legislative texts that we
recognize a divine force.   The word of the prophets also proved to be
true.   Chaps. 40—55 of Isaias rely upon the realization of the ancient
prophecies so as to announce new ones.   The oracles of Isaias which are
preserved by his disciples and serve as a springboard for new perspectives,
treat of the life of the community.   The Book of Jeremias, whose disciple

Baruch was entrusted by the prophet to reassemble his oracles (36, 32), also makes its influence strongly felt.

Upon return from the Exile the community is faced with new problems. The considerable importance of the Temple and of the sacred chant will bear with it the recognition of the divine character of the Psalms. The authority of the Books of Wisdom will find itself also canonized. The prophets were often in conflict with the scribes of their times. But after Jeremias and Ezechiel had announced a new structure of the community,[4] no longer based on collective retribution but on individual retribution, the psychological observations of the wise men, their manner of forming their disciples in an exact outlook on human life, and their very broad and penetrating humanism, now appear to have the primary importance. To be sure, these maxims and reflections are more and more explicitly linked to the Yahwistic tradition: " the fear of Yahweh is the beginning of wisdom "; but the increasing influence of the scribes also brings with it the canonization of the work of their masters.

Not that this canonization should be considered as an official act of an established authority. It is the very life of the people which leads the community and its leaders to recognize and to proclaim the unequaled authority of the holy books. The Jewish community of Alexandria, which spoke Greek, would acknowledge the need of having a translation of them and, about B.C. 130, the grandson of Ben Sira speaks to us in the prologue of Ecclesiasticus of a translation " of the Law, of the Prophets and of other books " which existed in his time. This is the first rough draft of the Canon. About the same time the first book of Machabees speaks of the " Holy Books " to designate a group of writings enjoying great veneration among the people. Finally, 2 Mc 2, 13 speaks of a library organized by Nehemias which does not, however, seem limited to only sacred books.

Thus there are still some hesitations on the exact establishment of the Canon in the first centuries which precede the Christian era. Palestinian Judaism tends to consider as having authority only the ancient books, particularly those written in Hebrew, and never those in Greek. This is the position of the Pharisees and of the historian Josephus, who echoes this in his *Contra Apion* (1, 8). The latter lists 22 inspired books separated into three groups. He thinks that the era of the composition of Scripture was finished with the epoch of the Persian king Artaxerxes, for, from this time on, the succession of the prophets became

---

[4] Cf. H. CAZELLES, " A propos d'une phrase de H. H. Rowley " in " Wisdom in Israel... , " *Suppl. VT*, III (Leiden, 1955), pp. 26-32.

uncertain. Here is this important text : " Through natural, or rather
necessary, consequence—since not everybody among us is allowed to
write history and our writings show no divergence, but since only the
prophets retold with certainty the remote and ancient deeds because
they had learned them through divine inspiration, just as contemporary
events were related by them as they occurred before their eyes—by a
natural consequence, I say, there does not exist among us an infinity
of books in disagreement and in contradiction but only 22 which contain
the annals of all times and receive just credence. These are first of all
the books of Moses, five in number, which comprise laws and tradition
from the creation of man until the death of Moses. It is a period of about
3,000 years. From the death of Moses until Artaxerxes, successor of
Xerxes to the throne of Persia, the prophets that came after Moses
recounted the history of their times in 13 books. The last four contain
hymns to God and moral precepts for men. After Artaxerxes until
our own days the events have been recounted, but these writings do not
receive the same credence as the earlier ones, because there was no longer
exact succession of the prophets. The facts show with what respect we
approach our holy books. After so many centuries have passed by, no
one is allowed to make any addition or any change in them. It is natural
for all the Jews from the time of their birth to think that the divine will is
contained in them, to respect them, and if need be to die for them with
joy. We have already seen many of them in captivity undergoing
tortures and all kinds of death in the amphitheaters rather than pronounce
one single word contrary to the laws and to the annals which accompany
them. "

Although this testimony may be debatable as to the historical
antecedents, it is most important in testifying to the faith of the Pharisees
contemporary to Christ. Josephus does not explain himself clearly in
regard to the names of the books inscribed in the Canon : Pentateuch,
Psalms, Proverbs, and Prophets are certainly included; as to the other
books, there is some hesitation. In any case, this position of Pharisaic
Judaism, which limited the Canon to the ancient traditional books,
was only one of the tendencies present. There were others also. The
Sadducean milieux (such as the Samaritans) only accepted the Pentateuch
as canonical. Besides, in the Alexandrian Diaspora as well as at Qumran, [5]
it was considered that God had not spoken His last word, and that
one still had the right to await an inspired message. Thus it happens
that in the Diaspora a real authority was recognized in books which are

called *deuterocanonical* by the Catholics, apocryphal by the Jews and Protestants. These are Sirach (Ecclesiasticus), Wisdom, Baruch, Judith, Tobias, the two books of Machabees and the Greek sections of the books of Esther and of Daniel. On the other hand, it is not impossible that the Jews of Qumran attributed like value to certain writings of their sect. We should at least maintain that in the time of Christ there were still some uncertainties about the Canon and the canonicity of books since nothing was yet defined.

In the Christian epoch

The Christian Church developed above all in the milieu of the Diaspora; therefore it will use the Greek OT, with the result that the NT often cites the OT according to the Greek translation made in Alexandria. It does not happen to cite *deuterocanonical* books as Sacred Scripture but other books, called *protocanonical* (Proverbs, Ruth, Ecclesiastes, Canticles). Actually, the apostles used the deuterocanonical books, for their Epistles contain some implicit citations from and traces of these books : Jas 1, 19 comes from Sir 5, 11; 1 Pt 1, 6-7 from Wis 3, 5. 7; Heb 11, 34 f. from 2 Mc 6, 18 to 7, 42; Heb 1, 3 from Wis 7, 26. Jude 14 even cites the Apocrypha of Enoch (1, 9).

But the apostles seem to have defined or promulgated nothing on this subject. Rejected by the Jews of Palestine, their ministry bore fruit in the Diaspora and they just employed the text in use. The first Fathers, called Apostolic Fathers, would do the same. St. Clement of Rome, writing to Corinth about A.D. 95, cites Judith and Tobias. Twenty years later, St. Polycarp of Smyrna (who knew St. John) cites Tb 4, 10 (*Ep. of Pol.* 10, 2) and places it on the same plane as Isaias. St. Justin, the Christian philosopher born in Palestine and teaching in Rome about A.D. 160, quotes the Greek fragments of Daniel. A famous document from the end of the 2nd century, called the Canon of Muratori, places a " book of Wisdom " (probably our Wisdom) among the writings having authority. Finally St. Irenaeus, about 180-200, is an excellent witness to the faith of his time; born in the East and living in Gaul, he also had close contact with Rome; he cites Baruch, Wisdom, and the Greek fragments of Daniel. Therefore the primitive Christian Church is in tranquil possession of a broad canon, without polemic or definitions.

The same is not true in Judaism. After the taking of Jerusalem by Titus in A.D. 70 and the destruction of the second Temple, it feels the need to be defined and reorganized on solid bases. It does so in the Pharisaic tradition at the synod of Jamnia held in Palestine near Joppe about 90-95. The Greek text used by the Christians became suspect;

moreover the drama of 66-70 cut Israel off from the Gentiles with the result that it fell back on its own heritage. The canon adopted at Jamnia is the strict canon; the text of Josephus cited above is an echo of the same tendency. Yet books like Baruch continue to be read in the synagogues in the 3rd century. In the same epoch the rabbinic tradition develops protective measures for the holy book. Certain rules establish the form and composition of the scrolls. It is forbidden to bring them into unclean places or to leave them upon a bed. They are said to " soil the hands, " like other sacred objects.

It was the *oriental Christians* who were most influenced by the rejection of the deuterocanonical books. The East was actually more in contact with the Jews than was the West. Some rather drawn out theological discussions obliged the Christian controversialists to invoke only the books recognized by those against whom they were arguing. The exigencies of apologetics came to interfere with the question of canonicity. Thus in his *Dialogue with Trypho* (n. 120), St. Justin affirms his intention of only using books " which are admitted among you on the consent of all. " In the middle of the 2nd century the first list of accepted books appears, that attributed to *Melito of Sardis* (*ca.* 160). This bishop addresses to his colleague Onesimus, in the guise of a dedicatory epistle to a collection of texts of the OT, and, it seems, upon his request, a list of books which " in Palestine " are " commonly accepted. " Now Esther and the deuterocanonical books are not included. Although it is neither an official catalogue nor an exact reflection of the practice of the Christian churches of Palestine, this list quite probably represents the terrain common to Jews and Christians, on which Onesimus could carry on the " battle for eternal salvation. "

At Alexandria *Origen* seems torn between the tradition attached to the complete Canon and the necessity of sticking to the Canon accepted by the Jews when discussing with them (*Ad. Afr.* 5, *PG* 11, 60). He actually cites Esther, Judith, Tobias, Wisdom, and Ecclesiasticus as Scripture. Thus if he marks the deuterocanonical passages with an obelus in his Hexapla and presents a Canon of 22 books, he does so more as a controversialist desirous of showing himself aware of the hesitations of the learned than because of a personal doctrine, even less so in the name of the practice of the Church. After him *St. Athanasius* makes the thought of his master more rigid. Likewise faithful to the complete Canon before 367, which was in the general practice of the Church, he becomes a theoretician of a peculiar notion of the Canon. The biblical books should be divided into two groups : first the " sources of salvation, " the official books in the Church, namely, 22 books of the OT (with Baruch,

without Esther) and all those of the NT. Then there were the books
which were not in the Canon but which the Fathers ordered to be read
to new converts. Then he cites Wis, Sir, Est, Jdt, Tb and Didache,
Hermas. These are the books " read. " Then he names the Apocrypha,
of heretical origin, outside the acceptable books. It has been asked
whether St. Athanasius denied inspiration to the second class of books.
He does not seem to have expressed himself clearly on this subject.
The creation of an intermediate class between the canonical books and
the apocryphal ones clearly shows lack of precision in the theology of
inspired books. Similar hesitations are found in St. Cyril of Jerusalem,
St. Gregory Nazianzen, St. Epiphanes, and in Syria with Theodore of
Mopsuesta, who is opposed by Theodoret. The 60th canon of the Council
of Laodicea v. 360 (*EB*, 8-9), much discussed, silent on the majority of the
deuterocanonical books of the OT and NT, might well reflect the thought
of Theodore of Mopsuesta. In fact, it is only after the Quinisext Council,
or " *in Trullo*, " of 692, that the East would adopt the complete Canon
of the two Testaments.

In the *West* the doubt over the canonicity of books excluded from
the Jewish Canon comes to light only with Rufinus and St. Jerome.
When at Rome, neither has any difficulty in using the books accepted
by the Latin Church. Both become champions of the restricted Canon :
Rufinus in the turnabout of his career after he has been influenced by the
thought of Origen whom he discovers, St. Jerome after he leaves Rome to
live in the East. When he praises the Canon of 22 books such as Origen
set down, *Rufinus* still regards the other books as " ecclesiastical, " but
does not believe them usable for confirming the dogmas of the Church.
And yet he believes in the inspiration of the LXX, which embraces
the complete Canon!

St. Jerome is more explicit than Rufinus, and in his prologue
" galeatus " (written about 390), a kind of warlike manifesto prefacing
his new translation from the Hebrew text, he declares " apocryphal "
all books not included in the 22 of the Jewish Canon. The term used was
equivalent to a denial of their inspiration. Jerome was to be the only one
in the West to hold this view. Such novelty would lead even
St. Augustine, his most famous opponent, to demand that clear positions
be taken in Africa; these will be in the Church the first official professions
of faith in the traditional Canon, although there were not definitions of the
Roman Magisterium.

The hesitations showing up principally in the East and, under
its influence, later and more sporadically in the West, evidently are the
doing of the scholars. They do not reveal a practical unanimity in regard

to a reduced Canon. Those who were hesitant did not always conform
their practice with their theories. Beyond the backwash at the end of the
2nd century, and in the 3rd and 4th centuries, the 5th century would
find once more the unanimity of the 1st and of the beginning of the 2nd,
except in Syria which has to wait until the 7th century.

II. THE CANON OF THE NEW TESTAMENT

In speaking of the criterion of inspiration, we have already stated the
motifs which led the churches to use and to reunite the writings from the
apostles or from their disciples, from the time when they judged the
reading of these useful for the community, even if this community was not
the direct recipient of them.   In 2 Pet 3, 16 we already note the use of
Pauline writings concurrently with other Scriptures.   In 1 Tm 5, 17 f.,
Lk 10,7 is cited with Dt 25, 4.   Among the Christian writings prior to the
second half of the 2nd century which have come down to us, the books
of the NT are cited with as much frequency and authority as those of the
OT, and those citations are already introduced by the formula " It is
written. "   Nothing should be lost which was bequeathed by the apostles.

But with the invasion of the apocrypha [6] no one wanted to admit
anything which was not of apostolic tradition.   When these apocrypha
were clearly heretical, they were quickly rejected.   This was not the case
if they were only intended to edify the Church.   Did not the Epistle
of St. Jude use the Jewish apocrypha?   Until about 150 we do not find
Christian apocrypha on the same footing with the Scriptures.   On the
other hand, all the books of the NT are already used as such except
for the small Epistles of St. John (2nd and 3rd), of St. Jude and of
St. Peter, of quite limited interest.

Beginning with 150 the question of the canonicity of the books
of the NT will be brought up.   Apocrypha are multiplied and two men,
Marcion and *Montanus*, will force the churches to become aware of
their traditional faith.

As a consequence of his dualist philosophy, *Marcion* comes to deny
the divine origin of the OT and, so as to separate the NT from the OT,
to deny everything which refers to it.   Thus only the Gospel of St. Luke
and certain Epistles of St. Paul find favor in his eyes, but not without
some mutilation.   St. Irenaeus and Tertullian rise up against him : they
are the champions of the traditional practice of the Church, the source
of which is to be found among the apostles themselves.   Inversely
Montanus and the followers of his sect, prophets of a new revelation

---

[6] Cf. LAGRANGE, *Histoire ancienne...,** pp. 22-23.

of the Spirit, threaten to introduce into the body of Scriptures their supposed revelations. Actually, although the Canon of Muratori points out two apocryphal pseudo-Pauline epistles of Marcionist inspiration, one to the Laodiceans, the other to the Alexandrians, it seems that the danger was not serious. Though a Montanist towards the end of his life, Tertullian did not depart from the principles pronounced in the struggle against Marcion. In all cases the question of the books to be accepted was brought up.

The first list of the accepted books of the NT springs from Rome. It is contained in what we call the *Canon of Muratori*, from the name of the scholar who discovered its first text in Milan around 1740. Zahn and Père Lagrange would be inclined to attribute its origin to Hippolytus. In any case the document is not an ordinance but a description of the Roman practice. The beginning is missing and we do not know what circumstance gave rise to it. The Epistle to the Hebrews is absent from this Canon. The state of the text leaves some doubts remaining over the mention of 2 Pt and Jas, which Père Lagrange believes to have been named. The Marcionist epistles already mentioned are excluded, as is the *Shepherd* of Hermas, too recent. The Wisdom of Solomon, called Philonian, is excluded. We are surprised to see it named with the writings of the NT. Is it really the canonical Book of Wisdom which is meant? Since we know that Hippolytus accepted Heb, 2 Pt and Jas, it seems likely that the Church of Rome had admitted the complete Canon at that time. Moreover Rome would not be affected by the doubts about the Apocalypse at Alexandria at the end of the 3rd century. As to Heb, whereas the West for a long time doubted its Pauline authenticity, St. Jerome believed it possible to invoke the legitimacy of its utilization and to sustain his own opinion favorable to its canonicity according to the practice of the " ancient writers. " [7]

Just as for the OT, the Alexandrians have certain doubts regarding the authenticity, then the canonicity, poorly distinguished at that time, of some books of the NT. On the one hand *Clement of Alexandria*, and the Canon of *Claromontanus* which seems to depend on him, even go so far as to admit the Epistle of Barnabas and the Apocalypse of Peter. The Canon does not name Heb but Clement accepted it. *Origen* expresses doubts relative to Heb, 2 Pt, Jude, 2 and 3 Jn. Yet he cites them and uses them. In the margin he points out certain books as good but of a private inspiration : Hermas, the Gospel according to the Hebrews, the letter of Barnabas, that of Clement of Rome, the Acts of Paul, and the

---

[7] Ep. CXXIX, cited in LAGRANGE, *op. cit.*, p. 153.

Preaching of Peter. But they are not, however, " apocrypha, " since these are to be rejected altogether.

Up to this point no doubt has affected the Apocalypse. In order to combat the millenarianism of Nepos who drew his argument from it, *Dionysius of Alexandria* overthrew its authority by attributing it to a John distinct from the Apostle. He did not reject it on that account from the number of inspired books, for Alexandrian practice was imposed upon him to that extent. At any rate he was not followed in Alexandria. Only the churches of Syria and of Palestine, under the influence of Eusebius of Caesarea, would suffer the consequences of the doubts uttered by Dionysius.

Eusebius, desirous of making himself the impartial echo of the doubts of the scholars rather than of the practice of the churches, has left us an account of his manner of viewing the question of the Canon. [8] He classes the books in four groups. There are the " approved " in which he places the Apocalypse " if that seems good "; the " disputed, " but well-known, for the greatest number, such as Jas, Jude, 2 Pt, 2 and 3 Jn; the " adulterated " such as the Acts of Paul, the Shepherd, the Apocalypse of Peter, the Epistle of Barnabas, the Didache and the Apocalypse of John " if that seems good "; finally there are the " heretical " writings : the Gospel of Peter, of Thomas, of Mathias, the Acts of Andrew, of John and of other apostles. It is difficult to say what distinction Eusebius made between the third and the fourth category. He himself did not seem to wish to give a personal opinion. His suffragant, St. Cyril of Jerusalem, would speak in different tones when " for the love of truth " he issued a list of accepted books in which only the Apocalypse was missing. He considered it a waste of time to linger over the disputed points.

Until the Quinisext Council, the East, more faithful to the Epistle to the Hebrews than the West, would show itself quite constant in excluding the Apocalypse which appeared neither in the 60th Canon of the Council of Laodicea nor in the Church of Antioch. On the contrary, Alexandria accepted it and St. Basil, St. Gregory of Nyssa, and doubtless St. Gregory of Nazianzen recognized it in Cappadocia. The Church of Antioch proved to be reticent also in regard to the small Epistles : 2 and 3 Jn, Jude, and 2 Pt, missing in the Syriac versions.

St. Jerome still echoes the scholarly misgivings concerning Heb, 2 Pt, Jude, Jas, 2 and 3 Jn. Nevertheless he firmly notes the universal acceptance of Heb. He is perhaps the first to distinguish in this case the questions of authenticity and canonicity. However, several times he

---

[8] Cf. *Ecclesiastical History*, III, 25.

seems to be confused about his subject matter. He even appears to contradict himself over the authenticity of the Epistles of John while being quite insistent about their canonicity.

There we might end the history of the controversies raised over the canonicity of certain books of the NT. In fact the first *official lists* were to appear in the Latin Church, and soon also the decisions of the Roman magisterium. The provincial Councils of Hippo in 393, then of Carthage in 397 and 418, and the Quinisext Council of 692 in the East, despite the ambiguity of the decision whereby it ratified rather diverse lists, several of them complete, put an end to the misgivings. We may consider as a document of the Roman magisterium the *letter of Innocent I* (405) to Exuperus, Bishop of Toulouse, pointing out to him the books accepted in the Canon, and condemning any others. [9] Similarly, without wishing to define the content of the Canon, the decree " pro Jacobitis " of the *Council of Florence* [10] is aimed at the Monophysites eager to return to the unity of the Catholic Canon. Finally, the *Council of Trent* ex professo repeats it and defines it against the Protestants, thereby referring to the traditional faith of the Church. Stressing the texts of the Orthodox Fathers, it affirms that the Council receives and venerates with equal piety and equal reverence all the books in the list which it then draws up. [11] Outside the Catholic Church, the Protestant Bibles which continued to omit the deuterocanonical books of the OT have not upheld the defiance of Luther for those of the NT. The latter have all been included. Only some critical marks still testify to scholarly hesitations about the authenticity of the last part of St. Mark (16, 9-20) and of a passage of St. John (8, 1-11).

§ 3. The Criterion of Inspiration and of Canonicity

Conscious of being the Mystical Body of Christ, animated and filled with life by her Spirit, the Church reads and interprets the Bible with Him whom she knows to be the author of it. Tradition is only her voice borne across the centuries. Guarding, protecting, commenting on Scripture, the Church does not submit it to herself as though it were under her tutelage, but sees in it the most sacred expression of her own thought. It is always the thought of the same Spirit of Christ who fixed it long ago in the inspired book and renews it from age to age in the Church which He assists.

---

[9] *EB*, pp. 21 ff.

[10] In 441, cf. *EB*. p. 47.

[11] *EB*, pp. 57-60.

How can the Church become aware of the inspired quality of one book to the exclusion of another? How will she be led to recognize with sufficient certitude that certain books are destined for her to regulate her faith and conduct? This is the whole question of the criteria of inspiration. Before proceeding on the historical level with the human course of events which have finally resulted in the solemn declaration of the Council of Trent, we must formulate the question on the theological level.

I. The internal criteria

This involved judging the worth of books, and since a book is evaluated when it is being read, one was led to inquire during the actual reading of the biblical books into some clue to their inspiration and, consequently, into the foundation of their canonicity. Already at the end of the 1st century of our era, if we can rely on the rabbinical traditions, when the *Synod of Jamnia* had to determine the body of Scriptures, some books of which were under discussion, the Jewish doctors proposed taking into consideration certain internal criteria : the more or less religious sense of the book, conformity with the Mosaic Torah. Thus Ezechiel, Canticles, and Esther were held in suspicion.

More recently, the biblical Canon was thrown once more into question by the Protestant crisis, and this was partly on the basis of considerations of the same order. Anxious to break away from the Roman magisterium and the concept of tradition which they ascribed to it, the Reformation theologians sought to find in Scripture itself testimony of its inspiration. It would be easy to remark upon the weakness and subjectivism of certain criteria proposed in their writings, but it would be erroneous to imagine Protestant biblical theology as fixed during this period. Theologians today do not believe they should settle for positions, really very unstable, which Luther took during the aggravation of his anti-Roman polemic. In fact, the present Protestant Bibles do not offer to their readers certain books of the OT which we call, employing a word which is unfortunate because it lends itself to ambiguity, the " deuterocanonical " [12] books and which the Protestants call, yet more unfortunately, the " apocrypha. " [13] We will borrow from the book of S. de Dietrich, written

---

[12] Cf. p. 37.

[13] The word means " hidden. " It actually designates non-canonical books which were often presented as having been written in very ancient times and kept hidden. The Protestants, by calling them " pseudepigrapha, " stress the intrusion of a borrowed name (name of a patriarch, prophet, or apostle). The fact is that the apocrypha are not all pseudepigrapha and there are pseudepigrapha among the inspired books (e.g., the Wisdom of Solomon).

to introduce the Protestant faithful to the reading of the Bible, the presentation of the official positions of the reformed churches. [14]

As for the writings of the NT, *Luther* classifies them " according to the greater or lesser importance which they give to the central message of the Redemption. " A book in which Christ is shown as the center of the Scriptures is acceptable. Perhaps apostolicity was also considered by him as a criterion of acceptance, at least for the NT; if he dissociates Heb, Jas, Jude and Apocalypse from the other writings, it would seem that this is due to their supposed non-apostolicity. To the question " Should Luther be accused of subjectivism? ", Suzanne de Dietrich does not give a clear answer. Yet she recognizes in him " sweeping judgments to which we could not subscribe, " and points out the variations in his thought. He approaches the two Testaments with what she calls " a spirit of faith and of liberty "; the question is not thereby solved. In short, the best we can say is that Luther judged the inspiration of biblical books according to a principle which is acceptable if it is only to give an orientation, but without any value for determining their content. We must also add that in certain circumstances where Luther expressed his disdain for such and such a book, he did so for reasons other than theological ones. The texts cited by Père Pesch in his treatise *De Inspiratione* [15] give proof of this.

Reflecting on the formation of the Canon of the NT and asking why only some of the writings of St. Paul and of the other apostles have come down to us, *Calvin* [16] answers : " In his admirable counsel, God has caused that, by public consensus, when all the other writings had been rejected, there remained no more than those alone in which his majesty shone forth. " Could this be the mark of inspiration? For him, it surely seems that the " public consensus " was the means by which God made known his " admirable counsel. " Therefore Calvin did not enunciate the following principle as clearly as one of his commentators pretends : " The formation of the Canon, and the inspiration of each of the books therein contained, derives therefore not from a decision of the Church, but from the sovereign decision of God. " In effect, the " public consensus " of which he speaks is not far distant from the Ecclesia of the Catholics, whose role in the selection of the inspired books " according to the admirable counsel of God " is by no means foreign to the later decisions of an organism of the magisterium. This does not create a new truth, but merely establishes the " consensus " of tradition.

---

[14] Cf. S. DE DIETRICH, *Le renouveau biblique* (Neuchâtel, 1949), pp. 21-28.

[15] Cf. p. 203, notes 3 and 4.

[16] Cited by S. DE DIETRICH, *ibid*, p. 37.

The later " Confessions " which attempt to formulate the common
Protestant faith show a more and more subjective orientation in the
choice of the criteria of canonicity. Thus article IV of the Confession
of La Rochelle gives second place to the " common accord and consent
of the Church, " insisting further on " the interior testimony and
persuasion of the Holy Spirit. " There is the same doctrine in the Confession of Westminster. To the " full persuasion, " defined as the " interior
work of the Holy Spirit who gives testimony by the word and with the
word in our hearts, " are added arguments of lesser objective value
(whatever way we become aware of the interior word of the Spirit!).
" We can be moved and induced by the testimony of the Church to
profess a lofty and reverent esteem for the Holy Scriptures; and the
heavenly character of the content, the efficaciousness of the doctrine,
the majesty of style, the cohesion of all the parts, the purpose of the whole
(which is to give glory to God), the fulness with which they reveal to
us the only way of salvation, and many other excellent things, their
all-round perfection, are the arguments by which they impose themselves
with abundant evidence as being the word of God. " [17] The composite
character of such a text manifests the perplexity of the theologians.
They must maintain at the same time the interior and personal testimony
of the Holy Spirit, the subjective criteria by which He is supposed to
formulate this testimony, and also the role of the Church, imposed by
custom.

For modern Protestant theologians such as Zahn and Harnack,
there is no need to seek a theological reason for the criterion of canonicity :
this can simply be deduced from practice. The only books preserved
would be those which were in practice required to be read, being suitable
to answer the need of edification of Christians. From this one would
conclude their inspiration.

The recent dogmatic renewal of Protestantism has led to new
positions. One of the most interesting is that of O. Cullmann. [18] He
declares himself " absolutely in accord with Catholic theology when it
insists on the fact that the *Church itself* has made the Canon. " But he
makes this Catholic position a bit more rigid by seeing in it a kind of
decree of the Church, whereas Catholic theology considers that it has been
only an explicit and definite recognition of the inspiration of the books.
This " decision " of the Church involving all its future existence had for
its aim, he states, the disentanglement of the apostolic tradition from its

[17] L. GOURNAZ, cited by S. DE DIETRICH, *op. cit.*, p. 27.
[18] *La Tradition* (Paris-Neuchâtel, 1953), pp. 41-52.

adventitious traditions; thus for him, the criterion of canonicity is apostolicity. "Among the numerous Christian writings, the books forming the future Canon *imposed themselves upon the Church through their intrinsic apostolic authority,* just as they still impose themselves upon us since the Christ-Kyrios speaks in them." ..."The OT has been received into the Canon as a testimony of that part of salvation history which prepared for the Incarnation. Thus it is that Jesus and the apostles understood the history of Israel. Therefore the Church was faithful *to the apostles* themselves by having the OT included in the *apostolic norm* which is the Canon." This is the position of numerous Catholics; further on we shall see that it leaves some difficulties unresolved.

Actually the taking of a position towards the biblical books on the part of the early Reformers was not the effect of purely theological reflections. The Reform is heir, on the one hand, to Catholic tradition, firm and tranquil for eleven centuries on the question of the Canon and, on the other hand, to the doubts deriving from literary criticism and stated by the Hellenistic and Hebraic scholars of the literary Renaissance. As other scholars had done in the early centuries, but in an atmosphere poisoned by the anti-Roman opposition, they came to confound questions of literary authenticity and of canonicity. They wished to return to the sources without being able to determine them easily. The rejection of the magisterium as a theological norm rendered a common doctrinal stand difficult. But usage, more strongly than theories, ended in imposing the acceptance of the Canon just as the Church handed it down to each of the faithful.

II. THE EXTERNAL CRITERIA

In regard to the Protestant Confessions, *the Catholic Church* has a precise doctrine : the faithful receive the sacred books from the Church and the Church receives them from the Holy Spirit by way of tradition. Being a work of the Holy Spirit, inspiration could only be revealed under His guidance. According to the promise made by Christ to His Church in order to confirm her in the faith, the Christian will normally find in her the testimony of the Spirit concerning His written work. It only remains to investigate by a historical examination how the Church was led to make her faith explicit and precise, the same faith of the apostles, as regards the inspiration of such and such a book with the exclusion of certain others.

While linking the faith of its faithful to the fact of the inspiration of specified books, and not only to the fact of biblical inspiration in general, whose precise object would remain open for each to determine, the Catholic Church really means to make this precision part of the revealed data. To pose the question of the criterion of canonicity, and fundamentally of inspiration, it is thus to ask what were for her the infallible marks of distinction of the sacred books. We cannot deduce them *a priori* from the notion of inspiration. An entirely interior pheno-menon, it neither entails nor demands, of itself, any apparent mark capable of revealing its existence in the writer or in his book. Rather, it would be necessary to inquire of the living voice of the Church, its Tradition, the only argument which the Council of Trent definitely invokes to put across its definition. It is just in the interpretation of the thought of tradition concerning the formation of the Catholic Canon that we meet two opinions worthy of consideration. To be sure, the conflict is limited to the formation of the Canon of the NT; this allows certain theologians of inspiration to brand this as a faulty orientation in the discussion. Since the inspiration of the OT and that of the NT are of the same nature, we do not see why, they say, the criterion acceptable for one should be declared insufficient for the other. Rather than closing the discussion, it seems fitting to present its points.

For the Old Testament

This collection was formed in the course of many centuries and the *formation of the Canon of the OT* is a complex process. It is not easy to state precisely the criteria which permitted Judaism to arrive at fixing its lists of sacred books. We have already had occasion to allude to the discussions of the doctors at the end of the 1st century of our era, but we are totally ignorant of what happened in the earlier centuries. Doubtless we know by history that the Jewish community previous to Christ manifests itself as a religious community, that of the Chosen People in which the revelation of the Holy Spirit is at work preparing the Gospel. Did men or organisms within this community receive a special assignment and light to maintain the sacred books and distinguish them from the others? Would this role have been incumbent upon the priests and prophets? No Jewish writer has told us so clearly, although Flavius Josephus seems to link the lack of prophetic succession with the closing of the Canon in the time of Artaxerxes I. [19]

In fact it was among the Jewish people that the books constituting the three collections were written, preserved, translated, and reassembled: the Law, the Prophets, and other books or Hagiographa, out of which

---

[19] Assuerus, he says. As in the Greek Esdras-Nehemias, it is question of Artaxerxes.

the Jews contemporary with the Christian era formed their Canon of Sacred Scriptures. Was the Mosaic, Davidic, Solomonic, and prophetic origin of certain books the reason for their transmission and for the consideration which they have enjoyed? This is quite possible. But such an illustrious origin was never maintained for many books which were treated, however, with the same respect. Thus the Chronicles are not linked to the group of prophetic writings as are the Books of Kings.

At the coming of the Messias, His followers would regulate their conduct according to His. Thus the Church received the Jewish Scriptures as He had accepted them. But for her Christ alone is the norm. Therefore it is understandable that the Christian Church considers itself in no way bound by the attitude of post-Christian Judaism even when one or another of her writers would allow himself to be influenced by what he believes to be the " *veritas hebraica.* " Thus she did not seek any criterion in regard to the OT. Or rather, faithfulness to the practice of Christ and His apostles, following along the lines of the small Yahwist communities, seems to be the sufficient criterion, tacitly admitted much more so than explicitly formulated.

For the New Testament

The question could not be so simply settled for the books which comprise our NT. They come into being after the death of Christ, a number of them are addressed to restricted communities, and several, such as the last two Epistles of St. John, are meant for very limited purposes. How can we look upon them as " Scriptures " just as the books of the OT? How can we distinguish them from the other Christian writings? Is it because they come from the apostles themselves, an opinion which our most ancient testimonies seem to reflect? Or else, can't we find another criterion than the affirmation of the living tradition of the Catholic Church which they founded?

Père Lagrange [20] believes the *apostolic origin* to have been for the Fathers the criterion of acceptance of a book as inspired Scripture. The apostles themselves, he says, were aware of possessing in normative, doctrinal, and moral matters an equal authority and, by very reason of their association with Christ, an authority superior to that of the ancient prophets. The Christians, for their part, recognized this authority. It followed that the writings of the apostles, in whom there was recognized a normative religious value, which " contain revelation without error " (p. 11), were for that very reason accepted as the word of God, and consequently as inspired and canonical. Thus to counteract the rejection

---

[20] *Histoire du Canon du N.T.*, pp. 8-14 and 171-175.

of certain books of the NT by Marcion, for example, as well as to vindicate their right to serve as a norm for the Church, one appealed to their apostolic origin.   The revelation of the canonicity of the writings of the NT, says Père Lagrange, was part of the power of the apostles invested by Christ with the mission of founding the Church.   In this mission " divine authority is directly included : whether it implies inspiration, it is a truth, perhaps revealed distinctly, but necessarily contained in the first.   Whoever really speaks in the name of God, with his authority, discerns the authority of God, confesses that he is His instrument and acts under His inspiration. "

Would there be here some confusion, already pointed out at the beginning of this study, between " divine authority " of a man or of a book, and " divine origin " of a book written under the special grace of inspiration?   It is true that the early Church did not base her reflections on canonicity on the theological concept of inspiration.   But from the text of the Fathers we cannot always conclude that their exclusive argument is the apostolic origin of the books.   Sometimes, alongside with or even independently from it, they defend the canonicity of the books in the name of tradition which has its source in the apostles, considered not so much as authors of books but as the first link in this tradition.   Thus St. Irenaeus and much later St. Cyril of Jerusalem, St. Athanasius, and Origen. [21]   Criticism today, even conservative, has some difficulty maintaining the attribution of 2 Pt and of the Epistle to the Hebrews to an apostle, and it is doubted whether James, the author of the canonical letter, is an apostle.   Therefore we cannot sidestep the objection of the non-apostolicity of certain books as easily as has been done with the writings of St. Luke and St. Mark.   For these, moreover, ancient tradition was quite hesitant to say whether they had been written under the control of an apostle or not.   Now in this theory, apostolic control is necessary for there to be canonicity.   To appeal to their authority as a condition and a mark of scriptural inspiration does not seem at all feasible for letters of such limited content as the last two Epistles of St. John or the one to Philemon.   It is not surprising that Père Benoit, and this is the opinion of the majority of the theologians of inspiration today, should recognize that the criterion of apostolic origin, outside the fact that " it seems to involve a difficult application in regard to the OT, does not even appear justified when the NT is under discussion. " [22]   In the behavior of the ancient writers, he would see

---

[21] Texts in *SDB*, I, col. 1037.
[22] *La Prophétie*, p. 296.

" the human and contingent preparation " for the dogmatic decision of the Church on the Canon, " an inquiry on the natural order as incongruous with her declaration of faith as the preambles and discussions of a Council are with the infallible decision resulting from it, " since this infallibility flows solely from the Holy Spirit. This is so true that the discovery of the non-apostolicity of a writing by critical methods, though its canonicity had long since been maintained by virtue of its apostolic origin, would by no means weaken the force of the ecclesiastical decision.

Therefore the only objective and adequate criterion is to be found in the *revelation made by the Holy Spirit to the Church and transmitted by the apostolic tradition.* It is evident that Our Lord and the apostles played a role of first importance in the transmission of the Canon of the OT by the use which they made of it. The same can be said for the apostles in the composition and transmission of the inspired writings of the NT, without having to attribute all the books to them. In referring to this apostolic role and practice, we have no other purpose but to plunge into the very sources of revelation. When in recent centuries appeal was made to the practice of the Church, the same argument was invoked. Through the Church founded by the apostles, we draw upon authentic revelation. Consequently, even when the inquiry seems to bear upon the apostolic authenticity of a writing, this authenticity will not be maintained in the name of literary criticism, but in the name of the tradition of the churches. We thus always return to this argument which has value, moreover, only in the theological sense of the word.

In that respect there is not after all a great difference between the Protestant and Catholic faithful. Practically all accept the sacred books of their Church because they believe in the link of this Church with Christ through the intermediacy of the apostles.

Conclusion : Extent of Canonicity and Inspiration

The Canon having been definitively fixed in the Church since the 7th century and the criterion of canonicity being the inspiration of the holy books as revealed to the Church, the Council of Trent was able to affirm the sacred and canonical character of the " entire books with all their parts. " Two important truths result from this; we must note them in conclusion before studying the second consequence of inspiration, the inerrancy of the Bible : inspiration extends to the whole Bible, and the whole Bible is the Word of God.

I. INSPIRATION EXTENDS TO THE WHOLE BIBLE

The Council of Trent was opposed to the dismemberment of the Canon
of Scriptures demanded by the Protestants. Once more the deuterocanonical books and passages were recognized as inspired. However, new
questions arose, and theologians or Catholic scholars could be found,
even after the Councils of Trent and of Vatican I, to bring up the problem
of the universality of the inspiration of the biblical text while wishing
to detract nothing from the Canon. Was it not fitting to restrict
inspiration only to the passages dealing with doctrine or morals? Was it
not necessary to deny the inspiring influx to purely historical narrations
(an idea of Lenormant who nevertheless does not deny to the biblical
historiographers some exceptional light...), or to passages containing
attempts at an explanation of natural phenomena (Rohling), or to the
obiter dicta, remarks of an occasional, personal, and quite secondary
nature, such as 2 Tim 4, 13 on the cloak left by Paul with Carpus (this
was doubtless the opinion of Newman)?

These hesitations could have had several reasons. Either there was
confusion about revelation by God concerning truths closely bound up
with the order of salvation and inspiration, or one took offense at the
presentations, very imperfect in our sense, of the history and the facts
relevant to cosmology or the natural sciences. Or yet it was not
understood how the mention of minute details could justify a special
intervention by God. These hesitations are without basis when we no
longer link the revealing intervention of God with inspiration. The
latter leads to the consignment of *writings* to the Church, writings by
authors quite diverse and quite diversely situated, destined to establish
revelation. Revelation itself has been entrusted by God to His people
within the manifold circumstances of their national life, by the words
of the prophets, the priests, the wise men, and finally, by the writings :
catecheses, psalms, midrashim, apocalypses, letters.... The literary
genre chosen by the author might admit of the insertion of words of
authors foreign to the Chosen People. The author of Proverbs uses
some Egyptian maxims; Esdras (5, 7) cites Persian documents; St. Paul
cites Epimenides (Ti 1, 12); the Epistle of St. Jude cites the book of
Enoch (v. 14). The biblical writers reflected current ideas when they
happened to mention certain cosmic phenomena : the origin of the
rainbow or the formation of the universe (Gn 1, 9 or Jb 38). If they were
writing to distant correspondents, they slipped into their letters personal
allusions to their works, to their health, to their projects, and they did not
leave out greetings or recommendations. The inspiration of these
authors did not bear on these details as such; they fell under its influx

as integral and normal parts of the book willed by God, according to its literary genre. We might say in the scholastic style : God wills " *primario* and *in se* the setting down in writing of religious truths, but *secondario* and *propter hoc* He wills the inspired books each according to its nature and with all the literary characteristics pertaining to it. " We should regard in the same manner the activity of the glossarists, the re-readers and, in some cases, of the translators, working under the inspiring grace as we have said previously.

It would no doubt remain to distinguish between the literary activity of an author in the strict sense of the word, and that of a compiler, of a historiographer working on written sources sometimes literally quoted, of a glossarist or of a translator, of a secretary drawing up his master's correspondence more or less in his own way. None of these activities is incompatible with the inspiring action which, not operating without man, adapts itself to the mode of his personal activity. But all these activities find their meaning in the accomplishment of the work which is the Bible; the Church believes in *the integral inspiration of Scripture, not in consideration of the literary activity of the writers but in consideration of the books which are the fruit of it.*

II. THE WHOLE BIBLE IS THE WORD OF GOD

Actually tradition has always seen in the holy books and in each of their texts the " Word of God. " This expression has the same force as another one : God is the author of all the Scripture. To make this mean that each word of the sacred book is a revelation of God, each word the object of a dictation of the Holy Spirit, each statement a divine truth, is an exaggeration from which the ancients did not always refrain. Whence an idolatry of the letter ending in the Cabala or, with more discretion but not without some semblance of superstition, in a literal allegorism too prone to make a ciphered book out of the Bible.

The Bible has preserved the vestiges of revealing interventions of God, whether they had been made to a prophet and then recorded in a book, or whether they had been made directly to the sacred writer. The religious truths thus entrusted by God are " the Word of God " in the highest degree. Further, the Word of God is the affirmative judgment, the teaching set forth by the hagiographer under the inspiring light, in a strict sense, for it is to such affirmations and to such teaching that inspiration is ordained by its very nature.

But everything that constitutes within the sacred books the vehicle of this Word of God in the strict sense, its arrangement, its expression, whether this concerns the style of the writer himself or the foreign citations he uses to translate his thought, all this is still the Word of God because it is willed by Him as a way of human expression of His message; this, as we have said, was written under the inspiring (but not revealing) action.

The distinction made by certain theologians between " the Word of God *ratione materiae,* " which we have called the Word of God in the strict sense and " Word of God *ratione consignationis,* " is perhaps not a fortunate one, at least in its expression. It is not by virtue of simple " consignation " into the Book that the literary accompaniment of the divine message is the Word of God, but in virtue of the meaningful expression of this message itself, of the accommodation of this message to the very diverse mentalities, full of nuances, of the readers. The only adequate distinction is the very one which we made above in speaking of the universality of inspiration, which extends to the truths willed by God in themselves, and to their translation willed and inspired in view of their communication to men.

This will be the task of exegesis to distinguish between the message and its coating, between the judgments of God, His teachings and their formulation, between assertions and opinions, counsels, allusions, illustrations of a truth under varying forms, quotations taken in hand or not by the author, all modalities of human language which the human expression of the Word of God did not find unacceptable.

CHAPTER IV

THE INERRANCY OF THE INSPIRED BOOKS

BIBLIOGRAPHY

G. COURTADE, " Inspiration et Inerrance, " *SDB*, IV (1949), cols. 520-559
G. CASTELLINO, *L'inerranza della S. Scrittura** (Turin-Rome, 1949).
A. M. DUBARLE, in *Initiation Theologique*,* I (Paris, 1952), pp. 63-71.
J. SCHILDENBERGER, *Inspiration und Irrtumlosigkeit der Hl. Schrift, Fragen der Theologie heute** (Einsiedeln, 1957), pp. 109-121.
J. FORESTALL, " The Limitation of Inerrancy, " *CBQ*, 20 (1958), pp. 9-18.
P. ZERAFA, " The Limits of Biblical Inerrancy, "* *Angelicum*, 39 (1962), pp. 92-119.

If all of the Bible is inspired, if it is entirely the Word of God, it immediately appears that error cannot be found in it : God can neither deceive nor be deceived. If the reader were exposed to learning error mixed with truth, he could not consider this text as a sure guide and the Church could not propose its Canon as a rule of faith and morals. Nevertheless, this question of inerrancy has greatly troubled people at the end of the last century and at the beginning of this one.

§ 1. The Doctrine

The Magisterium of the Church has never solemnly defined the fact of biblical inerrancy. This is a consequence of inspiration so unavoidable that such definition was never found necessary. Following Judaism in that respect, the Christian Church has constantly expressed its faith in the divine authority of the Scriptures; for any discussion, one practically always had recourse to the argument of Scripture. This was the procedure of Our Lord (Mt 22, 31 f.), that of the apostles (Acts 2, 16 ff.), that of the first Christians and of the Fathers. " You have pored over the Holy Scriptures, the truthful ones, " exclaims St. Clement of Rome (*Ep.* 45, 2). St. Justin does not admit of any contradiction in the Bible (*Dial. Tryph.* 65). St. Hippolytus is even clearer : " We will learn that Scripture cannot deceive us in anything " (*in Danielem* 1, 29). The great doctors of the 4th and 5th centuries hold the same doctrine, whether

St. Basil, St. John Chrysostom or St. Augustine : " That Scripture is truthful, no one but the infidel and the impious denies it, " says the latter (*De Genesi ad litt.* VII, 28, 42).   The statements of St. Jerome, albeit much aware of the difficulties of the text, are just as absolute : " Scripture cannot contradict itself " (*Ep.* XLVI, 6).   In the Middle Ages, St. Thomas Aquinas expresses the common opinion by writing : " We still must hold to this, that everything which holy Scripture contains is true. In other words, whoever would have a contrary opinion would be heretical " (*Quodlib.* XII, art. 26, sol. 1). [1]

Now modern discoveries have multiplied the difficulties which the Fathers had already encountered in regard to this dogma, difficulties of the scientific, historical and moral order.   In order to obviate these difficulties, some have sometimes sought to restrict the extent of canonicity or the scope of inspiration.   Others, such as A. Loisy, have renounced inerrancy and have even prided themselves on " torpedoing the old ironclad ship of biblical inspiration and inerrancy " [2] by the theory of " relative truth. "

Against these disestablishing explanations and the open denials by rationalism and evolutionism, the popes have maintained the doctrine of inerrancy.   In *Providentissimus* Leo XIII affirmed : " Those who think that in the authentic passages of the holy books any false idea can be contained, destroy the Catholic notion of divine inspiration, or make God Himself the author of an error. " [3]   Pius X condemned the modernist errors of A. Loisy.   Benedict XV treated this question in the encyclical *Spiritus Paraclitus.*   Finally at the beginning of the encyclical *Divino Afflante Spiritu,* par. 7, Pius XII wrote : " This doctrine which our predecessor Leo XIII has forcefully expressed, we also propose with our authority in order that it be religiously held by all. " [4]

§ 2. How to Apply the Principle?

We must first recall that only the inspired text enjoys inerrancy. Therefore, it must be determined first of all whether the copyist has not made a mistake.   When the text is a translation, we must be sure that it represents the original well.   The Latin translation in use in our liturgical books of the West, the Vulgate, enjoys a special privilege.   The

---

[1] Some patristic texts have at times been invoked in a contrary sense.   Their true sense can be found in G. COURTADE, *SDB*, IV, 526-527.

[2] Cf. *SDB*, IV, 523.

[3] *EB*, 126.

[4] *Ibid.*, 540.

Council of Trent has declared it " authentic. " But Pius XII has specified that this authenticity is not so much critical as juridical. That means that it is " absolutely exempt from all error in what concerns faith and morals, " but such a privilege is not as broad as that of inerrancy, as we shall see in this section. Finally we might add that the commentaries of the Bible which are, in short, developed translations, and all the interpretations stemming from them, can make mistakes.

Once that is said, we must recall some rules of human language which prevent attributing to the sacred authors errors which they have not committed.

1. Every word can signify several things, and we must be quite precise about what the author wishes to signify by it according to the psychological context in which he puts it. When we say " the sun *rises,* " the expression does not have the same sense at all as in this other phrase : " Napoleon *rises* and makes his plan of battle. " Now the Bible is rendered in a very concrete language in which image-making words abound but can serve to express very different ideas.

2. The statement itself changes in meaning along with the context in which it is inserted. The classic example has been given with reference to Ps 53 (v. 2). We find in Scripture the following affirmation : " There is no God. " Happily the context teaches us that this erroneous opinion is not that of the author, but of the impious. In that case there is what is called an *explicit citation* : the opinion expressed is not to be imputed to the author.

A decree of the Biblical Commission, of February 13, 1905, further admits that there can be *implicit citations* in the Bible. We indeed happen to cite authors without feeling any need to specify that we are citing. But naturally there must be valid reasons to see in the words of an author an implicit citation and not an expressed affirmation on his part : normally a person thinks what he writes. There again, it is the context which permits the question to be settled. These simple examples are sufficient to show that the study of the context is much more necessary than is often believed. Even in a dry demonstration we are obliged to use several phrases in a row which clarify one another. Now the Bible is comprised of things other than demonstrations. It is only by the context that we can truly render an account of what the author wishes to say in each of his phrases and of the import we must attribute to his expressions.

3. All the phrases of the book and all the expressions chosen by the author, as a result, depend on his general line of thought. In order to apply the principle of inerrancy to them, it must be stated quite precisely in what genre of book they figure. A phrase about Napoleon like the

one cited above has an entirely different import depending on whether it figures in a history book, signed by Thiers or Madelin, or in *The Red and the Black* of Stendhal. The import of the phrases, their value for assertion, depends on what is called the *literary genre* of the book itself.

In the last resort, everything depends on the *judgment* borne by the author when he writes the phrase in question. Whence the adage : *truth is in the judgment*. It is not in the word, which does no more than evoke it. It is not in the phrase itself, independently of the general ordering in which the author situates it. In order to understand its exact import we must put ourselves in the perspective in which the author intended to place himself. It is because of their lack of the religious sense proper to biblical authors that many otherwise penetrating minds have sometimes called into question the truth of their judgments. In fact they did not arrive at the plane on which the thought of those authors was moving.

§ 3. The Applications

God has given men an intellect so that they might use it; He did not intend to replace this natural endowment of reason by the supernatural gift of revelation, recorded in Scripture, which would dispense them from any further inquiry. Therefore one must not seek in the Bible *natural* truths about man, the world and even God; for those, it pertains to reason to acquire them painfully by methods proper to science and philosophical reflection. The sacred authors composed their works according to *supernatural* truths, inaccessible in themselves to reason; moreover it has sometimes happened that in so doing they have also thrown in relief certain natural truths necessary to the order of salvation, for example, monotheism. Such a distinction, which seems elementary to us, has not always been clearly apparent, notably in the time of the great controversies which set Catholic apologists in opposition to rationalist thought during the last two centuries. It was then that difficulties of several categories—moral, scientific, historical—were raised, dispelled with great difficulty by an apologetic which let itself be carried off onto the terrain of its adversaries. Let us give some examples.

I. In the moral order

It was especially in the 18th century that the rationalists (Voltaire) emphasized the moral weaknesses recorded by the Bible. They insisted on the " lies " of the patriarchs, on the cruelties of the Jewish conquest,

on the equivocal attitude of Judith with Holofernes.... In most of
these cases it can be established that the author does not approve of the
conduct of the men or women in the fabricated instances. He does not
make saints out of the patriarchs; they are men whom the grace of God
must aid and assist. The strict orders given to Josue are explained
either by human weakness which God must protect against corruption,
or by the literary genre. In spite of the loftiness of the moral principles
which the Bible contains, it is something different from a moral code;
it bears witness to the action of a condescending God who must measure
His action to human weakness (cf. Mt 19, 8). Such is the explanation,
in the last resort, of the moral imperfections which are pointed out in the
biblical heroes. The Bible relates a divine *pedagogy* and a *progressive*
pedagogy. God has taken on men in a lowly intellectual and moral state
so as to lead them up to the Gospel. He has revealed their ideal to them
little by little, and it is not surprising that in the first stages of sacred
history they do not manifest an understanding of the divine laws which
comes up to the level of the Sermon on the Mount. [5]

II. IN THE SCIENTIFIC ORDER

The scientific discoveries of the 19th century have given a world picture
far different from that which the Israelites could have had. Since Galileo,
it has been known that the earth revolves around the sun and not conver-
sely; geology uncovered the stages of creation throughout all their
duration, species appeared to have come successively upon the earth,
and the length of prehistoric times could no longer fit in with the chronological framework of Genesis.

J. Didiot and Msgr. d'Hulst had suggested a solution of the problem
which restricted inerrancy to matters of faith and morals. The
Magisterium rejected this avenue of conciliation. It did not so much
as adopt the " concordism, " which tended to identify the days of Genesis
with the geological periods, and discovered in 2 Pt 3, 5 " the modern
theory which leads the composition of bodies back to hydrogen. " The
concordists were obliged to adapt their commentaries to the evolution of
scientific theories, and " Moses, stubbornly concerned with keeping
himself informed, submissive to the teachers of the moment, changed
his opinion in two editions of the same commentary. " [6]

---

[5] Cf. E. GALBIATI and A. PIAZZA, *Mieux comprendre la Bible,** Fr. tr. (Paris, 1956), pp. 279-302; L. JOHNSTON, " O.T. Morality, " *CBQ* (1958), pp. 19-25.

[6] F. PRAT, *Bible et histoire,** p. 24.

In his encyclical *Providentissimus*, [7] Leo XIII recalled the traditional doctrine. " The Spirit of God who spoke through the sacred writers did not wish to instruct men on these things which are without usefulness for salvation, " said St. Augustine, and Cardinal Baronius echoed him : " Scripture teaches us how to go to heaven and not how the heavens go. " St. Thomas had offered more precise formulae : " Moses ... spoke according to sensible appearances " (I^a Pars, q. 70, art. 1, sol. 3) and in regard to Job (26, 7) : " This is said according to the estimation of the public, as is the custom in Scripture. " Leo XIII resumed this traditional doctrine. The authors use the expressions and images of their times without being preoccupied with correcting the scientific inaccuracies of them : " The ordinary language first and properly expresses what falls under the senses; the sacred writer did not do otherwise, for he too was bound by sensible things, that is to say, by those which God Himself, in speaking to men, had pointed out in a special human manner so as to be understood by them. " The Bible does not produce science and science does not produce theology. No conflict is possible if each remains on its own ground. Even where their two domains clash (for example, in what concerns biblical miracles or the unity of the human species), there is no opposition to fear, provided that the Bible be correctly understood according to the laws of its own language, and science not force the meaning of its positive declarations by setting up systems less founded on facts than demanded by philosophical postulates inimical to revelation.

It follows from this that when biblical writers speak of the vault of the heavens, of the properties of the spleen to cure the eyes and of wine for the stomach, of the hare as ruminating, and of the waters of a fountain coming from a great lower abyss, it is their way to express themselves in speaking of something entirely different from the physical or geological constitution of the world. When they describe creation, they are not concerned with natural history; they are giving a theological definition of man in the organized universe.

III. In the historical order

After discussing the scientific questions and giving the principles summarized above, Leo XIII added : " It will be good to apply these same principles to the related sciences and especially to history. " In fact people began questioning themselves on the reality of certain things which up to this time seemed to follow from the obvious reading of the Bible. These difficulties did not stem any longer from an antireligious

[7] See also *Divino Afflante Spiritu*, par. 6.

prejudice against the Bible (as in the rational criticism of miracles), but from a confrontation between the biblical text and the history of the Near East, such as it could be scientifically reconstituted with the help of Babylonian, Assyrian, and Egyptian documents now dug up and decipherable. Why does the Book of Daniel make Balthazar the son of Nabuchodonosor, when his father was Nabonidus, the fourth successor of this king? Why does the Book of Judith make Nabuchodonosor a king of Assyria, when he doubtless never set foot in Ninive? Why does the Book of Jonas speak of a conversion of Ninive, totally ignored in the cuneiform tablets? Besides, the attentive study of the biblical text itself presented statements scarcely compatible among themselves, if one assumes a historical point of view. Should the conquest be pictured as a series of campaigns of a unified Israel directed by Josue, or as a series of undertakings of distinct tribes, according to the description in the first chapter of Judges? Did the sojourn of the Israelites in Egypt last 430 years (Ex 12, 40), or a little more than four generations (Gn 15, 16)?

For a moment a solution was believed to be found by admitting that the biblical author was speaking about history " according to appearances, " in the same way as he spoke about nature " according to appearances. " In this case the appearances were the traditions or documents which were at his disposal. The facts could then be false, but it didn't matter; the author was speaking according to the current opinions around him. This system, extended to the entire Bible as a principle of general explanation, was rejected by Benedict XV in the encyclical *Spiritus Paraclitus* : " Those who think that the historical parts of Scripture rely not on the absolute truth of facts but on what they call the relative truth, do away with the doctrine of the Church; they have no fear about drawing this conclusion from the very words of Leo XIII, because he said that principles established for the natural sciences could be applied to historical sciences. Therefore they maintain that the hagiographers, having spoken according to appearances in these matters, also reported through ignorance the facts as they appeared according to the popular version or erroneous evidence. " [8]

The disapproval of the system comes from the fact that the Judeo-Christian religion is bound up with history. Scripture is a testimony on the action of God on history; in it, He comes to bring salvation to men and to found His kingdom. If the Bible relied upon nonexistent facts when it retraces *sacred history*, the faith and hope of men would rest in a vacuum.

---

[8] *DB*, col. 2187. Cf. *Divino Afflante Spiritu*, par. 35.

But the essentially *religious* angle under which the Church envisions the facts which she teaches, well indicates the extent of the condemnation of the system of " historical appearances. " The facts reported by the sacred authors are attested by them as truthful in the measure in which they wished to rely upon them to make men grasp the mystery of divine action here below, in the measure in which they are directly linked to the history of salvation. Now this does not exactly cover over the secular or political history of Israel. Certainly, if Moses, David, and the Exile were not historical realities, the holy books would be no more than imagination without consistency. But that the hagiographers were bound to give all the details on every fact in order to hand down their message, is a demand which takes no account of the purpose of their work, and which, moreover, does not correspond to the facts of human psychology. In many cases they could be satisfied with approximations in which details were left quite in the background. It is an approximation of this sort which, for complex reasons, led to calling Balthazar, his successor, the " son of Nabuchodonosor " (Daniel).

We must also guard against wishing to reduce the Bible to a simple history : it records a revelation; it is therefore just as much a religious and theological book as a history, and God owed it to Himself to inspire books other than historical ones. Thus Job has appeared more and more as a book of Wisdom, consecrated to the problem of evil and to the suffering of the innocent, and not as a dialogue historically realized between Job and his friends. The wealth of divine thought is thus expressed in a great variety of writings, and each of them must be interpreted according to the laws of its literary genre.

§ 4. The Literary Genres and the Expression of the Divine Thought

Pope Pius XII, in the encyclical *Divino Afflante Spiritu*, completed the work of his predecessors by forcefully recalling that " in order to express what they had in mind, the eastern people did not always use the forms and manners of speaking that we use today, but much rather the ones whose use was accepted by the men of their times and of their countries " (par. 35). As we pronounce the word *history*, we think of our modern books which strive to reconstruct the past with all the exactness desired. Now this preoccupation was not that of the ancients; among the Assyrians and Egyptians we would find nothing that corresponds to it, in spite of all their culture. In these ancient civilizations, the laws are less a command of a legislator than the solution of concrete difficulties where there was a conflict of interests; morality is less the expression of an absolute than the observation of experience. In regard to literary forms, as an answer from the secretary of the Pontifical Biblical Commission recalled it to Cardinal Suhard apropos of the first eleven chapters of Genesis, " they do not respond to any of our classic categories and cannot be judged in the light of the Greco-Latin or modern literary genres. We cannot deny or affirm their historicity as a whole without unduly applying to them the norms of a literary genre under which they cannot be classified. " [9]

In our times we rank the literary genres into history, novels, legends, poems.... These classifications correspond to our mentality, but the biblical authors had other categories in mind. Their preoccupations were indeed quite different. They had to make understood the action and invisible being of God to very " materialistic " contemporaries. There were annalists of their times to relate the campaigns of the king and like things. They, on the contrary, had to start from the observed facts, national or individual, so as to lead their readers, in suitable images, to discern the action of divine grace. Thus we will necessarily find in them a mixture of real facts and of images intended to give the religious dimensions of these facts. The portion of one or the other will vary along with the end pursued; the literary genre adopted will correspond to each type of teaching. With the sacred author, the theoretical (truth to be grasped) and the practical (literary genre adopted) could not err because of the grace of inspiration. But we must identify his genre before grasping the truth he wishes to express. In the case of the succession of David, the literary genre adopted is very close to what we call history; court dramas and civil wars with the psychological chain of events. In the case of Job, on the contrary, the real idea is the existence of a just man of old, known by popular tradition, and, along with this, the concrete experience of the suffering of the innocent; but the details of the dialogue and even of the prologue are the concern of a writer who wants to render perceptible to the imagination the religious problem he is discussing.

The question of literary genres far surpasses that of the historicity or non-historicity of the holy books. [10] It is possible that difficulties raised by the study of the texts forced to pose the question. But the determining of the literary genres seems to be in our days a prime requisite, not of apologetics, but of understanding the Word of God. If we wish to grasp the judgments of the author and understand his thought (divine

---

[9] See our *Introduction to the Old Testament*, pp. 125 ff.

[10] F. GALBIATI and A. PIAZZA, *Mieux comprendre la Bible,** pp. 32-39.

thought for believers), we must make this inquiry in a very objective manner. " To meet well the actual needs of biblical studies, " further states the encyclical *Divino Afflante*, " let the Catholic exegete, in explaining Sacred Scripture, in proving and defending its absolute inerrancy, use this resource prudently; let him inquire into how the manner of speaking or the literary genre, used by the hagiographer, can lead to the exact interpretation, and let him be convinced that he cannot neglect this part of his task without a great detriment to Catholic exegesis. " [11]   All the literary genres of eastern antiquity may have been used in the Bible " provided that the genre employed is not in any way repugnant to the holiness and truth of God " (par. 37).   Actually there will be less concern in that case with the genre itself than with the way it was used.   It would be quite easy to imagine in our times that God had inspired a novel packed with human and religious truth, such as written by Dostoevski; we could not imagine that He could have inspired a pornographic novel.

Conclusion

From these considerations it follows that the sacred book, inspired by God, communicates divine truth to us, but that we will not discover this truth except by entering fully into the judgments of the sacred writer who was the intelligent instrument of the book whose principal author is God.   Since this book is addressed to men in the manner of men, it can only be understood with all the resources of human intelligence. The theology of inspiration and inerrancy itself demands that we study the methods used for the interpretation of ancient texts, that of textual, literary, and historical criticism.   But since this concerns a text that the Church considers as inspired and has in custody, we will also have to see what rules she gives us to use these methods correctly and arrive at the true meaning of the Bible. [12]

---

[11] *EB*, 560.

[12] On the various aspects of this question, one can also consult J. P. WEISENGOFF, " Inerrancy of the Old Testament in Religious Matters, " *CBQ* (1955), pp. 248-257; J. T. FORESTELL, " The Limitation of Inerrancy, " *CBQ* (1958), pp. 9-18 and the " Tables " of the *DTC*, 5 (1956), cols. 1104-1105 (Paris, 1956).

THE RULES OF RATIONAL CRITICISM

by H. Cazelles and P. Grelot

What then is a book? Let us reflect on this apparent triviality. A book is a discourse that is drafted, read, and copied. Its text is *written* (once engraved, now printed); but one only *reads* if he *understands*. [1] It appears as a collection of written symbols, but it is above all a thought, and the symbols are there to communicate this thought.

Such is the Bible. It is not enough that our eyes distinguish the symbols which make it up; beyond this material reading we must grasp what the biblical authors had in mind, when they put their work down in writing, or when they altered or completed that of their predecessors. Now the reader can often supply in them ideas which they did not have, and project his own opinions into the texts. Such a danger is not imaginary; it even exists when we have before our eyes a contemporary text, written for us in the milieu we live in, according to our immediate needs. What errors are possible in the reading of a simple poster! Now understanding the Bible is an infinitely more delicate task. The very detail of the difficulties to overcome will show us the method to follow in its rational study.

1. Let us resume the example of the poster. The poster is there under my very eyes; its text imposes itself upon me without my willing it. We could not say the same for the biblical text. Of course, the Bible is spread throughout the entire world in millions of copies; but most of these printed texts are only translations. The biblical text is not that text. It is rather the text of the Bibles printed in Hebrew and Greek, which is infinitely less widespread. A rational study demands first a recourse to this original.

2. But are we really dealing with the original? I can speak of an original when I receive a letter. The poster I read in the street is already no longer the text itself written by the author; printing flaws could have slipped into it. Knowledge of the authentic text is even more delicate when the author has long since died, the copies written by his hand are lost, and there is nothing left to correct the errors which copies allow! Now, like all other books of antiquity, the Bible is no longer actually known except through copies of copies. " We never run into an original from Greek and Latin antiquity, " writes Dain. [2] An unusual stroke

---

[1] St. John Chrysostom : " The purpose of our efforts is to make you well understand the meaning and power of the sacred text. " Homily *In genesim* VIII.

[2] A. DAIN, *Les manuscrits*, p. 90.

of luck caused the discovery, in 1952, of two manuscript letters from the leader of the second Jewish revolt against the Romans in 135, [3] but this is not a biblical text. The printed Bibles, since that of Gutenberg (1452-1455), are only copies of manuscripts. The first task of the biblical scholar is to return, beyond the first printed texts, to the oldest and best manuscripts, in order to draw nearer to the original text.

3. Here a new difficulty arises, for variants are ascertained from one manuscript to another. Most often it is only a question of material faults of the copyists, distracted or negligent, or, on the contrary, too zealous. But sometimes the variants are such that we can infer two editions of the same text. Those are the problems with which *textual criticism* is occupied; whence its importance : starting with the manuscripts, it proposes to establish the true texts that the authors intended.

4. This establishing of the text already demands that one have recourse to the skills of the paleographers; one must take into account what the writing was at the time when the author lived and at the following ages during which his work was copied. But there is more. Once he has fulfilled this job of an archivist, the biblical scholar must become a philologist, for he must *study the language* in which the author was writing. There are three biblical languages : Hebrew, Aramaic and Greek. These are three dead languages, for neither the modern Hebrew spoken in Israel nor contemporary Greek are in all points similar to biblical Greek and Hebrew. The syntax and morphology have evolved a great deal, and the vocabulary even more. Thus we must establish the laws of the written language of old, without forgetting that this written language depended on the spoken language and that the ancient languages have changed with the centuries and the milieux.

5. The language itself is rooted in the living context of a psychology. A text, like a discourse, expresses an idea or, at the very least, a state of soul; the words are arranged according to an intellect, a will, a sensibility. Therefore philological research emerges forcibly into what is called *literary criticism*. This is touchy, but inevitable. It obeys two sets of laws. There are the general laws of human psychology. A man who speaks and who writes joins his phrases according to a determined thought. When there are gaps or inconsistencies in the thought, we might imply that it is a matter of two texts that have not been drafted at the same time and for the same purpose. We have no right to attribute incoherent

---

[3] J. T. MILIK, " Une lettre de Siméon bar Kokheba, " *RB* (1953), pp. 276-294. cf. p. 264.

nonsense to the author. But there are also special laws of composition which are related to the milieu and thought patterns. To make himself understood, the author must group his phrases and developments according to certain frameworks demanded by the problems and social customs of the present time in which he is writing. These frameworks, flexible and varied besides, in which the thought must be patterned in order to be understood, are called literary genres. So literary criticism has a double purpose : to determine the *literary units*, and to state precisely their *literary genre*.

6. Such a task places the biblical scholar in the presence of an author and his milieu. This is no more yet than a first approximation in order to situate the text in history. For if the whole text is not necessarily historical by its literary genre, at least it belongs to a moment in history. One can only understand it well if he relives in spirit, with the author and his whole milieu, the circumstances in which it was written. *Historical criticism*, therefore, is indispensable to the study of a text, even when this text communicates eternal truths; its eternal value is recognized only through the present moment when it was thought and written. So we find ourselves obliged to study the social structures of the epoch; there, too, there are found general laws of sociology, but there is also a host of particular and fortuitous circumstances. Only a good acquaintance with eastern societies, with their troubles and their aspirations, can allow the biblical scholar to understand the literary works which were born in this setting. Pushing even further, he will try to determine the author of the text, if not by name (often hard to uncover), at least by his psychology, his reactions, his intentions. Sometimes he will even be able to pin down the date of the composition of the text.

7. The work does not stop there. If criticism wishes to study a work in all its dimensions, it must situate it within the cultural history of entire humanity. A text, whatever it is, inherits a past and prepares a future. It is a witness in one stage of human development; it gives evidence of an event, perhaps of a purely psychological order, through which the profound life of the human species can be discerned. Therefore, through ancient, it has a lasting value; it is not just a dead thing to us. We know only too well how our present depends on our past, and how, therefore, this past conditions our future to some extent. A human text, no matter what the century, only takes on its full meaning when it reveals in total objectivity a law, an orientation, or a possibility of the human life. Such is the perspective in which biblical criticism must finally be placed.

CHAPTER I

THE TEXT OF THE BIBLE

A. The Manuscripts of the Old Testament

§ 1. The Building Up of the Collection of Books

BIBLIOGRAPHY

A. M. HONEYMAN, " Semitic Epigraphy and Hebrew Philology, " *OTMS*, pp. 264-282.

J. KENNEDY, *An Aid to the Textual Criticism of the Old Testament* (Edinburgh, 1928).

D. DIRINGER, *Le iscrizioni antiche-ebraiche palestinesi* (Florence, 1934).

B. J. ROBERTS, *The Old Testament Text and Versions* (Cardiff, 1951); " Text, Old Testament, " *IDB*, IV, pp. 580-594.

S. MOSCATI, *L'epigrafia ebraica antica* (Rome, 1951).

I. J. GELB, *A Study of Writing* (Chicago, 1952) (also paperback, 1963).

G. R. DRIVER, *Semitic Writing*[2] (London, 1954).

E. WÜRTHEIN, *The Text of the Old Testament* (London : Blackwell, 1957).

F. G. KENYON, *Our Bible and the Ancient MSS* (London, 1958).

M. COHEN, *La grande invention de l'écriture* (Paris, 1958).

J. FÉVRIER, *Histoire de l'écriture*[2] (Paris, 1959).

When one wishes to study a text, the first task is to assemble the witnesses to that text; then it becomes necessary to classify them. For the Bible, this undertaking is more difficult than for the profane texts of the ancient Greco-Roman world; we have many more manuscripts, and older ones, of the biblical books than we have of the ancient historians, the tragedians, or even Homer. By contrast with Egyptian or Assyro-Babylonian literature, on the other hand, the Israelite texts are both fewer and more recent. The Bible has its setting where these two cultural spheres of ancient times meet; hence it will be useful to review its composition and the transmission of its text against that background, taking particular note of the way in which the art of writing developed.

The Near East was far in advance of other cultural centers in its use of writing. Chinese writing, for example, is known to us only from the end of the second millennium B.C., though its origins are certainly older than that. [1] But both Egypt and Sumer had established systems of writing by B.C. 3000, and Minoan Crete by B.C. 2500 at the latest. The early scripts of Sumer and Egypt, [2] which have been deciphered and again read in modern times, are cumbersome and unwieldy; they include a multiplicity of signs: word-signs of pictographic origin, and syllabic signs often with more than one possible value. Their complexity made them the preserve of a caste of professional scribes.

A decisive forward step was made by those northwestern Semites at the crossroads of the three great Near Eastern civilizations who, in the middle of the second millennium B.C., invented the alphabet. The first traces we have of it are the inscriptions incised in stone in archaic characters, presumed to be alphabetic, by the Semitic-speaking workers employed in the Egyptian mines at Sinai. These " proto-Sinaitic " inscriptions have been variously dated between B.C. 1850 and B.C. 1500. [3] Well on in the 14th century B.C., the kings of the various Chanaanite city-states were still using the cuneiform syllabary for their correspondence (the Tell el-Amarna tablets) with Pharao, their overlord. But this was based on the persistence of diplomatic custom, for it is virtually certain that an alphabet derived from that known at Sinai, and which in turn is the ancestor of all the later scripts of the West and of India, was already in use on the Phoenician coast in the 15th century B.C. The Greek alphabet broke off from it in about the 9th century B.C.

Of some thirty consonantal signs that allowed for indicating (with a certain indifference to the vowels) the full range of phonemes into which the syllables could be broken down, the Phoenician system finally kept 22; this script had already penetrated into the south of Palestine by the 11th century B.C. (arrowheads from el-Hadr, near Bethlehem). Parallel to this, another derivative of the proto-Sinaitic script with a larger complement of individual letters was borne along the desert trade-routes to southern Arabia at about the same time. Lastly, at Ugarit, near Lattakia in modern Syria, local scribes of the 15th—14th centuries B.C., accustomed

---

[1] J. FÉVRIER, *Histoire de l'écriture* (Paris, 1948,) p. 69.

[2] See plate 8 (Fr. ed.)

[3] The earlier date is still maintained by A. GARDINER in *Journ. Eg. Archaeol.*, 48 (1962), pp. 43 ff.; these same quasi-pictographic characters persisted until the 13th-century, however, at Lachish in Juda and at Hasor in Galilee. For a 15th century discovery, also from Lachish, that argues for a more recent origin of the script, see F. M. CROSS in *Harvard Theol. Review*, 55 (1962), p. 239. W. F. ALBRIGHT (*BASOR*, 110 [1948], pp. 6-22) and CROSS (*BASOR*, 160 [1960], pp. 21-26) hold for about B.C. 1500 at Sinai, and " the end of the Middle Bronze age " for the origin of the script.

to the use of clay tablets, adapted the alphabetic principle for use on that material, imitating the Phoenician system. Several abecedary tablets from that site attest to the letters of the alphabet in the order still familiar to us today, though with a certain number of supplementary signs (30 in all). [4]

Practically all of the texts written in Chanaan before the days of the Israelite kingdoms were on perishable materials, and have disappeared. Many compositions, besides, were handed down only by word of mouth, as in the case of the war poems of the period of the Conquest, of which some traces are still to be found in the Bible   The tablets from Ras Shamra (Ugarit), however, and some Phoenician inscriptions such as that of Ahiram, give us an idea of the orthography of texts in this early period, of the arrangement of certain classes of text (*v.g.*, lists; compare Jgs 8, 14), and even of the formulation of certain compositions prepared for recording on ʋtone.   Albright, Cross and Freedman have made vigorous efforts to recover from such sources the primitive characteristics of the oldest biblical texts. [5]   This is the cultural milieu for the work of Moses, and for the religious life of Israel in the period of the Judges; but for lack of documents, one can hardly be more specific.

From the period of the monarchy (10th—6th centuries B.C.), we have still no actual biblical text, but we do have certain Israelite writings and inscriptions. [6]   There is the " agricultural calendar " of the tenth century, found on a slab of stone at Gezer.   There are the dockets or reports from Samaria at the end of the 9th, or in the 8th, century.   Then there is the Siloe tunnel inscription, by the diggers of that aqueduct (end of the 8th century), and the palimpsest [7] papyrus document of the same period found at Murabbaat in Judea.   There are the petition and other texts recently recovered, on potsherds *(ostraca)*, from Yabneh-by-the-Sea and Tell Arad; and others written on the same material by Jewish military personnel at the time of the seizure of Lachish by Nabuchodonosor, at the beginning of the 6th century.   To these should be added the

---

[4] The principal styles of writing from the ancient Near East which are of value for illustrating the Bible and its transmission may be seen reproduced in J. B. PRITCHARD, *ANEP* (Princeton, 1954); ID., *The Ancient Near East: an Anthology of Texts and Pictures* (Princeton, 1958), illustrations, pp. 51-83; D. J. WISEMAN, *Illustrations from Biblical Archaeology* (London and Grand Rapids, 1958).

[5] F. M. CROSS and D. N. FREEDMAN, *Early Hebrew Orthography* (New Haven,

[6] *DB Suppl., IV*, pp. 409 ff.; T. C. VRIEZEN and S. HOSPERS, *Palestine Inscriptions* (Leyden, 1951).

[7] A palimpsest is a manuscript whose earliest text has been more or less effectively obliterated, and a new one written in its stead on the same surface.

Moabite stone, recounting the conflict of King Mesha (9th century) with Israel; and the letter on papyrus, recovered at Sakkara in Egypt, sent by a prince from the Palestinian coast to Pharao at the end of the 7th century B.C. in the face of the Babylonian threat. From these one can gather an idea of the manner in which the writings of the 8th and 7th century prophets were set down. [8]

The Sakkara papyrus already shows an abandonment of the old Phoenician script (plate 5). An Aramean script derived from the older one tends to replace it along the Mediterranean coast, where international influences are strongly felt. Both Jews and Egyptians call this an Assyrian script, since it comes to them from Mesopotamia; and in fact, it has been documented from Assyria itself in the mid-7th century, on a large ostracon written in Aramaic. This same script appears again in numerous Aramaic documents (papyri and ostraca) left by the Jewish colony at Elephantine from the end of the 6th down through the 5th century B.C. [9] Fourth century documents in the same script have recently been recovered from the Wadi Daliyed in Palestine; they originated in the city of Samaria. From these facts one can reasonably infer that the Aramaic script was used after the Exile for the writing down of a number of biblical books composed in that period, and for the copying of the older books; but we have no actual example of a biblical text from this period either. Though it ceased to be the script of everyday, the older Phoenician script by no means vanished from the scene. It persisted among the Samaritans, separated from the Jews most of the time from the 4th century B.C. onwards; much later, they made of a developed form of it the standard script for copying the Mosaic books, though their actual manuscripts now preserved are all medieval or later. The Jews, too, kept this script alive for certain purposes down into the following period.

§ 2. At the Turn of the Christian Era

About the 2nd century B.C. a further transformation took place. The Aramaic script employed by the Jews of Palestine took on definite local

---

[8] J. NAVEH, " A Hebrew Letter from the Seventh Century B.C., " *Israel Explor. Journal* 10 (1960), pp. 129-139; " More Hebrew Inscriptions, " *ibid.* 12 (1962), pp. 27-32; A. DUPONT-SOMMER, " Un papyrus araméen d'époque sainte... " *Semitica* I (1948), pp. 43-68.

[9] The bulk of these materials is to be found in A. COWLEY, *Aramaic Papyri of the Fifth century B.C.* (Oxford, 1923); E. G. KRAELING, *The Brooklyn Museum Aramaic Papyri* (New Haven, 1953); G. R. DRIVER, *Aramaic Documents* [2] (abridged ed.) (Oxford, 1957).

characteristics which paved the way for what is known as the square-letter script—a name specially appropriate if one has in mind texts carved on stone, such as the name of Tobias on the rock face at his stronghold of Araq el-Emir in Transjordan, or the printed text of our Hebrew Bibles. This square characteristic is far less developed in the manuscripts found since 1947 in association with Khirbet Qumran, near the Dead Sea, which range in time from the late 3rd century B.C. down to about A.D. 68 [10]; nor is it to be found conspicuously in the Nash papyrus of the Decalogue, of about the mid-2nd century B.C.

Despite the considerable furor of controversy when they were first discovered, the Qumran texts are now definitively established as coming from the period we are discussing. Among the archeological data furnished by the excavation at the site are included evidence of a room used for scribal purposes, with plaster-finished writing tables and a pair of inkwells, one of bronze, the other of pottery.

Biblical materials from this source are written on prepared skins, first ruled for the transcribing of the text in columns, and ultimately sewed together into scrolls. The columns of writings of the large Isaias scroll (1QIs[a]) [11] vary between 4 ½ and 6 ½ inches in width, and have approximately thirty lines to the column. The individual letters are suspended, as it were, from the ruled lines previously traced with a dry point. There are erasures, corrections, and also additions above the line, a number of which are by later hands and give evidence of " critical " rereading, such as is indicated also by dots above or below certain letters to cancel them from the text. To represent some of the vowels, the letters *y, w, aleph* and *h* are inserted into the consonantal text, to be read as *i, o* or *u, e* and *a* respectively, in most cases. These pseudo-consonantal " mothers of the reading " *(matres lectionis)* are employed rather lavishly in a part, only, of the Qumran manuscripts, and the system of reading aids which they present seems to be of Aramaic origin. Ligatures in the script are not uncommon, but are still by no means as frequent here as in the contemporary inscriptions of the Nabateans (Arab speakers whose epigraphic texts, however, are in Aramaic). Certain scrolls at Qumran, mainly but not exclusively copies of the Pentateuchal books, are written still in the archaic Phoenician script, comparable to that on the coinage

---

[10] F. M. CROSS, " The Development of the Jewish Scripts, " *The Bible and the Ancient Near East*, ed. G. E. WRIGHT (New York : Doubleday, 1961), pp. 133-202; J. T. MILIK, *Ten Years of Discovery in the Wilderness of Judaea* (London and Naperville, Ill., 1959), pp. 133-136; F. M. CROSS, *The Ancient Library of Qumran*[2] (New York : Anchor Books, 1961), pp. 117-122 and *passim*.

[11] See plate 1.

of the Asmoneans from the days of John Hyrcanus to the end of the
dynasty (135-37 B.C.).   Texts of the Herodian period and the
1st century A.D. employ Phoenician letters for the writing of divine
names (El, Elohim, Yahweh, etc.) both for biblical and non-biblical
passages otherwise copied in the normal square-letter script.   Biblical
books comprise roughly one-quarter of the manuscripts known to us from
Qumran; the bulk of the non-biblical material is religious in character,
including compositions proper to the sectarian group, though there are
also graffiti on pottery, practice alphabets, etc.

Nearly all the Old Testament books have been identified at Qumran
(exceptions : Esther, Judith, Wisdom, Baruch 1-5, Machabees, the
additions to Daniel), though sometimes from fragments of quite limited
size. [12]   There is no question, of course, of the Bible as one book; the
various books formed a series of scrolls, written on one side only, often
with a blank column or more at the conclusion of the text to serve as a
protective covering.   Though the standard practice (cf. Lk 4, 20) may
have been to roll up the text with its concluding portion at the outside,
the actual documents as found are sometimes better preserved toward
the end, and sometimes toward the beginning, of the text.   When rolled
up, sometimes wrapped in linen, they might be deposited for safekeeping
in a cylindrical jar large enough to hold a number of them.   At this time,
a clear-cut Old Testament canon was perhaps not so firmly established
to the exclusion of other literature as later on; the rabbis of Palestine
made their definitive selection of the scriptural canon they would recognize at the end of the 1st century A.D.   However, the three principal
categories of sacred books, the Law, the Former and Latter Prophets, [13]
and the Writings (or Hagiographa) had already become traditional by
the 2nd century B.C. (see the Prologue to Sirach, and Lk 24, 44).   It will
therefore be convenient to use this classification in making a rapid
inventory of the biblical manuscripts found at Qumran.   The totals
given will be for the eleven separate caves in which manuscripts had been
found by February 1956; but manuscripts from the 2nd century A.D.

---

[12] Summaries in *RB*, 63 (1956), pp. 49-67 (translated in *Bibl. Arch.* 19 [1956],
pp. 76-96); also in P. W. SKEHAN, " The Qumran Manuscripts and Textual
Criticism, " *VT Suppl.* IV (Leyden, 1957), pp. 148-158, and in the books of MILIK
(Ten Years) and CROSS *(Ancient Library)* cited above, n. 10.   But what is given
in the text above, subsequent to the publication of *Discoveries in the Judaean Desert
III : Les petites grottes de Qumran*, ed. M. BAILLET, J. T. MILIK, R. DE VAUX,
2 Vols. (Oxford, 1962), is statistically more precise regarding the total number
of published and unpublished biblical manuscripts from caves 1 to 11 inclusive
(166 in all).

[13] See *above*, p. 7.

sites (Murabbaat, etc.) will not be included, nor will the various phylacteries and mezuzas that contain passages from the Mosaic books.

Of the books of the Law, Genesis is to be found in 15 manuscripts
(2 of these in paleo-hebrew, and 1 which may have included Ex by the
same scribe); Exodus, also in 15 copies (2 of them in the old script;
plus the copy of Ex that continues Gn by the same hand). Leviticus
occurs in 8 manuscripts, 4 in the ordinary script, from cave 4 (one combined with Nm), and a copy each in the paleo-hebrew script from caves 1,
2, 6, 11. There are 4 manuscripts of Numbers (plus the copy in a hand
that transcribed also Lv). Deuteronomy is the most frequently attested
biblical book, with 25 copies (2 in the old script), plus 1 text of the song
in Dt 32 written separately. One of the paleo-hebrew Exodus manuscripts
is the recension of the text preserved in later times exclusively by the
Samaritans. Besides these original texts, there are also a midrashic
paraphrase of Gn in Aramaic that mixes elaborated stories with quite
close renderings, a bit of a targum of Lv, a commentary in Hebrew on
Gn 49, and parts of two LXX manuscripts of Lv and one each of Ex
and Nm. It should perhaps be emphasized again that the amount of
text preserved in most cases is relatively small—sometimes barely
enough to make the identification certain; and this is true for all parts
of the OT.

Among the " Former Prophets, " there are present fragments
from 2 manuscripts of Jos, 3 of Jgs, 4 of Sm, and 3 of Kgs. The " Latter
Prophets " are better represented : 1 complete manuscript of Isaias,
and 11 fragmentary ones, along with bits of several commentaries on the
book; 4 manuscripts of Jeremias, one of them in the short recension
known up to now only from the LXX translation; 6 of Ezechiel; and
8 of the Minor Prophets, for some of which again partial commentaries
exist.

The evidence is thinner for some, though not all, of the Hagiographa.
Of psalm manuscripts, there are 18, plus 3 of psalm 119 that may not
have contained other psalms. There are 3 manuscripts of Job, plus a
fourth in the archaic script (!). Of Proverbs, there are 2 manuscripts;
of Ruth, of Canticles, and of Lamentations, 4 each; of Ecclesiastes, 2;
of Daniel, 8; of Esdras, Paralipomenon, and Sirach, one each. The
" Letter of Jeremias " (Bar. 6, *Vulg.*) is present in one Greek fragment;
there are 3 Aramaic, and 1 Hebrew, copies of Tobias. Of all the Hebrew
texts, only one manuscript of Daniel and one of Kings are on papyrus
(and a bit of Isaias, perhaps from a commentary, not counted); the
Greek texts, and the Aramaic of Tb, appear both on papyrus and on
leather. Of the later Jewish canon, only Esther is missing; and Sir,

Letter of Jer, and Tb go beyond that canon. The Aramaic of Tobias appears to be the hitherto lost original form of the text.

Despite the very fragmentary character of these manuscripts, which makes it difficult to form an idea of the state of the text of complete books other than Isaias (after which Ex, Nm, Sm, Ps are best represented), one can still appreciate from them the circumstances of copying and transmission of the Old Testament in the period before the destruction of the Temple. This does not give us a direct insight into the procedures of learned and scribed groups elsewhere in Judaism, and in particular among the Pharisees; but the comparison of these Qumran texts with the texts from the period of the second Jewish revolt under Bar Kosiba (Bar Kochba) can be very instructive for identifying the techniques by which, in the course of time (see *below*), the manuscript tradition was fixed *ne varietur*. Qumran itself was destroyed and abandoned before A.D. 70; in the following periods Judaism reorganized its communal life and intensified its efforts to transmit the books of a fixed canon with ever greater safeguards for their exact preservation and understanding.

§ 3. From the Ruin of the Temple to the Massoretes

BIBLIOGRAPHY

S. A. BIRNBAUM, *The Hebrew Scripts :* II. The Plates (London, 1954-1957).

B. J. ROBERTS, *The Old Testament Text and Versions* (Cardiff, 1951).

E. WÜRTHWEIN, *The Text of the Old Testament* (Oxford, 1957).

P. KAHLE, *The Cairo Genizah*[2] (Oxford, 1959).

F. KENYON, *Our Bible and the Ancient Manuscripts*[5] (London, 1958).

M. GREENBERG, " The Stabilization of the Text of the Hebrew Bible, Reviewed in the Light of the Biblical Materials from the Judaean Desert, " *Journ. Amer. Orient. Soc.* 76 (1956), pp. 157-167.

Texts : Annual of the Hebrew University Bible Project, I (Jerusalem, 1960—).

With the destruction of the Temple and the end of its priesthood, the Bible becomes the one source for later Judaism that has unquestioned authority. A succession of rabbinical " doctors of the Law " (Hillel, Ishmael, Eliezer, Akiba) were concerned with providing more and more exact norms *(middōt)* for its interpretation, while a parallel work of collating and recording oral traditions led on the one hand to the legal compilations, the Mishna and the Tosephta, and on the other to the earliest collections of *midrashim*, mainly edifying stories that shed an indirect light on the biblical books. But for a unity of faith and discipline, it was especially necessary under these conditions to be able to refer to a definitive text. The recensional variants and the carelessness and inexactitude of private copies, still evident in the texts from Qumran, had to be suppressed. While the process of compiling oral laws and homiletic materials went on in the academic centers of Galilee and Mesopotamia for centuries after the extinction of Jewish national life in Judea with the Second (Bar Kochba) Revolt in A.D. 135, it is becoming increasingly clear that the standardization of the Bible text and of the norms for its transmission was already an accomplished fact, in all essentials, well before that same date.

The evidence for this fixing of the consonantal text between the two revolts, presumably in connection with the meeting at Yabneh (Jamnia) which determined the Jewish canon toward the close of the 1st century, is not as copious as that for the preceding period, but it is still noteworthy. From two series of caves in the Judean desert, in the Wadi Murabbaat in Jordan, and in the Wadi Khabra just inside the Israeli occupation border, have come fragments of Gn, Ex, Nm by one scribe; of another copy of Gn, three more of Nm, two of Dt, and one each of Ps, Is, and the Minor Prophets. [14] Making limited allowances for the Psalm manuscript, which seems to come from the second half of the 1st century A.D., all these texts present a fixity of script, of format, of orthography and of content which argues for the existence of a definitive standard by which their production was guided. To be expected, perhaps, for the books of the Law and of Isaias, the definitive character of this text is most notable in the case of the Minor Prophets, of which very substantial portions are preserved in the Murabbaat manuscript, with

---

[14] There are also, as for the previous period, phylacteries (passages from the Law transcribed to be worn in a small leather container on the forehead or the wrist) and mezuzas (similar excerpts to be attached to doorposts) among these 2nd-century finds—once again, with a notably standardized text. A singular Palestinian recension of the Minor Prophets in Greek (the LXX brought closer to the normal Hebrew text), dating from the first century A.D., is another feature of these discoveries, and a part of the cumulating evidence for " critical " study of the Bible text both in Hebrew and in Greek at an early date. See the article of M. GREENBERG referred to above, p. 77; also *Discoveries in the Judaean Desert II : Les grottes de Muraba'ât*, ed. P. BENOIT, J. T. MILIK, R. DE VAUX, 2 Vols. (Oxford, 1961); J. T. MILIK, " Le travail d'édition des manuscrits du Désert de Juda, " *VT Suppl.*, IV, *Volume du Congrès, Strasbourg 1956* (Leyden, 1957), pp. 17-26; Y. YADIN, " New Discoveries in the Judaean Desert, " *BA*, 24 (1961), pp. 34-50, 86-95; *Israel Explor. Journal* 11 (1961), pp. 40, 78, 81; *Yedi'ōt* 26 (1962), p. 206; D. BARTHÉLEMY, *RB*, 60 (1953), pp. 18-29; B. LIFSHITZ in *Yedi'ōt*, 26 (1962), pp. 183-189.

only three meaningful variants and only one of these notable (though not an improvement), from the received text in our printed Bibles. How this work of standardization was accomplished, we do not know at all well. The Talmud describes a process of collation dependent on three manuscripts preserved in the Temple, from which the text was established by conforming always to the reading on which at least two of the three agreed. While this is suggestive, and might have some application especially for texts of the Law, it is in general more likely that the authority of particular scholars, rather than a numerical majority of manuscripts, was the determining factor. The process was a convergent one, in which not all variations in detail were finally excluded for all books of the Old Testament; but the work was thorough, and though in certain books the choices made leave something to be desired, in general, from the critical point of view, it must be adjudged a success.

In addition to a remarkable series of documents touching on family life, real estate, and military orders left in the desert caves by refugees of the Bar Kochba revolt, and the biblical texts mentioned above, there are a variety of Hebrew and Samaritan inscriptions (funerary, from synagogues, etc.) known from the following period. At Dura-Europos on the Euphrates were found liturgical fragments including some biblical verses, dating to the first half of the 3rd century. The papyri from Oxyrrhynchus in Egypt include some Hebrew texts of the 4th or 5th century, but not biblical ones. The oldest materials recovered from the Geniza (a storeroom or repository for discarded texts of a sacred character : biblical texts, and others containing the divine Name written in Hebrew) of the synagogue in Old Cairo date from the 7th or 8th century. The two collections of material gathered by Firkowitsch a century ago in the Crimea certainly contain early texts, now in Leningrad : though Harkavy justly cast suspicion on the colophons (appendices to the text, naming the copyist and dating his work) as having been tampered with or forged. An indirect witness to the extent of standardization of the text comes from its various translations, which will be discussed later. A number of these can be dated rather closely : and " the more recent they are, the closer they come to the Hebrew text we have. "[15] We may call to mind the second column of the Hexapla of Origen, which gave the Hebrew text in Greek transliteration, before A.D. 240 (see *below*, the section on the Greek versions and the work of Origen).

The scribes who transmitted the text between the 3rd and the 6th centuries A.D. handed on, in addition to the consonants themselves,

---

[15] P. CHEMINANT, *Précis d'introduction à la lecture et à l'étude des saintes Ecritures,* II (Paris, 1940), p. 50.

a few critical markings the function of which is not always clear to us, and some of which are already employed in the texts from Qumran. There are, for example, the dotted letters *(neqûdôt)* of certain words or phrases : ten in the Pentateuch, and five elsewhere in the Bible; the function of the dots is to cancel (according to the tradition which imposed them) the letters over which they stand. The inverted letters *nun* in Nm 10, 35-36 and in several passages in the Psalms are of a similar character, serving like our square brackets. When the orthography of words in the text went against the normal practice, these same scribes listed the more usual forms as *sebîrîm*, the unexpected. They proposed alternative readings or scribal corrections *(tiqqûnê sôferîm)* for some eighteen passages of which the received wording appeared to them strange, sometimes on theological grounds. The verse divisions and the paragraphing for liturgical and other purposes became stabilized during this period, with spacings between sections marked off by the letters *pe* for longer, and *samekh* for shorter, units. In the Qumran texts the paragraphing shows, on the other hand, the same freedom and inconsistency as does the wording itself.

This work of transmission by the scribes was succeeded, from about the 6th century, by the work of the Massoretes, or " men of tradition ", who set themselves to reduce to writing a large body of detailed information relating to the text that had thus far been developed and transmitted orally. They belonged to a variety of schools : the Eastern Massoretes, with centers such as Sura and Pumbeditha in Mesopotamia; and the Western or Palestinian Massoretes, of whom two families, Ben Nephthali and Ben Asher, achieved exceptional prominence, with the Ben Asher tradition finally preempting the field.

The Massoretes thought it necessary to provide special signs to indicate the *vocalization* of the text. The oral tradition in this regard before their time had been eked out very inadequately by the *matres lectionis*, of which the standard consonantal text made rather limited use. For use with Syriac, a set of diacritical points to indicate special features of pronunciation of consonants and vowels had taken its rise as early as the beginning of the 4th century, and had developed into a system thereafter; it is exemplified in a manuscript of A.D. 411. [16] Other systems succeeded this one, on into the 7th century; notably the use of small Greek vowel-letters above and below the consonantal text. The first attempts at creating a vowel system to accompany Hebrew texts seem to be of 7th-century date. It is possible that the fixed redaction

---

[16] J. B. SEGAL, *The Diacritic Points and the Accent in Syriac* (Oxford, 1953).

of the Koran (though at first without vowels) in the edition of the Caliph Othman may have hastened the process of defining in written form the pronunciation of the biblical text among the Jews.

Of vowel systems, the Eastern Massoretes experimented with several. The first was a " simple " system derived from the Nestorian Syriac arrangement; it allowed for six vowels written, as usual in these Eastern systems, above the line of consonants (hence, " supralinear "); the consonants themselves were written with intervals between them. In the 8th century, under the influence of the Karaite sect (a Jewish group acknowledging the Scriptures but repudiating Talmudic tradition), they adopted a new supralinear system, more complex. This involved the use of tiny Hebrew consonants to represent certain vowels, with dots used for others. The first manuscript with an Eastern vocalization studied by modern scholars came from the Yemen; the major portion of it was acquired by the Prussian State Library of Berlin in 1878, while 7 stray leaves of it are in New York. But the discovery of the Cairo Geniza furnished more ample materials, and made possible the researches of Paul Kahle. [17] The prolegomena to the Kittel-Kahle *Biblia hebraica*[3] give a detailed listing of the numerous extant portions of Eastern manuscripts now dispersed in Cambridge, Oxford, Budapest, Berlin, Leningrad and New York. The Leningrad manuscript of the Prophets, originally transcribed in A.D. 916, has been furnished with a supralinear vocalization : but it is one accommodated to the Western (Tiberian) standards. Students of Kahle, including A. Diez-Macho, are continuing to work with these materials, which call for a good deal of further study.

The activities of Western Massoretes ran parallel with those in the East. Kahle [18] distinguishes three systems of vocalization used in Palestine; for these the evidence from the Cairo discoveries is much smaller in quantity. Some additional texts of this type have lately been identified by Diez-Macho in New York and in Strasbourg. It was seemingly once more a Karaite impulse which led to the development, beginning in the 8th century out of an existing Palestinian system, of the vocalization which became standard after reaching its final form with the scholars of Tiberias in the early 10th century A.D. This system allows for seven different vowel qualities marked by a variety of dots beneath the consonants of the text (except for *ô*, represented by a dot

---

[17] P. KAHLE, *Masoreten des Ostens* (Leipzig, 1913); A. DIEZ-MACHO, " Nuevos manuscritos biblicos babilónicos, " *Estudios Biblicos*, 16 (1957), pp. 235-277.

[18] *Masoreten des Westens*, I-II (Stuttgart, 1927-1930); " The Massoretic Text of the Bible and the Pronunciation of Hebrew, " *Journal of Jewish Studies*, 7 (1956), pp. 133-154.

above and to the left of the consonant it follows, and *û*, written as a dot within the *mater lectionis*, when a *w* is present for that purpose). This notation combines with the existing *matres lectionis w, y* and *h* already present in the text for the representation of long vowels. There are also special signs for three different extra-short vowels, and for an extremely reduced vowel of obscure quality.

To this provision of a vowel system, the Massoretes added other helps for the reading of the text. They provided indications for the hard or soft pronunciation, and for the doubling in pronunciation, of certain consonants. They also standardized the recitation of the text by furnishing a system of cantillation marks or accents that determine, among other things, whether a word is to be joined with (conjunctive accents), or separately phrased from (disjunctive accents) the word that follows it. A distinct " poetic " system of accents governs the reading of Ps, Prv, Jb. When the traditional manner of reading the text called for a departure from the written consonants as they stand, the Massoretes noted that what was to be read (the *Qerê*) was different from what was written (the *Ketîb*).

A whole series of varied observations were recorded in the margins. To the right of each column of text was placed the " smaller Massora "; it indicates such things as the uniqueness of a word in the Bible, its frequency of occurrence if it is rare, whether or not an optional *mater lectionis* is actually used in writing a word on a given occurrence of it, how many verses in the Bible begin with the identical phrase that begins the verse being annotated, etc., etc. On the outer margins of the text the " larger Massora " is disposed : it takes note of words that recur in identical or similar pairs, parallel passages, variations in accent on identical phrases, etc. At the end of a book, the " final Massora " gives the total of its number of verses, and the like.

This same technique was applied with slight divergence in their traditions of pronunciation by the two families Ben Asher and Ben Nephthali; the phrase " in Israel, " for example, was pronounced *beyisrael* by the one group, *bísrael* by the other. Manuscripts authentically reflecting the Ben Nephthali tradition are scarce; and Kahle's classification of such materials as exist has lately been called into question : much of the work commonly associated with Ben Nephthali is alleged by Diez-Macho and others to be older in its origins than hitherto supposed, and to be an outgrowth of the older Palestinian vowel system antedating the developed Tiberian.[19] Such a codex is the *codex Reuchlinianus*, written

---

[19] A. DIEZ-MACHO, " A New List of So-called ' Ben Naftali ' Manuscripts..., " *Hebrew and Semitic Studies presented to G. R. Driver* (Oxford, 1963), pp. 16-52.

in A.D. 1105, once owned by the famous humanist Reuchlin, and now preserved at Karlsruhe. [20] The work of the Ben Asher family is easier to trace, and five generations of its scholars are known. Thus the oldest complete manuscript of the Prophets now extant was the work of Moses ben Asher, who wrote out its text in A.D. 895; it is currently preserved in the Karaite synagogue of Cairo. None of the Massoretic manuscripts is a scroll, after the ancient manner; they are codices with leaves folded, stitched, and with text on both sides, like our modern books. The scroll form, with the consonantal text alone, is henceforth associated all but exclusively with liturgical use.

The oldest complete text of the Bible, and at the same time the most strictly authentic representative of the Ben Asher tradition in its definitive form, was the codex preserved up to a few years ago in the synagogue of the Sefardic Jews (i.e., Jews with ancestry from Spain or Portugal) in Aleppo; it was written originally, vowels and all, before A.D. 950. So jealously guarded (though a photograph of one page had been printed in 1887) that even Jewish scholars such as the late M.D. Cassuto could have brief access to it only with the greatest difficulty, it was thought for a time to have been destroyed altogether during rioting in Aleppo in 1947. More recently, it has been announced that this codex, sadly truncated and damaged, has passed into Israeli hands, and is to become a basic source for a Bible publication project centering at the Hebrew University. [21] In default of this witness, the much used Kittel-Kahle *Biblia hebraica* has been based on the Leningrad codex B19a, written in A.D. 1008; the argument for identifying this codex, in its present, corrected form with the Ben Asher tradition is indirect, but adequate, and has been outlined several times by Kahle, notably in the prefatory material to the edition itself (many printings since 1937). Another notable codex, limited to the Pentateuch, is the British Museum MS. Or. 4445 (Gn 39, 20—Dt 1, 33); its massora cites Ben Asher as an authority, and Kahle ascribes the entire manuscript to the lifetime of Aaron ben Mosheh ben Asher in the 10th century (C.D. Ginsburg had supposed the consonantal text a century older than the vowels). The second Firkowitsch collection, now in Leningrad, has 3 Pentateuch manuscripts, 2 of the Prophets, and 1 of the Hagiographa, going back to the 10th century. From the 11th century onwards, the extant manuscripts are more numerous. Only after the Renaissance and the establishment of a received text by the work of Jacob ben Chayyim for the second Rabbinic Bible, published by D. Bomberg in Venice,

---

[20] Facsimile edition (Copenhagen, 1946).

[21] See *above* the *Textus* volume in the bibliography; *CBQ*, 23 (1961), pp. 70-71.

A.D. 1524-5, did the systematic classification of the medieval manuscripts begin. Certain highly esteemed texts, such as the *codex Severi*, known from a medieval list, and the codex of Rabbi Hillel ben Mosheh, said to have been written about A.D. 600, are no longer extant. In the 18th century, B. Kennicott saw to the collation of over 600 manuscripts and editions; G. Bernardo de Rossi, of more than 800 additional manuscripts and still other editions. When, in 1908, C.D. Ginsburg completed a new collation, mainly of British Museum manuscripts, he observed that the variants from the Ben Chayyim text were relatively insignificant. Neither the collating base (Ben Chayyim's received text) nor the techniques employed in these enterprises correspond to present-day scholarly requirements. Ginsburg's collation is the least useful, de Rossi's the most instructive.

As far as the text itself is concerned, two editions of the Hebrew Old Testament can claim to reflect the Ben Asher Massoretic tradition with sufficient accuracy to be called " critical " : the Kittel-Kahle edition, in which the arrangement is the modern editors' endeavor to reflect the poetic structure of the original; and the edition of N. H. Snaith, [22] which conforms strictly to the practice of the Massoretes with regard to the spacing and arrangement, as well as the substance, of the text. Only the Kittel-Kahle edition purports to supply alternative readings in a double critical apparatus drawn from Hebrew manuscript sources, the ancient versions, and modern scholarly conjectural reconstructions. Except for one Isaias manuscript and two chapters of Habacuc (from a commentary), the Qumran and second-century evidence, as yet largely unpublished, has not been taken into account; besides, the control of their complex sources, and the critical judgment exercised, on the part of the various collaborators to the Kittel-Kahle edition is subject to varying degrees of challenge on the part of other Old Testament scholars.

Appendix: the Samaritan Pentateuch

The break between the Samaritans and the Jews is commonly ascribed to the 4th century B.C. As far as concerns a separate tradition for the text of the Pentateuch, which the Samaritans also recognize as authoritative, the change cannot, however, be placed before the days of Johu Hyrcanus in the end of the second century B.C. The particular

---

[22] After careful study, N. H. Snaith, on behalf of the British and Foreign Bible Society, settled upon a 15th-century MS from Lisbon (B.M.Or. 2626-8) as the basis for his edition published in 1958; the results are generally quite close to the Kittel-Kahle text.

repetitious and simplified recension of the Law preserved at a later date only among the Samaritans is verifiable at Qumran in an expanded text of Numbers, in a paleo-hebrew manuscript of Exodus, and in other traces of the same type of text that seem to have no specially Samaritan sectarian connections. Certain passages in the New Testament (cf. Acts 7, 2, 32) are cited in the " Samaritan " form. Our earliest written texts from the Samaritans themselves (apart from some 4th century B.C. business documents lately discovered) are synagogue and other inscriptions from early in the Christian era, mainly the 4th century A.D. These contain the Decalogue and other biblical texts.

The Samaritan community at Nablus possesses a scroll of the Law alleged to date from " the thirteenth year after the conquest of Chanaan by Josue. " The oldest portion of this scroll, written by one Abisha, dates from the 11th century A.D.; it has recently been published by F. Perez Castro. [23] A list of known Samaritan Pentateuch manuscripts has been drawn up by E. Robertson. The first to come to the attention of European scholars was acquired in Damascus in 1616 by Pietro della Valle. The better copies of this Samaritan text range between the 12th and the 14th centuries. The first printed edition of this material was done in Paris in 1632; the most recent is that of von Gall (1914-1918), but some prefer to his the edition of Blayney (1790). This is, of course, a text written in Hebrew like the Massoretic text; but the script is distinctive, a contorted offshoot from the old Phoenician script. Though the Samaritans know a system of vocalization like that of the Babylonian Massoretes, their biblical texts are normally without vowels. Like the Qumran texts, they have an expanded orthography with a generous use of *matres lectionis*. In the 19th century Petermann endeavored to record in transcription the manner in which the Samaritans read the Pentateuch to place in evidence their oral tradition regarding the vowels. More recent studies have emphasized similarities between the Samaritan pronunciation of Hebrew and certain peculiar features of the orthography of the Qumran manuscripts; the matter is of interest for the historical pronunciation and the grammar of biblical Hebrew. [24]

B. THE VERSIONS OF THE OLD TESTAMENT

In addition to the text itself, whether in Hebrew or in Samaritan script, there are other documents which enable us to pursue our quest for a

---

[23] F. PEREZ CASTRO, *Sefer Abiša'*, *edicion del fragmento antiquo...* (Madrid, 1959).

[24] See M. BAILLET, " La récitation de la Loi chez les Samaritains, d'après Z. Ben Hayyîm, " *RB*, 69 (1962), pp. 570-587.

detailed and precise knowledge of the inspired wording : namely, the translations made from it at various times. It is quite often not too difficult to recover through them the basic Hebrew forms that stood before the translator. We need to be acquainted, therefore, with the manuscript tradition of the principal ancient versions of the Old Testament : the Greek, Aramaic, Syriac and Latin versions, of which the Greek is by far the most important.

§ 1.   The Greek Versions

BIBLIOGRAPHY

H. B. SWETE, *Introduction to the Old Testament in Greek*,[2] revised by R. R. Ottley (Cambridge, 1914).

F. G. KENYON, *Recent Developments in the Textual Criticism of the Greek Bible* (London, 1933); *The Text of the Greek Bible* (London, 1937).

H. M. ORLINSKY, *The LXX, the Oldest Translation of the Bible* (1949).

Msgr. R. DEVREESSE, *Introduction à l'étude des manuscrits grecs* (Paris, 1954).

J. COSTE, " La première expérience de traduction biblique : la Septante, " *La Maison Dieu*, 53 (1958), pp. 56-88.

F. KENYON — B. J. ROBERTS, the works listed *above*, p. 77.

The Septuagint

After the fall of Samaria and of Jerusalem in the 8th—6th centuries B.C., the Jews began to spread to various parts of the world : this is the well-known development of the Diaspora. The establishment in Egypt antedated the 5th century B.C., and was enlarged as a result of the conquests of Alexander. In contact with the Hellenistic world, which regarded them with distaste tempered by curiosity, the Jews began to speak its language. For the practice of their faith, therefore, and for giving an account of it to the Greeks, a translation of the sacred books became necessary. The legend embodied in the letter of the pseudo-Aristeas [25] describes the manner in which seventy-two Jewish doctors of the Law are purported to have produced this translation at the bidding

---

[25] Translation and notes in R. H. CHARLES, *Apocrypha and Pseudepigrapha of the Old Testament* (Oxford, 1913), II; text in H. B. SWETE, *Introduction...*; see *above*. R. TRAMONTANO, *La lettera di Aristea a Filocrate* (Naples, 1931); H. G. MEECHAM, *The Letter of Aristeas* (Manchester, 1935); M. HADAS, *Aristeas to Philocrates* (New York, 1951); A. PELLETIER, *Lettre d'Aristée à Philocrate* (Sources chrétiennes) (Paris, 1962).

of Ptolemy Philadelphus; its name of Septuagint (LXX) loosely reflects
the number of the translators as seventy.   In theory, this tale and
the name that goes with it have to do only with the rendering of the
Mosaic books; in fact, " Septuagint " now serves as a label for the entire
biblical corpus in Greek as it existed in the time of Christ.

However fanciful the tale now is, it still seems to reflect rather
precisely the date at which the first efforts at translation actually took
place.   The grandson of Ben Sira, the author of Ecclesiasticus, in
furnishing a prologue, about B.C. 116, to his Greek rendering of his
grandfather's work, was already acquainted with translations of the Law,
the Prophets, and the " other books. "   He does not strongly endorse
these translations, but he knows the difficulty of the undertaking.   Are
we to posit, not only a multiplicity of translators for the various books,
but a variety of translations of the books individually?   For a long time
the position of P. de Lagarde was accepted without challenge.   According
to this, the manuscript evidence we have can be sifted for the faults of
transmission and of careless citation by which a single original translation
has been deformed.   P. Kahle, on the other hand, has supposed that
there were in the earliest stage a variety of independent renderings,
so that the quest for *the* original Septuagint is illusory.   H. Orlinsky
continues to argue for a proto-Septuagint in the spirit of Lagarde.   The
biblical text employed by Philo for his numerous citations of the Pentateuch is difficult to determine from the manuscripts of that author;
their divided evidence has been employed by Kahle to support his position, but P. Katz [26] reaches directly contrary conclusions.   Both the
Hebrew and the Greek evidence from Qumran confirm the existence
of the same rendering contained in our later manuscripts (see *below*)
as having circulated, and having even been subject to some critical
reworking (notably, but not only, the Minor Prophets) in pre-Christian
times. [27]   The problem of the relation between the Old Testament
citations in the New Testament and the current Greek OT text of the
first century A.D. is even more complex than the question of Philo's
text. [28]

With Thackeray, we can agree that the pre-Christian Greek renderings
were made to meet liturgical, and occasionally apologetic, needs.   There
were no dictionaries, grammars, or concordances in existence; and the

[26] P. KATZ, *Philo's Bible* (Cambridge, 1950).

[27] See provisionally F. M. CROSS, *Ancient Library of Qumran...* (New York :
Anchor Books, 1961), pp. 163-194 (especially the note on pp. 170-172).

[28] W. DITTMAR, *Vetus Testamentum in Novo* (Göttingen, 1903); L. VÉNARD,
" Citations de l'A. T. dans le N. T., " *SBD*, 2 (Paris, 1934), cols. 23-51.

translators were not all equally fitted for their task. They were often
preoccupied with edifying the reader; at a minimum, they were determined not to upset him in his faith in the one, spiritual and transcendent
God. Often therefore they toned down the language of the original text.
Sometimes they misread, sometimes they mistranslated; one of them
would opt for a particular term, another for a different one in dealing
with an identical Hebrew original. Where there were difficulties, double
renderings might be offered from the first, or creep in later. The standards and the diligence of the various translators differed. To quote
A. Vaccari, the rendering of Canticles and of Ecclesiastes is servile;
that of the Psalms and the Prophets is mechanically literal; in the Pentateuch and the historical books we find faithful translation; in Job and
Proverbs, much greater freedom. Occasionally it is a new text which
emerges, colored by the doctrinal traditions of the translator's day. [29]
The Pentateuch seems to have been both the most carefully dealt with
portion of the original text, and the best understood by the translators.
But even in their errors, the translators give us precious evidence of what
they saw, since normally they strive to render, word for word, each
Hebrew word by a standard Greek equivalent. To isolate the Hebrew
phrase supposed by a particular Greek expression, one need usually
do no more than consult a well-organized concordance such as that of
Hatch and Redpath, [30] which provides for each Greek term all the
Hebrew expressions it was selected to render, with detailed references.

The number of Greek OT manuscripts available for study has been
augmented considerably in the last few decades. The oldest we have
is the Greek papyrus 458 of the John Rylands Library in Manchester,
England. Its fragments give us 15 verses of Deuteronomy, dating from
the 2nd century B.C. Another fragment of Dt in Egypt (pap. Fouad 266)
is of approximately the same date. Then there are the fragments on
leather and on papyrus found in the desert of Juda (Exodus and the
Letter of Jeremias in Qumran cave 7; two MSS. of Lv and one of Nm in
4Q; and most important, substantial fragments of a Greek scroll of the
Minor Prophets of the 1st century A.D. from the Wadi Khabra, offering
a text related to the citations of St. Justin in the 2nd century). [31] There

---

[29] J. COSTE, " Le texte grec d'Isaie XXV, 1-5, " *RB*, 61 (1954), pp. 35-66.

[30] E. HATCH and H. A. REDPATH, *Concordance to the Septuagint* (Oxford,
1897-1906) (facsimile reprint, 1954).

[31] P. W. SKEHAN, " The Qumran Manuscripts and Textual Criticism, " *VT
Suppl.*, IV (Leyden, 1957), pp. 148-158; M. BAILLET in *Discoveries in the Judaean
Desert III*, pp. 142-143; D. BARTHÉLEMY, *RB*, 60 (1953), pp. 18-29; B. LIFSHITZ
in *Yedi'ot*, 26 (1962), pp. 183-189.

are also fragments of Nm, Dt, Jer on papyrus from the 2nd century A.D. discovered in Egypt, purchased by Chester Beatty, and currently in London. Other Beatty papyri of the 3rd century furnish substantial parts of Gn, Is, and of Ez—Dn—Est (of which latter group supplementary parts of the same MSS. purchased by W. H. Scheide are in the United States). Also from the 3rd century are 33 leaves of a codex of the Minor Prophets in the Freer collection in Washington, 4 leaves from a Genesis codex from Oxyrhynchus now in Oxford, and some Psalm materials from the Fayûm presently in London. With the 4th century, the papyri become still more numerous. Already in 1933, P. L. Hedley counted 174 different fragmentary papyri of the Old Testament up to the 7th century A.D.

The earliest nearly complete copy of the ancient Greek rendering is the Vatican manuscript referred to as B; it is of the 4th century A.D., and on parchment. At the beginning most of Genesis (1, 1 to 46, 28) is lacking, along with some verses of 2 Sm 2, and about 30 Psalms; the books of Machabees were never contained in the MS. The date is based on paleographical considerations; its " uncial " (rounded capital) script is usually ascribed to the middle of the 4th century, though the history of its preservation until the 16th century is quite unknown to us. The uncial script remained standard for copying biblical manuscripts from the 4th century till about the 10th. The Sinaiticus MS. (known as S or ℵ), only slightly later than B, had somewhat more bizarre adventures. In 1844 it came to the attention of C. Tischendorf, in the monastery on Mount Sinai where, as he told the story, he recovered 43 leaves of it in a wastepaper basket. These he brought to Leipzig. By 1860 he had persuaded the monks to make a gift of the rest of the MS. (156 leaves) to the czar; from the home they thus acquired in St. Petersburg (Leningrad) they were eventually purchased in 1933 for the British Museum, where they now are. The same institution houses the codex Alexandrinus (A), a 5th-century MS. which lacks only a few verses from Gn and from 1 Sm, and a group of Psalms. Another 5th-century MS., the codex Ephraemi (C), in the Bibliothèque Nationale in Paris, contains only a part of the sapiential books as the under-writing in a palimpsest, imperfectly effaced to provide for the later copying on the same leaves of a series of theological treatises of St. Ephrem the Syrian, in their Greek translation. A 7th-century Isaias MS. in Dublin (O) is also a palimpsest. There are preserved remains of more than ten other uncial manuscripts, most of which, like the codices already mentioned, were " pandects, " containing the whole of the Old and of the New Testaments. The 6th-century Marchalianus codex (Q) contains only the Prophets; there is in Vienna a sumptuous illuminated MS. (L) of Genesis, of the 5th or 6th century. Other fine uncial MSS. are now divided among libraries in different countries : of the 5th-century Sarravianus (G) 130 leaves are in Leyden, Holland, 22 in Paris and 1 in Leningrad. The 10th-century Genesis codex of the Bodleian Library at Oxford is continued by a leaf now in Cambridge, which shows on its verso the change to a minuscule script; in this altered guise, the MS. is continued by leaves preserved in Leningrad and London.

From the 10th to the 15th century, the normal hand in biblical MSS. was a cursive minuscule script. Early in the 19th century, Holmes and Parsons collated some 300 such manuscripts; F. Kenyon knows of a total of 1560 of them.

Printed editions begin with the Spanish one in the Complutensian polyglot, 1514-1517, sponsored by Cardinal Ximenes. The Aldine edition from Venice, 1518, and the Sixtine text of 1587, from Rome, were noteworthy. The progress of critical study has made necessary extensive compilations, such as that of Holmes and Parsons (1798-1827). The two major critical editions now in progress are the Cambridge Septuagint of Brooke, Thackeray, MacLean, etc., which since 1906 has furnished all of the historical books (including Tb, Jdt, Est) except Machabees; and the parallel Göttingen *Septuaginta* of Rahlfs and Ziegler, which has published all the Prophets (including Daniel), as well as Psalms, Wis, 1-3 Mc, with Sirach to appear shortly. The Göttingen enterprise, which includes less significant sample publications of Genesis and Ruth, not only collates all variants, but presents as its running text the form judged to be basic and earliest by the modern editor; the Cambridge basic text is usually that of B, even in the books (such as Dt) where it is known to be inferior. An extensive edition of Josue, not yet completely published, was prepared by Max Margolis. Hand editions, of less value for critical work but convenient for handling and preliminary consultation, are those of H. B. Swete, *The Old Testament in Greek*, 3 Vols., Cambridge, three editions and various reprints since 1895, and A. Rahlfs, *Septuaginta*, 2 Vols., Stuttgart, since 1935.

Aquila, Symmachus, Theodotion and Origen

The confidence of the Jews in their ancient Greek translation (or translations) ebbed rapidly as it came to be adopted by the Christian Church. About A.D. 130 a Jew from Pontus, Aquila, prepared a new rendering, literal in the extreme. With the purpose of reproducing explicitly each word of the original, even to the untranslatable particle used to mark the object of verbs, he did violence to the Greek language. This labored procedure makes Aquila's rendering a good witness for the underlying original, and Origen used it as the third column in his Hexapla, next to the transliteration of the Hebrew into Greek letters. The translation of Aquila has survived, like the other later Greek renderings, only in a fragmentary way. In 1875, H. Field published his *Origenis hexaplorum quae supersunt* (Oxford, 2 Vols.), furnishing a large number of gleanings from Aquila and the others, found in certain hexaplaric MSS. such as Q, in patristic citations and in certain rabbinic sources. Other survivals of Aquila's work came from the Cairo Geniza—fragments of 3-4 Kgs published in 1897 by F. C. Burkitt, and a series of Psalms which C. E. Taylor edited in 1900. More Psalm evidence has been published from the Ambrosian palimpsest (see *below*).

About A.D. 170 (thus Mercati and Schoeps), a Christian named Symmachus, member of an Ebionite sect, familiar with the LXX and with Aquila, made a new rendering aimed at readability; it was held in great esteem by St. Jerome. Our sources for it are limited to the margins of Q, to patristic citations, and to similar fragmentary indications.

Theodotion, at the end of the 2nd century, provided another text which, in the judgment of many (*e.g.*, J. A. Montgomery) was no more than a revision of existing LXX material. The usual text of Daniel, and many verses worked into the rendering of Job, are ascribed to him; and we have also the various hexaplaric *marginalia* and patristic citations to work from. Since " Theodotionic " readings occur in earlier Fathers and even in the New Testament, his recension must be thought of as closely linked with earlier tradition. Origen seems to have known three other anonymous translations, a *quinta*, *sexta*, and, for the Psalms, a *septima*. There are extant fragments of the *quinta*, for which there is alleged a connection with Nicopolis in Epirus; and also of the *sexta*, which is linked to Jericho in a way suggestive of the Qumran finds. These renderings were apparently of certain biblical books only, not of the whole OT.

Origen (d. A.D. 253-254) produced no new translation; he comes at the term of a long development of which the names of the three revisers mentioned above are only symptomatic. [Nothing has been said, for instance, of the critical reworking of Greek texts in pre-Christian Palestine-Syria which is now known to underly the so-called " Lucianic " recension of the LXX.] But " from the moment one comes in contact with the Old Testament in Greek, Origen is always present " (Devreesse). Concerned as he was with apologetic and theological controversy, Origen felt the need not merely for copying, translating, and commenting texts, but also for confronting the existing manuscript traditions one with

another. Msgr. Devreesse represents the work of Origen as twofold.
For one thing, he took the received text of the LXX as a base, and edited
this by marking with an obelus (÷) passages he found lacking in the
Hebrew, while inserting after an asterisk (×) such passages as he thought
necessary to introduce on the basis of the Hebrew and the evidence of the
other Greek renderings. His second and major undertaking was the
disposing in four (Tetrapla), and then in six or more columns (Hexapla)
of a wide variety of parallel texts and renderings : the Hebrew in Hebrew
characters, the same transliterated into Greek, then Aquila, Symmachus,
the LXX, Theodotion. This huge labor of collations, preserved at
Caesarea in the library founded by the martyr Pamphilus, was known
to St. Jerome, but had disappeared by about A.D. 600. However, traces
of it remain, and a fragmentary palimpsest Psalter from the Ambrosian
Library in Milan, identified by Cardinal G. Mercati in 1896 as a copy of a
number of hexaplaric columns, omitting the first in Hebrew characters,
has recently been seen through the press by G. Castellino and published
after the Cardinal's death. [32]

§ 2. Targums in Aramaic

The Greek rendering of the OT is copiously represented in modern
libraries. Less so are the Jewish translations into Aramaic, though
these also are of considerable significance. Called " targums, " a name
that means simply translations, they have the advantage that their
language is very much akin to the Hebrew original.

Aramaic became widespread among the Jews from the time of the
Exile. From Nehemias we have the complaint that, as a result of mixed
marriages, the children of alien mothers no longer spoke Jewish, that is,
the Hebrew of Judea (Neh 13, 24). It may even be that, in the days of
Esdras, the solemn reading of the Law was accompanied not merely by
explanations as to what the Law required in detail, but also by an oral
rendering to make it possible for the listeners to grasp the meaning of the
very words of the text (Neh 8, 4-8); if so, this would be the first known
instance of a Targum being provided. In any case, the " Passover
papyrus " from Elephantine, with its numerous allusions to the priestly
legislation, is composed in Aramaic and dates from about the same time. [33]
In the centuries that followed, though the precise chronological develop-

---

[32] *Psalterii hexapli reliquiae, I,* ed. Joh. Card. MERCATI (Biblioteca Vaticana,
1958).
[33] See our *Introduction to the Old Testament,* pp. 162 f.

ment can no longer be traced, the custom took root of having an oral rendering into Aramaic follow the liturgical reading of the text in Hebrew. The " targumist " came at last to have an official standing; he " interpreted, " verse by verse when the Law was being read; though he was forbidden to do this while actually looking at the Hebrew text itself. Hebrew always remained the sacred language; even at Qumran, the bulk of the non-biblical texts are written in Hebrew. Yet at certain periods Aramaic made notable inroads, as is evident from Daniel 2—7, from the dossier in Esdras 4, 6—6, 18, and from the Aramaic materials at Qumran : Tobias, Enoch, the Testament of Levi, the Genesis apocryphon and other texts. The Asmonean period no doubt prompted a renewed emphasis on Hebrew; to what extent this affected the mass of the population we do not know. Recent insistence that Hebrew rather than Aramaic was the primary language employed by the common people at the time of Christ [34] is no doubt a little extreme. Be that as it may, during the 2nd century A.D. Aramaic was clearly dominant in Palestine, and targums became indispensable.

The origins of oral targum tradition are thus easy enough to trace; but much greater problems surround the written targums, with respect to the time, place and circumstances of their composition. The Talmud gives us reference to a Targum of Job, which is alleged to have been proscribed, with the burial of a copy of it, by Gamaliel the Elder, the teacher of St. Paul. And in fact a fairly literal Targum of Job has been one of the discoveries of cave 11 at Qumran, in 1956. [35] A bit of Aramaic rendering of Leviticus has been recovered from Qumran cave 4; and in Mk 15, 34, a quotation of Ps 21 (22), 2 is in Aramaic. The Genesis apocryphon from cave 1 at Qumran, already mentioned, contains in addition to midrashic expansions on the various adventures of the Patriarchs, a rendering into Aramaic of a number of chapters of the canonical book. The third person narrative beginning with Gn 14, in particular, is a quite close paraphrase of the Hebrew, and could easily be classified as a targum. [36]

At the beginning of the 20th century, G. Dalman maintained that the Targum " of Onkelos, " which he dated to the 2nd century A.D., was the oldest targum known to us. The work of P. Kahle on the materials from the Cairo Geniza has led to a shift of emphasis : he characterizes the Onkelos Targum as a late scholastic exercise based on older materials

---

[34] H. BIRKELAND, *The Language of Jesus* (Oslo, 1954).

[35] See provisionally *CBQ*, 25 (1963), pp. 122-123, based on an account by J. van der Ploeg, O.P.

[36] N. AVIGAD and Y. YADIN, *A Genesis Apocryphon* (Jerusalem, 1956).

from which he postulates that a wealth of midrashic elements has been excised. The form of Palestinian targum materials known from the same Geniza is " closer to midrash than to translation proper " (R. Bloch); and these materials are of considerable antiquity. They are now scattered among the libraries of Oxford, Leningrad (the Antonin collection), Cambridge (which has portions of what seems to be a 6th-century copy), and elsewhere. Some have been identified and in part published only recently by A. Diez-Macho. [37] It seems likely that the targums of Palestine have their roots in pre-Christian Judaism; but before this can be deemed certain, a better edition of the materials is called for than is represented by Ginsburger's edition (1899 and 1903); also an attentive comparison with the materials contained in the early midrash collections should be carried out. [38] Ginsburger's work is based on recensions of the Palestinian Targum to the Torah independent of the Geniza fragments : a *Targum Yerushalmi I* or pseudo-Jonathan targum which in its present form seems dependent on the Targum Onkelos; and a fragmentary targum known as the *Yerushalmi II*, which seems to represent an earlier stage of the same rendering. There are also scattered *tosephtas* of the Palestinian Targum, which are liturgical excepts, seemingly rather late; and finally, a complete copy of the Yerushalmi Targum in what is alleged by A. Diez Macho, who is preparing it for publication, to be a 2nd-century form of it, was recently identified in the *codex Neofiti I* of the Vatican Library (the manuscript itself is late medieval). Even the Samaritans preserve written Aramaic targums in their fossilized archaic script : there is no consistency in the manuscript tradition of these. In general, the question of what is truly ancient among these texts has implications beyond the realm of Old Testament criticism; since it involves indirectly the nature of the Aramaic background of the New Testament, the language of Christ and of the apostolic preaching in Jewish Palestine.

Only the Onkelos Targum carries the official endorsement of the Jewish scholars of Babylonia, where it seems to have been finally edited. The name of its putative author as given in the Talmud is presumably borrowed from the history of the Greek Bible and the translator Aquila. Similarly, the accepted rendering of the Former and Latter Prophets of the Jewish canon is ascribed to one " Jonathan, " which could be a Hebrew equivalent for the name Theodotion. These are both the fruit

---

[37] " Nuevos fragmentos del Targum palestinese, " *Sefarad*, 15 (1955), pp. 31-39.

[38] R. BLOCH, " Note méthodologique pour l'étude de la littérature rabbinique, " *Rech. sciences relig.*, 43 (1955), pp. 194-227; " Note sur l'utilisation des fragments de la Geniza du Caire pour l'étude du Targum palestinien, " *Rev. ét. juives*, 14 (1955), pp. 5-35.

of collaboration by many hands, and are rather late in the form we have, though based on much older sources. For the Prophets, A. Diez Macho has turned up samples of a quite different recension from the usual one. For the hagiographa (except for Daniel, Esdras, Nehemias) the extant targums are rather of the expanded, paraphrastic type; the targum to Proverbs is simply the Syriac Peshitta rendering transposed into the squareletter script, and has no independent value, while the targum to Job is in no way connected with the ancient one recovered at Qumran.

The earliest editions of the targums are from the 16th century; they then appear both in rabbinic Bibles and in the 16th-17th century polyglots. Critical studies by Kahle and his pupils, looking toward more definitive editions, have yielded partial results, but much remains to be done. [39] For textual criticism, the targums offer advantages in such measure as they contain genuinely ancient material that purports to translate, rather than to exegete the text; B. Roberts illustrates this from Gn 4, 1; 12, 6; 14, 19; 15, 2. Sometimes, too, the citations of the Old Testament in the New show kinship with the targum tradition.

§ 3. Syriac and Other Oriental Versions

BIBLIOGRAPHY

F. KENYON—B. J. ROBERTS, as cited *above*, p. 77.

B. BOTTE, L. LELOIR, G. VAN PUYVELDE, " Orientales (Versions) de la Bible, " *SDB*, VI (1960), cols. 807-884.

G. MERCATI, *Nuove note di letteratura biblica e cristiana antica** (Rome, 1941).

Syriac is a literary dialect of eastern Aramaic, the fruit of a long development; whereas the targums are written for the most part in less standardized western Aramaic forms. Also these latter were written for Jewish communities, whereas the Syriac translation of the Old Testament has come down to us ultimately through the Christian Church. Its origin, however, remains obscure. Certain links between the Palestinian Targum to the Pentateuch and the Syriac version have been pointed out [40]; it is possible that a line of transmission existed by way of the province of Adiabene, whose royal dynasty became converts to

---

[39] J. F. STENNING, *The Targum of Isaiah* (Oxford, 1949); A. SPERBER, *The Bible in Aramaic I, II, III* (Leyden, 1959-1962) (Pentateuch according to Targum Onkelos; Former and Latter Prophets according to Targum Jonathan).

[40] D. M. ENGBERG, *The Peshitto of Second Samuel* (Philadelphia, 1949), pp. 74 ff.

Judaism about the beginning of the Christian era, while the same province subsequently became the center for a flourishing Christian community. Toward the turn of the 2nd-3rd centuries, we know of two recensions of the Syriac Pentateuch, one quite literal, the other more free. Corrections based on the Septuagint crept in at an early date. Yet the full history of this text remains uncertain, and critical opinion is divided as to whether the earliest rendering was of Jewish or Christian origin.

There is extant a Syriac manuscript of the Pentateuch (British Museum Add. 14425) with a colophon from the " year of the Greeks 775, " i.e., A.D. 464. An incomplete Isaias MS. discovered by Cardinal Tisserant is some four years older. At this period Nestorius had already been deposed from the see of Constantinople (A.D. 431), and the Syrian Church was in process of breaking up into Nestorians, Jacobites, Melkites and Maronites. Each of these communities has its own biblical tradition; the Nestorian copies seem to be the more conservative and important. Various revisions are known, culminating in a standardized text about the 8th century. More than 15 6th-century MSS. exist. The Ambrosian manuscript from Milan, published by Ceriani, shows that the Peshitto (" simple ") text was substantially the same among 6th-century west Syrians as the received form of modern printed editions. These begin with Gabriel Sionita in the 16th century, and include the work of S. Lee in 1823, the Protestant mission at Urmia in 1852, and the Mosul Dominicans in 1887-1891. Further critical work is called for, and the activity of W. E. Barnes, G. Diettrich, and J. Bloch has paved the way for a full-scale critical edition, on which an international group of scholars is currently engaged.

Other Syriac translations followed the Peshitto. For liturgical purposes, between the 4th and the 6th centuries, the sections employed in the public readings of Antioch and Jerusalem, along with a *horologion*, were put into " Syro-Palestinian " western Aramaic and preserved thenceforth among the Melkites. Of a version made at the insistence of Philoxenos of Mabbug in the early 6th century for the monophysite (" Jacobite ") west Syrians, practically nothing survives. A third version, the Syro-hexaplar, was produced early in the 7th century by the bishop Paul of Tella and a group who collaborated with him. This is better known, thanks to an 8th-century MS. now in Milan, published (like the Peshitto one mentioned above) by Ceriani, and a number of other portions published by H. Middledorpf, P. de Lagarde, and others. This is a useful witness to the work of Origen, from whose Hexapla it preserves the *sigla* in the text (obelus and asterisk, see above). All three of these later Syriac renderings are secondary versions from the

Greek, and it is to the Greek OT and its problems that they introduce us finally.

The same may be said for the Coptic versions (for which the textual evidence goes back in part to good 4th-century papyri), and the Ethiopic, Armenian, Georgian, Slavonic and Gothic versions : with whatever cross-influences from other sources, it is mainly to the Greek tradition that they carry us back. The same could be said respecting the Arabic versions (except the 10th-century one of Saadia, and certain others based on the Peshitto), and the Latin versions other than the Vulgate. The influence of the various Latin Bible texts in the western Church, their antiquity, and their closely literal character, however, make it advisable to deal with them separately.

§ 4. The Latin Versions

BIBLIOGRAPHY

B. BOTTE, " Latines (versions) antérieures à saint Jérome, " *SDB*, V (Paris, 1957), cols. 334-347.

F. STUMMER, *Einführung in die lateinische Bibel** (Paderborn, 1928).

A. BEA, *Le nouveau Psautier latin* (Paris, 1947).

Till the end of the 2nd century, the Roman Church spoke Greek. But even before it changed over to Latin, its missionaries to northern Italy and the Church in Africa used Latin of necessity, and Latin renderings began to appear. They are remarkably divergent, as can be seen in the various patristic citations. In endorsing the *Itala*, St. Augustine was no doubt contrasting the texts he had known in Europe with those circulating in Africa (so Schildenberger). Between the 2nd and the 5th centuries, there are many obscure points in the history of the text, or texts. Of some books there were probably several translations, all made from the Greek and preserving traces of this source in their vocabulary. Unmistakable contacts with the Palestinian Targum open up the question as to whether certain elements of the Latin Bible may not have had their origins in a Jewish translation prior to the Christian activities in this matter. No early text has come down without retouches. The Psalter, the most widely circulated text, was revised in Africa in the mid-4th century (Dom Capelle).

The manuscripts go back no earlier than the 5th century. A listing of the extant material has been published by the monks of Beuron Abbey, who are also engaged in a long-term project for the publication of a

Vetus latina [41] edition that will replace the 18th-century one of
Dom P. Sabatier. One of the best manuscripts of this rendering that is
available is the rather late (7th century) Heptateuch in Lyon, published
by U. Robert. A lectionary from Wolfenbüttel dates from about A.D. 500,
and from the fifth century we have fragments of a Vienna palimpsest
now in Naples, some palimpsest fragments from Würzburg, and parchment
fragments in London and Florence. There is also the important 9th-
century text in Madrid which was used for the Alcalà polyglot.

The Psalter has to be considered separately. The Beuron list gives
over 150 copies of it. One of the most noted is the 5th-6th-century
Psalter originally from the abbey of S. Germain des Prés, now at the
Bibliothèque Nationale in Paris. A Lyon Psalter is of the 5th-6th century, one from Verona of the 6th-7th (this contains the form of text
familiar to St. Augustine), those of St. Gall and of Corbie (now in
Leningrad) of the 8th century. A group of manuscripts of English
origin, the earliest being of the 8th century, gives us the Roman Psalter
still employed in the Missal, and at St. Peter's in Rome. Another group,
of Spanish (" Mozarabic ") origin, is of the 9th and later centuries [42]; a group
of "Ambrosian" Psalters from Milan goes back as far as the 10th century.

At the request of Pope Damasus, St. Jerome made a first revision
of the Psalter about A.D. 382; the *psalterium Romanum* mentioned above
is sometimes alleged as the product of this revision, but the justice of
this view has been in dispute since it was challenged by Dom
D. de Bruyne. [43] A second revision by St. Jerome was made presumably
in A.D. 386, after he had consulted, so it would appear, the Hexapla of
Origen in the library of Caesarea in Palestine. This edition won widespread favor. From Gaul (whence it acquired the label *psalterium
Gallicanum*) it spread throughout the western Church and became a
fixture in the Breviary; in complete Latin Bibles of the customary
" Vulgate " variety, it appears in a multiplicity of manuscripts, of which
one of the most notable is the *codex Amiatinus*, prior to A.D. 718, now in
Florence. Both these Psalters have in recent years received excellent
critical editions. [44]

---

[41] So far, in addition to the *Verzeichnis*, or check-list of witnesses, Genesis
and certain New Testament Epistles have been published.

[42] Collated and edited as *Psalterium Visigothicum Mozarabicum* by T. Ayuso
MARAZUELA for the Madrid polyglot (1957).

[43] See our *Introduction to the Old Testament*, p. 378, n. 3.

[44] *Liber psalmorum ex recensione S. Hieronymi*, Rome, 1953, contains the
" Gallican " Psalter as vol. X of the Benedictine Vulgate project (see below); *Le
psautier romain et les autres anciens psautiers latins*, ed. R. Weber (Coll. bibl. latina,
10) (Vatican City, 1953).

Jerome had learned Hebrew during his retirement to the desert of Chalcis (A.D. 373-378); he took up the study of it again at Bethlehem, and sought instruction from Rabbi Bar Anina. After 392 he undertook a new rendering of the whole Old Testament directly from the Hebrew; this he finished in 405. Except for the Psalter, this translation has become the Vulgate Latin text. His final rendering of the Psalter, known as the *Psalterium juxta Hebraeos* [45] has been transmitted with his collected works, but is known only rarely in conjunction with other biblical materials (in an eighth century Psalter, Vatican 11, by a Merovingian hand, along with the Gallican Psalter; and alongside the Old Latin Psalms from Corbie, as well as the Gallican Psalter, in a MS. now in Leningrad).

Besides the *Amiatinus* already mentioned, a number of manuscripts of the Carolingian period give us the Vulgate text. The many times this was copied made some recensional work necessary quite early, and one who undertook this task was Cassiodorus, the one-time minister for Theodoric, who retired (in the 6th century) to the south Italian monastery of Vivarium. Yet even by Carolingian times we can distinguish three recensions and as many families of manuscripts : those of Alcuin, those of Theodulf of Orleans, and the Spanish family of MSS. connected with the 8th-century *codex Toletanus*. In the course of its long history, this Latin text underwent renewed critical study in Paris in the 13th century. In the main it was a Paris text that Gutenberg followed for his " 42-line Bible " of 1452. The Alcalà (Complutensian) Bible of 1518 and the edition of R. Stephanus (Estienne) in 1528 presented different texts. Printed editions multiplied with the rise of Protestantism; and the Council of Trent decided on editing an official, critically sound text. The edition of Sixtus V in 1590 was unsatisfactory; with corrections, it became the Sixto-Clementine text of 1592 and all later editions. This text, too, had its limitations, and in our day a sustained effort over decades on the part of the monks of the Benedictine abbey of St. Jerome in Rome, commissioned for the task by the Holy See, has gone into the production of a definitive edition; Genesis appeared in 1926, and the eleven volumes in print by 1963 include all of St. Jerome's translations from Hebrew and Aramaic except the Prophets, still to be published. [46]

---

[45] *S. Hieronymi psalterium juxta Hebraeos*, ed. Dom HENRI DE STE.-MARIE (Coll. bibl. latina, 11) (Vatican City, 1954).

[46] The Psalter in this edition is the " Gallican " one; see *above*. A useful Vulgate *editio emendatissima* with the Clementine text, and with critically selected variants to both the Old Testament (except the Prophets and some " deuterocanonical " Books) and the New, furnished by the members of this same Benedictine foundation, was published by Marietti (Turin and Rome) in 1959. It contains three Psalters : the Gallican, the *juxta Hebraeos*, and the 1945 breviary version.

C. THE NEW TESTAMENT

Except for the Aramaic original of St. Matthew's Gospel, no longer extant, and sometimes questioned as to its ever having existed, the New Testament was composed in Greek. In the Greek manuscripts which we possess, it is usual to find the whole Bible, sometimes with a few non-canonical compositions included. Yet the fact remains that in such Bibles the Old Testament is no more than the copy of a translation, whereas the New Testament is a copy of the original text itself. Thus even when these separate parts are placed side by side, the questions of textual criticism of the New Testament must be approached on different terms than those referring to the Old.

§ 1. The Greek Text

BIBLIOGRAPHY

The works of F. KENYON, R. DEVREESSE, etc., cited *above*, pp. 77 and 86.

P. COLLOMP, *La papyrologie* (Paris, 1927).

L. VAGANAY, *Initiation à la critique textuelle néo-testamentaire* (Paris, 1934) (Eng. trans. *Introduction to the Textual Criticism of the New Testament* [St. Louis, 1937]).

H. W. ROBINSON (ed.), *The Bible in its Ancient and English Versions* (1940).

D. W. THOMAS, " The Textual Criticism of the Old Testament, " *OTMS*, pp. 238-263.

M. DAVID — B. A. VAN GRONINGEN, *Papyrological Primer* (Leiden, 1946).

D. R. AP-THOMAS, *A Primer of Old Testament Text Criticism* (1947).

B. BOTTE, " Manuscrits grecs du Nouveau Testament, " *SDB*, V. cols. 819-835.

A. SOUTER, *Text and Canon of the New Testament* (1954).

F. G. KENYON, *Our Bible and the Ancient MSS* (London, 1958).

M. M. PARVIS, " Text, New Testament, " *IDB*, IV, pp. 594-614.

J. DUPLACY, *Où en est la critique textuelle du Nouveau Testament* (Paris, 1959).

B. BOTTE, " Papyrus bibliques, " *SDB*, VI, cols. 1109-1120.

Manuscripts on papyrus

Since the New Testament texts were composed, almost without exception, during the second half of the 1st century A.D., it is hardly surprising that we should now possess neither an original nor a copy dating to that earliest period. On the other hand, discoveries from the sands of Egypt make it possible to envision quite clearly the form in which a letter of St. Paul, or a note such as that which he addressed to Philemon, would have been prepared. A. Deissmann [47] is among those who have studied the question most in detail. Texts of some length were still being written in columns on one side only of scrolls; shorter texts were prepared on single leaves. Between the various churches, texts circulated very quickly; before the end of the century there was already a collection of Pauline Epistles (2 Pt 3, 16). A type of text begins to circulate at this time whose influence is traceable in the 2nd century both in the Latin world and in the Syriac-Christian milieu. This text, especially of the Gospels and Acts, more popular, and more " Semitic " than other forms, is not necessarily the better for that; and it is certainly not the single oldest form.

By the 2nd century the " codex " or regular book form of manuscript (see *above*, p. 83) is in vogue, and New Testament texts of this type and date have been recovered. The oldest is the Papyrus Rylands 457 (Jn 18, 31-33. 37. 38), written on both sides (see figure 3). Various considerations, in the main paleographical, make it necessary to date this fragment in the first half of the 2nd century, fifty years at most after the publication of the fourth Gospel. This is an evidence of the rapid diffusion of the Gospel from Asia Minor to Egypt, where the fragment was found and purchased in 1920. This impression is reinforced by more recent discoveries : first, that of a papyrus copy of John (pap. Bodmer II, *ca.* A. D.200) also from Egypt, known as P[66] in the standard list of New Testament papyri, and fully published, its first 14 chapters nearly intact, and the chapters 15-21 in more fragmentary state. [48] Then there is the notable MS. P[75], also in the Bodmer collection, from Egypt, and dating *ca.* A.D. 175-225, containing in its present form most of Luke and about the first two-thirds of John. [49] An extra-biblical document which must be mentioned here is the papyrus Egerton 2, dating from about A.D. 180, and containing citations of our canonical Gospels, intermingled with other material of undetermined origin; this has been the subject of lively

[47] A. DEISSMANN, *Licht vom Osten* 4 (Tübingen, 1923); translated from an earlier edition as *Light from the Ancient East* (London, 1910).

[48] *Papyrus Bodmer III, Évangile de Jean chap. 1-14; Supplément, chap. 14-21...
avec reproduction photographique... (chap. 1-21)*, Geneva, Bibliotheca Bodmeriana (1956-1962).

[49] *Papyrus Bodmer XIV-XV, Évangiles de Luc et Jean*, I-II, Geneva, Bibl. Bodmeriana (1961).

discussion since it was published in 1935. [50]   Of late 2nd-century date are also some fragments of Matthew, part in Oxford and part in Barcelona (P⁶⁴, P⁶⁷). [51]

Of 3rd-century date are our earliest copies of Jude and 1-2 Peter, by one same Egyptian hand, [52] and known jointly as P ⁷². From about A.D. 220 comes a vellum fragment of about 14 lines of text of the *Diatessaron*, or harmonized Gospel, of Tatian, in Greek, found at Dura-Europos on the Euphrates. A little later are the Oxyrrhynchus papyri now in the British Museum, containing fragments of John (P⁵) and Hebrews (P¹³); and a fragment of Acts (P⁴⁸) in the Laurentian library in Florence. The most notable group of 3rd-century papyri are those of the Chester Beatty collection. The first of them (P⁴⁵) contains 30 of an original 220 leaves of a codex of large format, with 2 leaves of Mt, 6 of Mk, 7 of Lk, 2 of Jn and 13 of Acts, in a rather tiny script. Of P⁴⁶ there were originally 104 leaves, the full papyrus sheets being folded twice to produce these leaves, rather than once only as in the preceding MS. The content is the Pauline Epistles, and the 86 leaves which remain are divided between the Beatty collection (56 leaves) and the University of Michigan (30 leaves). The Epistles were grouped in the now traditional order, but with Heb placed between Rom and 1 Cor. F. Kenyon was of the opinion that 1-2 Tm and Titus, the " Pastoral Epistles, " were not contained in this codex. [53] The third of this group of Beatty papyri (P⁴⁷) contains chapters 9—17 of the Apocalypse. [54]

Copies on parchment

With the 4th century, papyrus MSS. become more frequent; we may mention in particular P³⁸, at the University of Michigan (pap. Mich. 1571), containing two chapters of Acts. In addition to the various reviews of papyrology, such periodicals as *Biblical Archeologist*, *J.B.L.*, and *Chronique d'Egypte* (Brussels) take notice of new discoveries and publications in this field. For the 4th and later centuries, however, our principal interest shifts to less fragmentary evidence in the great biblical

---

[50] H. I. BELL and T. C. SKEAT, *Fragments of an Unknown Gospel* (London, 1935).

[51] R. ROCA-PUIG, *Un papiro griego del evangelio di San Mateo 2* (Barcelona, 1962).

[52] *Papyrus Bodmer VII-VIII, Épître de Jude, Les deux Épîtres de Pierre*, Geneva, Bibl. Bodmeriana (1959).

[53] G. ZUNTZ, *The Text of the Epistles…* (London, 1953).

[54] F. KENYON, ed., *The Chester Beatty Biblical Papyri, II-III and Supplement* (London, 1933-1937). The accepted numbering of N.T. papyri is that currently being continued by K. Aland in *ZNW*.

codices on parchment.   The Vaticanus (B) has lost its last leaves, and with
them the Pastoral Epistles, Hebrews and the Apocalypse.   The Sinaiticus
(S, or ℵ), slightly later and already equipped with the divisions of the
Gospel text proposed by Eusebius of Caesarea (*d.* 340), contains the whole
NT, and in addition two early Christian texts, the *Epistle of Barnabas*
and the *Shepherd of Hermas*.   The Alexandrinus (A), later than
St. Athanasius, and presumably of the beginning of the 5th century, has
suffered some damage : it lacks most of Mt, two chapters of Jn and eight
of 2 Cor; it includes, outside the NT canon, the *Letter of Clement of Rome*.
Given to James I of England by the patriarch of Constantinople Cyril
Lukaris, the manuscript had been brought by the latter from Alexandria.
The palimpsest MS. *codex Ephraemi rescriptus* (C), now in the Paris
Bibliothèque Nationale, was once the property of Catherine de' Medici.
Its 5th-century biblical text is more complete for the New Testament
than for the Old; even so, only 145 leaves of an original 238 for the NT
are preserved, and nothing is left of 2 Thes or of 2 Jn.

The *codex Bezae* (D), probably also of 5th-century date, is a quite
different type of MS.   It contains only the Gospels and Acts, with a Latin
text facing the Greek at each opening of the codex.   The Greek text in D
varies notably from that of the uncials named above, and brings to light
again the popular text underlying the ancient Syriac and Latin renderings,
already spoken of.   It takes its name from the fact that after the sack
of Lyon it was given by the French Huguenots to the Reformer Théodore
Beza, who in 1581 gave it to Cambridge University.   The Washington
codex (W) in the Freer Gallery, also 5th century, contains only the
Gospels, with a supplementary " logion " at Mk 16, 14.

Several uncials date from the 6th century.   Like those already
listed, these later MSS. are often designated by capital letters (a different
system was proposed by Gregory and von Soden).   The Claromontanus
in Paris (D2) contains only the Pauline Epistles in Greek and Latin;
E2, the Laudianus at Oxford, has only Acts; H3, the Coislinianus, of
which the fragments are scattered in Paris, Leningrad, Moscow, Kiev,
Turin and Mount Athos, contains the Pauline Epistles and an important
colophon saying that the MS. was collated with that of the library in
Caesarea; N, in Leningrad, is a copy of the Gospels on purple vellum;
O, which was brought from Sinope in 1899 by a French military officer,
is the Gospel of St. Matthew in gold lettering on purple; P2, the Porphyrianus from Wolfenbüttel, contains the Gospels; Q, in the same library,
has Luke and John; R, in the British Museum, is fragments of Luke;
T, in the Vatican, fragments of Luke and John; and Z, in Dublin, Matthew
only.   Of uncials later in date, the Koridethi MS. (Θ, in Tiflis) deserves

to be mentioned for its text-critical significance, as it seems to be the direct copy of an extremely ancient manuscript.

In all, 212 uncial manuscripts at least of the NT, some complete, many fragmentary, are known for the period from the 4th century to A.D. 1000. How copious this evidence is can be appreciated when one reflects that for Homer not a single uncial exists. Were it not for the papyri, ranging from the 2nd century B.C. to the 7th A.D., which have yielded some 13,500 out of 15,693 lines of Homer, we should be limited for our oldest witness to the codex Venetus 454, a 10th-century minuscule! For Aeschylus, the codex Mediceus in Florence is from about A.D. 1000, and the Paris ms. is of the 13th century. For Herodotus and Plato, we are dependent on two or three 10th-century manuscripts. Virgil, for whom a 5th-century manuscript exists, is quite exceptional in that regard.

The minuscule script begins to make its way while the uncial is still being regularly employed. Thus the Uspensky Gospel ms. in Leningrad, the oldest dated ms., is a minuscule of A.D. 835. With time, this script came into constantly greater favor, and in the end replaced the uncial script, which persisted for several centuries only as a vehicle for liturgical texts. A first series of minuscules, including the Uspensky Gospels, was produced in the Stoudion monastery in Constantinople in the 9th and 10th centuries; those are followed by others from Italian scriptoria. Known as *codices vetustissimi*, these texts are followed in the 10th to the 12th centuries by *codices vetusti*, which are succeeded by the latest products of the manuscript period, from the 13th century till the spread of printing in the 16th. In all there remain to us an accumulation of some 2,500 biblical codices, plus about 1,500 lectionaries for liturgical purposes (1,200 of these being Gospel lectionaries) from sources in the East. To utilize a mass of evidence such as this, classification of the manuscripts by families is a first necessary step. Such classification, in turn, cannot be carried out without taking into account the testimony of the ancient versions, which we will survey next.

§ 2. The Versions

BIBLIOGRAPHY

    See the works of KENYON and VAGANAY, and the articles by B. BOTTE,
      L. LELOIR, G. VAN PUYVELDE, cited *above*, pp. 77, 86 and 95.
    A. VÖÖBUS, *Early Versions of the New Testament* (Stockholm, 1954).

Christianity spread with great rapidity to the various regions of the Roman Empire. Earlier not only than the codices Vaticanus and Sinaiticus, but even than the Chester Beatty papyrus codex of the Epistles of St. Paul, was the work of translation, based on manuscripts now lost, of the whole New Testament into Syriac, Coptic and Latin for the faithful of Syria, Egypt, and the West.

Putting to one side the disputed question as to whether Tatian composed his Gospel harmony, the *Diatessaron*, in Greek or in Syriac, [55] our knowledge of the oldest continuous Syriac translation of the Gospels is currently based altogether on two manuscripts, which are far from presenting an identical text. The one, recovered from a monastery in the Nitrian desert of Egypt, was published in 1858 by W. Cureton, after whom it is usually called the Curetonian version. It comprises eighty folios of a Gospel lectionary of 5th-century date, in which Jn precedes Lk. The other was discovered by Agnes Smith Lewis in 1892 in the monastery of St. Catherine at Sinai, whence it is known as the Sinaiticus Syriac. It is a palimpsest, in which the under-writing is a 4th-century Gospel book providing about three-fourths of the entire Gospel text. This ancient Syriac " separated Gospels " *(da-mepharreshê)*, so called to distinguish it from the mixed, or harmonized, *Diatessaron*, may have originated about A.D. 200. It was followed by another, which became the official version in all parts of Syriac-speaking Christianity, the " Peshitto, " or " simple " version, which has been transmitted with remarkable consistency and faithfulness since the 5th century. The British Museum contains one, and there exists another, 5th-century MS. of it; and from the 6th century we have extant a dozen more. Though the name of Rabbula of Edessa, bishop there from A.D. 411 to 431, has been connected with the origins of the Peshitto, it seems to be rather a 5th-century revision of earlier texts, supplemented perhaps by a fresh translation of Jas, 1 Pt and 1 Jn, not contained in the earlier versions. The Peshitto did not originally include 2 Pt, 2-3 Jn, Jude or the Apocalypse. A 6th-century revision from the Greek for Philoxenos of Mabbug supplied these books and reworked the others; this was followed in the 7th century by further modifications, the extent of which is not clearly known, by Thomas of Harkel. Of the Philoxenian-Harkelian version there are at Rome a MS. of the 7th century, and another of the 8th.

Coptic is a developed stage of the language of Pharaonic Egypt, in part transformed by Greco-Roman influences, and written in Greek

---

[55] Whatever the original language of the Diatessaron, a Syriac form of it was the text commented on by St. Ephrem (d. 373); until recently, this commentary was known only from an Armenian translation. The greater part of the original Syriac has been found in a unique manuscript in the Chester Beatty collection, and edited by L. LELOIR, *Saint Ephrem, commentaire de l'évangile concordant* (with Latin translation) (Dublin : Hodges Figgis and Co., 1963).

letters with a few supplementary characters for phonemes alien to Greek. There were a number of dialects of Coptic : Fayumic, Akhmimic, Sahidic, Bohairic, Middle Egyptian, etc. The New Testament in Sahidic, the dialect of Upper Egypt, seems to have a literary priority over the others. Its oldest extant witnesses are 4th-century copies of Jn and Acts. Recent discoveries of early material promise to give us a 4th-century copy of I Peter, also in Sahidic, and good Middle Egyptian evidence for Mt and for the " Western " text of Acts. In Bohairic, for which early evidence has until lately been confined to a few verses from Rom and Phil, and the first verse of Jn, a substantial manuscript containing most of Jn (along with Gn 1-4, 2) in a form related textually to the Sahidic, differing from the later Bohairic texts, and suggesting that it has been handed down through Gnostic hands, has been published by R. Kasser (Louvain, 1958). In general, given the profusion of manuscript (and especially papyrus) discoveries from Egypt, one may anticipate that further exploration of the remains of the Coptic versions will continue to prove most instructive for the history of transmission of the NT text. Indirect light on the use and transmission of the New Testament in Egypt is also shed by a group of Gnostic texts in 4th-5th-century papyri from Nag Hammadi (Chenoboskion), notably an apocryphal *Gospel of Thomas* and an *Apocryphon of John*, both of which to some degree reflect 2nd-century origins. [56]

The New Testament was translated into Latin very early, somewhere in the neighborhood of A.D. 150. Citations by St. Cyprian enable us to learn of an African form of this text; those of Novatian and others, of a text that circulated in Europe. There was probably a 4th-century revision undertaken in Italy, prior to St. Jerome. Of this old Latin version there survive some fifty manuscripts and fragments; critical citation of these is done by means of small letters in italics. Of " European " witnesses to this text, the most important is the 4th-century *codex Vercellensis (a)*, which has the four Gospels in the western order (Mt, Jn, Lk, Mk). The Verona codex *(b)* of the 4th-5th centuries is in better condition than *a*; later MSS. are those of Corbie *(ff2)*, 5th century; and of Brescia *(f)*, 6th century. The Epistles and Acts are contained in later copies. " Among the MSS. which basically represent the African group of texts, we must refer to the Bobbiensis *(k)* of the 4th-5th centuries, and the Palatinus *(e)*, 5th century, for the Gospels; for Acts, the Catholic Epistles and the Apocalypse, the Floriacensis palimpsest (6th century);

---

[56] For a discussion of these, see W. C. VAN UNNIK, *Newly Discovered Gnostic Writings* (Studies in Biblical Theology) (London and Naperville, Ill., 1960); cf. *CBQ*, 23 (1961), pp. 91-92.

and for St. Paul, the Freising fragments *(r)* of the 6th-7th centuries "
(Vaganay).

This ancient text was to be replaced in the Latin Church by the
Vulgate, of which the witnesses are numerous and the use was widespread.
St. Jerome did not produce a new rendering, but a revision of the Italian
text of the Gospels.   The oldest manuscript, that of St. Gall, from about
A.D. 500, is unfortunately quite fragmentary.   6th-century copies are
scarce; the Fulda codex (from A.D. 541-546) contains the whole NT,
the Gospels in a harmony based on the *Diatessaron*.   A Milan MS. and the
Harley MS. are also of the 6th century; the Amiatinus (already referred
to for its OT part) is of the 8th; and with the 9th century, copies become
numerous.   The critical edition of the Vulgate NT by Wordsworth and
White cites also Old Latin readings in its apparatus; the *Vetus latina*
from Beuron and the work of Jülicher and Matzkow give partial editions
of Old Latin texts.

To conclude we may mention briefly, as for the OT, the Gothic,
Ethiopic, Armenian and Georgian versions.   For the two last-named, the
interesting critical problem is their basic relationship to the Old Syriac. [57]
From this point of view they have some significance in the realm of NT
textual criticism.

---

[57] S. LYONNET, *Les origines de la version arménienne et le Diatessaron* (Rome,
1950).

CHAPTER II

TEXTUAL CRITICISM

Textual criticism has as its goal the reconstitution of the original state of a text of which one has only copies extant. Every copy is more or less faulty. When one has a number of copies, the variants he observes between them are an occasion for seeking out the genuine reading in each place. Even when there is but a single copy available, there may be manifest errors in it which compel the reader to assume as the original a text other than what the copy offers him. Present-day textual criticism is more chary than that of earlier generations in accepting conjectural emendations not based on a manuscript tradition. A better knowledge of the ancient Near East and its languages has currently made understandable a number of passages which had long appeared to be without ascertainable meaning.

§ 1. General Principles

BIBLIOGRAPHY

P. COLLOMP, *La critique des textes* (Paris, 1931).

L. DENNEFELD, " Critique textuelle de l'Ancien Testament, " *SDB*, II, cols. 240-256.

H. J. VOGELS and L. PIROT, " Critique textuelle du Nouveau Testament, " *SDB*, II, cols. 256-274.

Dom H. QUENTIN, *Essais de critique textuelle* (Paris, 1926).

Moshe LAZAR, " Alfonso de Zamara, copiste, " *Sefarad*, 18 (1958), pp. 314-323.

Textual criticism is a science with a history. It was pursued actively in ancient times when, for example, the classical authors, and Homer in particular, were edited by Alexandrian scholars. It was these scholars who invented the system for indicating textual defects that was later employed by Origen. Since the Renaissance, this type of study has been again brought to the fore and extended to texts of every sort; the endeavor to systematize it with valid rules has most often been connected with its application to the text of the Bible. J. J. Griesbach formulated a set of fifteen rules; K. Lachmann, in editing a text of the New Testament in 1842, outlined a technique for textual work; and in preparing for the first volumes of the Benedictine edition of the Vulgate, Dom Quentin did the same. Similarly well known are J. Bédier, for his work on medieval texts, and L. Havet, dealing with the text of the Latin classics.

Textual criticism is a necessary component of the study of a text and its transmission. It is a historical science, which looks to the intellectual satisfaction that comes from detailing the facts that account for the present state of the text being studied, with such faults as it may contain. The difficulty with this science comes from the basic ignorance we have, at the outset of our research, as to what the author of the original text had in mind, and as to what the successive copyists who transmitted the work did and thought during their scribal endeavors. We do not even know, as a starting point, how many times a particular text has been recopied between the author's autograph and the copies from which we begin our study. Yet all along the line certain *historical* and *psychological* factors have been at work, the nature of which we need to discern and bear in mind.

I. HISTORICAL FACTORS

1⁰ We should know to begin with the conditions in which the *copyists* did their work. Did they copy a text which they themselves read while they copied; or one which was read to them by someone else? In the first case, their mistakes must be accounted for as visual ones; in the latter case, faulty hearing may have been involved. Both kinds of errors are known to us, with examples from Greek and from Egyptian literature. [1] We can therefore expect to encounter similar faults on the part of copyists of the Bible.

Even more, we need to go back to the very origin of the text, and to understand the conditions under which an ancient work was composed. St. Paul dictated his letters, and thanks to other collections of literary correspondence in antiquity, that of Cicero in particular, we can form an estimate of the way he went about it. The author would, to be sure, reread his letter; but oral style would permit him certain turns of phrase, and certain syntactical liberties, that should not in consequence be presumed to be errors of later copyists. [2]

---

[1] B. VAN DE WALLE, G. POSENER, *La transmission des textes littéraires égyptiens* (Brussels, 1948).

[2] G. A. ESCHLIMANN, " La rédaction des Épîtres pauliniennes, " *RB* (1946), pp. 185 ff.

It should also be recognized that in antiquity a body of texts might be compiled from unrelated, even disparate, works. In a number of instances, in Egyptian school texts of the New Empire period (16th to 12th centuries B.C.), the " Satire on the Trades " is juxtaposed with the " Teaching of Amenemhet I " and the " Hymn to the Nile. " Other evidence tells us that Egyptian compositions were divided into paragraphs, each of which was designated by its opening words, or *incipit*. The aspiring pupil was taught this series of incipits, which then recur in a fixed order in the copies.

Another factor that needs be known is how copies of the text, once made, were preserved. Our fullest information on this score comes from Assyro-Babylonia, thanks to the 7th-century library of Ashurbanipal. Certain texts had been standardized for a long time, many since the Cassite period in the mid-second millennium B.C., into fixed series of tablets, within which each tablet carried a number reflecting its place in the series, as well as a " colophon " giving the date of the copy and the name of the scribe. If the prototype was damaged and the copyist was unable to read it, he sometimes noted the fact in his copy, unaware of the wry smiles this would bring to modern readers of it. The paucity of documents from Palestine makes knowledge of the methods of trans-mission in Egypt and Mesopotamia especially valuable for its sidelights on the obscure situation in the Israelite territory. Egypt is the more significant, in that there, as normally in Palestine, texts were copied on perishable materials by preference to the clay tablet; and though the humidity in Palestine has destroyed its early written texts, the desert sands and dry climate of Egypt have preserved an abundant docu-mentation.

2⁰ The work of the copyist was from time to time supplemented by that of *recensions. A recension is a deliberate revision made by a student of the text who is endeavoring to meet the problem of variants and defects he sees in the copies available to him*. About recensions of the Old Testament, which for particular books assuredly took place, we are practically without information. The long work of the Massoretes preliminary to the introduction of the vowel points must be regarded as a recension, which we are currently in a better position to appreciate. The Massoretic text of Isaias, for which the earliest complete copies are of the 10th century A.D., must be regarded as on the whole better than the Qumran scroll 1QIsᵃ, a thousand years older.

We are somewhat better informed regarding the Greek Bible, from the letter of St. Jerome to Pope Damasus. Jerome knew three recensions of the Septuagint : that of Hesychius in Egypt, that of Lucian in Constantinople and Antioch, and that of Origen in Palestine. Elsewhere he cites only Origen and Lucian of Antioch, and seems to see in the Lucianic texts rather an older version previous to Origen. P. de Lagarde was satisfied he had identified this Lucianic recension, which he saw as a " seventh translation, " in texts from the Middle Ages. He identified variants marked in certain manuscripts with a Syriac *lamed* or a Greek *lambda* as being proper to the Antiochene patristic texts, and saw in the letter *l* the initial of Lucian. This identification is regarded by many, however, as insufficiently founded. [3] The great recensional undertaking on the Septuagint in Christian times remains that of Origen at Caesarea. [Further study of the " Lucianic " evidence, however, increasingly relates it to deliberate revision of the Alexandrian Septuagint under Jewish auspices in Syria-Palestine in pre-Christian times to bring it more into conformity with the Hebrew text of the late 2nd or early 1st centuries B.C.]. Origen undertook no corresponding activity for the New Testament. He did, however, have several copies of it in his library at Caesarea, which was later expanded by the priest Pamphilus before his death as a martyr in A.D. 310. This library survived the storm of persecution under Diocletian, and it was from Caesarea that Bishop Eusebius sent 50 copies of the Bible to Constantine.

3° Any given recension would have an authority of its own, and could give rise to a series of copies that would become a *family* of manuscripts. Yet the notion of manuscript family does not correspond directly to that of recension. As in the case of Lucian of Antioch and his reputed recension, it is sometimes difficult to identify the family of manuscripts which was the product of a particular recensional effort. Yet though the manuscript family does not always point unerringly to the character of a given recension, it normally does yield helpful indications. A " family " is in practice a group of manuscripts with the same specific characteristics : identical passages added or missing in the texts, identical " common " faults. In the agglomeration of Greek minuscule manuscripts of the New Testament, the Irish scholar Ferrar was able to isolate the group known as " family 13. " All its manuscripts share the following features : 1) exceptional readings in Mt 1, 16 (Joseph is not called Mary's spouse), and 12, 14; 2) transpositions of Lk 22, 43-44 (the bloody sweat) after Mt 26, 39, and of Jn 7, 53—8, 11 (the woman taken in adultery) after Lk 21, 38; 3) a concluding summary not only of the number of *stichoi* in the Gospels, but before this also of the number

---

[3] Msgr. DEVREESSE, *op. cit.*, p. 120.

of words. It has been possible also for Kirsopp Lake to identify another
similar group of NT manuscripts, " family 1. "

Any such family supposes an " ancestor " or basic manuscript,
usually no longer extant, from which the whole family derives; this is
labeled the " archetype. "

4⁰ Along with recensions, a manuscript tradition includes *contaminations*. Either a copyist works with a number of texts, or he compares
his chosen prototype with another text from which he accepts readings
when he thinks it opportune. Such procedure leads to an eclectic text.
The situation occurred frequently in the Middle Ages, and gave rise to
great difficulties for the demonstration of how manuscripts are related as to
prototypes and families. In place of a theoretical filiation of manuscripts
such as in (I) below, the result is an actual relationship like that in (II),
in which it has become quite difficult to disentangle the web of relationships and to arrive at a recognition of the missing archetypes A, B and C.
How is one to isolate c and d, which are of family A contaminated with B,
from e, a direct descendant of B; or from f, copied from C, but contaminated by B', which in turn derives from a mixture of A and B?

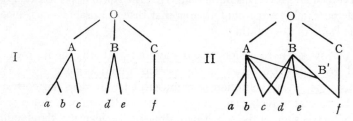

5⁰ Finally, subsequent to the recensions, there have often been
what are known (still among manuscripts) as *editions*. These are procedures for fixing certain external features of the text so as to standardize
the length and number of its lines (stichometry) and its division into
paragraphs. The oldest manuscripts, such as Vaticanus, were copied
(except for the poetical books) in unbroken lines that left no room for
sense divisions. Since all the lines have then roughly the same number
of letters, it becomes possible to identify places in which a particular
copyist, through inadvertence, has lost the number of letters in question
by skipping a line of his prototype. The edition of Eusebius included
for the Gospels a division into numbered paragraphs (for which cross
references were furnished by means of the " Eusebian canontables "). [4]
The canon and paragraph numbers were placed in the margins and did

---

[4] Cf. A VACCARI in *Mélanges Furlani** (Rome, 1957), pp. 433 ff.

not affect the arrangement of the text itself. The edition of Euthalius was quite different, since he arranged his text in sense units, *per cola et commata.*

II. PSYCHOLOGICAL FACTORS

We have thus far reviewed the principal matters regarding the milieu and the techniques of the copyist which might have some influence on the text he produces. To these must be added certain *psychological factors* which will affect the individual copyist in degrees peculiar to himself :

1º The copyist is exposed to certain indeliberate errors : for example, he may confuse one letter with another—in Greek, A with Δ or Λ; in Hebrew, *resh* (r, ר) with *daleth* (d, ד). This latter case is the more frequent for the fact that during several centuries, in the Aramaic script, these two letters were practically indistinguishable. The copyist may duplicate a letter which he has already copied (dittography), or he may on the other hand neglect to copy one of two identical letters that stand in close connection in the parent text (haplography). In this latter alternative, the eye of the copyist, moving from the text being copied back to the prototype, may be caught by the identical letter, but not in the correct place. He may in this way be led to skip a whole phrase of some length, if a similar combination of letters recurs at a short interval, either at the beginning *(homoiarkton)* or at the end of a word *(homoioteleuton).*

The ends of lines in the prototype are the point at which faults of this kind occur with the greatest frequency. Sometimes too, if the text being copied is not in perfectly straight lines, the copyist may be led to attach a line-ending of this kind to some following line, thus giving rise to a transposition (of this a clear-cut case from a Phoenician inscription has been pointed out by Dupont-Sommer); though transpositions can also occur in other circumstances.

2º Copyists are also liable to the impulse to " harmonize " parallel texts. In a chapter of Chronicles dealing with the reign of David, a copyist may introduce the text of the parallel passage from the book of Samuel (2 Sm 23, 25. 34); in Mk 3, 14 (Jesus choosing the Twelve), the Sinaiticus introduces the parallel choice of the apostles from Lk 6, 13. These harmonizations could occur automatically, simply because the copyist had the parallel passage in his memory. They could, however, come about more or less purposefully. They are particularly numerous in citations, the copyist deeming it his duty to rectify what appeared to him to be a faulty transcription on the part of his predecessor, when what he read seemed to him not to match up with what he knew.

3⁰ The scholarship, or would-be scholarship, of the scribe could be at the bottom of multiple errors in transmission, above all by way of addition to the text. He would tend to transform a text which he did not understand into a sequence of letters materially close in appearance to that which it replaced, but yielding in his judgment a more suitable sense. This is what is known as the " easier " reading. For example, depending on where they supposed Emmaus to be located, the copyists varied its distance from Jerusalem between 60 and 160 stadia in the text. Proper names were similarly manipulated in a number of cases. A further step has to do with the copyist's supposition that a specific text is contrary to received doctrine. It is not impossible that the Massoretic text has for such reasons blurred the Messianic implications of certain Old Testament passages adduced by Christians [though the only place where a choice between already existing variants seems actually to have been made on some such premise is in Ps 22, 17—translator]. It is certain that some passages in the Gospel of St. Mark were altered by copyists who saw them as out of harmony with the divinity of Christ. So, the copyists of the Verona and Palatinus codices were unwilling to admit that Christ " was astonished " (Mk 6, 6), and suppressed the disconcerting phrase. The uncials D (Bezae), W and Koridethi would not admit that the relatives of Christ said of Him " He has gone mad " (Mk 3, 21). Other copyists would not have it that the Son " does not know the day " of the final cataclysm. Others set out to efface the Jewish coloration of the Gospels.

III. RULES OF TEXTUAL CRITICISM

Based on these historical and psychological factors, and their influence on the transmission of a text, certain rules have been formulated which, however, must always be applied with discretion. As propounded by L. Pirot, the rules are seven :

1⁰ The reading which is the harder to understand is to be preferred, unless it is out of harmony with the context : *lectio difficilior.* Easier readings are normally attributable to the copyist.

2⁰ The shorter reading has preference over the longer, since the scribe's tendency is to explain and to gloss; but this rule can be reversed if it is possible to verify a haplography, a homoioteleuton, or the skipping of a line of text. *Lectio brevior potior.*

3⁰ That is the original reading which best accounts for the origin of the alternate readings.

4⁰ Any variant is to be rejected which gives the effect of a deliberate correction.

5⁰ In parallel passages, readings which are verbally divergent are to be preferred, given the tendency of scribes to harmonize.

6⁰ The reading which best squares with the diction and the outlook of the particular sacred writer is always to be preferred. There may, of course, be room for doubts with regard to this presumed diction or outlook : so that, for example, many critics will not accord priority to the readings of codex Bezae in spite of their more Semitic cast.

7⁰ Before accepting a variant, one must take into account the special characteristics of the particular manuscript in which it appears. From the manuscript taken as a whole we come to know the abilities or limitations of the scribe, the model from which he copied, its layout (in length of lines; in number of glosses), and the manner in which he consulted it.

§ 2. New Testament Textual Criticism

BIBLIOGRAPHY

Cf. the works cited on p. 108.

M. J. LAGRANGE, *Critique textuelle du Nouveau Testament, II : La critique rationnelle* (Paris, 1935).

L. VAGANAY, *Initiation à la critique textuelle néotestamentaire* (Paris, 1934).

H. J. VOGELS, *Handbuch der Textkritik des neuen Testaments* (Bonn, 1955).

I. CHOICE OF A TEXT

New Testament textual criticism is difficult because the manuscripts are so many. The first task of critics was to ascertain the scope of the material; the present results of such a survey we have reviewed above. The next step is the comparing and collating of manuscripts. The scriptural data include uncials, minuscules, liturgical books (lectionaries), papyri, ostraca (texts copied on pottery fragments), amulets, and in addition the various early versions and the citations in early writers, both of which have to be studied for text traditions of their own. The sheer quantity of all this transcends the data for any other ancient text whatsoever; and has given evidence of some 150,000 variants. Most of these are meaningless variations in spelling, or slips of the pen. Westcott and Hort, to whom we owe the figure in question, themselves affirmed that nine-tenths of the text is certain, and that variants of any significance relate to only a minimal part of the whole. Substantial variations there are, however, such as the pericope (i.e., paragraph) about the adulterous woman (Jn 7, 53—8, 11), the mention of the bloody sweat at Gethsemane (Lk 22, 43-44), the doxology at the end of Romans (16, 25-27). Ordinarily variants are less extensive than these; as when a series of manuscripts omits the title " Son of God " given to Christ at the beginning of Mk, or when another group of manuscripts omits mention of any particular church in the address of the Epistle to the Ephesians.

In the face of variants such as these, what text is to be preferred? For a long time it was the text of Erasmus, made popular through the editions of Robert Estienne, that was accepted. But Erasmus hardly did more than reproduce the manuscripts in the friary of the Dominicans in Basle, and the inadequacy of his text was recognized quite early. Bengal (1687-1752) was the first to undertake the grouping of manuscripts into families on the basis of recognized variants. He saw two fundamental types, or families, of manuscripts. This was too little. Griesbach (1745-1822) identified three families. Hug and Lachmann gave primacy to the early manuscripts. But it was Tischendorff who furnished the first critical edition (*Ed. octava major*, Leipzig, 1869-1872), abandoning the " received text " and giving priority to the family of the Sinaiticus, which he had discovered. Westcott and Hort offered identifications for the three families and the three recensions acknowledged by St. Jerome; their edition was based on the Vaticanus, which belongs to the same family as the Sinaiticus. The later work of Kirsopp Lake and of Streeter eventuated in the recognition of a fourth family, at least for the Gospels. Indeed, Père Lagrange came to distinguish different family groupings when there was question of the Gospels on the one hand, or of Acts, the Pauline Epistles, the Catholic Epistles or the Apocalypse as other, distinct, units. In the sketch that follows we will limit ourselves to characterizing the four great family groups of manuscripts, for which there are particular witnesses to be found in each of the several groupings of New Testament books.

II. Four families of texts

The first family studied by Père Lagrange is that which was long and mistakenly considered to be a " Western text, " because the evidence for it comes especially from the older Latin versions. Though its principal representative is a manuscript presumably of the 5th century (the Greek-

Latin codex D), this type of text is one of the earliest attested. It is present already in certain papyri (P³⁸), and in a parchment fragment of the 4th century from which derive the Old Latin and Old Syriac versions and which is cited by such Church writers in Greek as Marcion, St. Justin and St. Irenaeus. L. Vaganay connects with this type of text the uncials W, in Mk 1-5; E, in Acts; F and G in the Pauline Epistles; and several minuscules. This ancient text-type had a wide distribution in the 3rd and 4th centuries; but its homogeneity has been questioned. One would hesitate to restrict it, with Lagrange, to a limited number of witnesses; or to see in it, with Vaganay, " a mass of unrelated ancient variants " that has been considerably reworked.

The codex Bezae (D) tends to transform expressive but unexpected turns of phrase into banalities (thus in Mk 7, 19 *ocheton*, " drain, " replaces *aphedrōna*, " privy "). It is concerned for clarity, and does not admit of anyone's going to a desert place by boat (Mk 6, 32). It occasionally employs a slight modification (Mk 2, 26) to obviate a difficulty in the text. It tends to moderate the style of Mk by supplying conjunctions, suppressing redundancies, avoiding historical presents and collective plurals. It harmonizes, reproducing St. Matthew's *Our Father* in the Gospel of St. Luke (11, 1-4), and the evangelical golden rule in the decree from Jerusalem (Acts 15, 29). It introduces into the text biblical and theological preoccupations of its own, as when it omits, among other things, the mention of Abiathar the high priest (Mk 2, 26) which seems to disagree with 1 Sm 21, 3-4. It includes longer readings which in general are to be regarded as additions; thus, after Mt 20, 28, " But you, seek to become great starting from littleness, and starting from greatness, to become little " (after which follows the equivalent of Lk 14, 8-10). What attracts attention to this text type is its rather strong Semitic cast. The Latinisms it has been alleged to contain seem more questionable.

The second family is that of the great manuscripts, Vaticanus and Sinaiticus. Westcott and Hort saw in this a " neutral " text, which had not been corrupted like the others. It is today regarded as a recension especially well done, but not without faults of its own. Witnesses to this recension are to be found among the papyri, in a series of uncials, in various minuscules, in the Coptic versions (which has led to an Egyptian attribution for this text type), and in citations by Greek Fathers living in Egypt, such as SS. Athanasius and Cyril of Alexandria. It aims to give " what is ancient, short, correct. " In case of doubt, the copyist suppresses the doubtful element; thus for example, neither the woman taken in adultery nor the bloody sweat is given. Harmonizations and tendentious corrections are rare.

The third family is by far the most widespread. From an origin at Antioch, it traveled to Constantinople, and from there it was disseminated throughout the Greek world. The bulk of the minuscule manuscripts belongs to this recension, but it can count also certain important uncials, such as A (Alexandrinus), E (Basiliensis), K, Ω. It is the text of St. John Chrysostom. " In general, what characterizes this recension is a solicitude to be elegant, smooth, complete. It takes great pains with literary correctness : it offers better balanced phrasing, a better chosen diction, and in sum, a text for the use of the cultivated reader. It evinces also a notable concern for clarity, extending itself to explain in any possible way passages that are obscure. It also shows concern to have no element of the sacred books passed over, running together materials from parallel passages. This yields a fuller text, but one replete with serious flaws. Yet it is by no means a text without value. It has preserved, in one or another of its older witnesses, a goodly number of readings that were current in Syrian circles from the earliest centuries. " [5]

The fourth family is the Palestinian one, going back to the martyr Pamphilus († 310), a disciple of Origen. But this 3rd-century Palestinian recension is difficult to distinguish. The families 1 and 13 would be branches of it, as would the two oldest groups within the Georgian version. Another good representative of it would be the uncial manuscript Θ from Koridethi in the Caucasus, of the 8th or 9th century. All these texts are related to what we know of the text employed by Origen; but the witnesses within this family of manuscripts have been so contaminated by the Byzantine text that the evaluation of them is a singularly complex problem.

III. CRITICAL PRINCIPLES FOR A CHOICE OF HEADINGS

We no longer have, at present, the archetypes of these several families in their pristine state. Within a given family, certain good readings of the archetype may possibly have been preserved only in isolated manuscripts, or only in citations, the importance of which has of late become increasingly evident. The choice of the correct reading, whether it is made on the level of individual witnesses or on that of manuscript families, should be governed by critical principles : what principles?

This cannot be a choice based on numerical majority. Just as one single manuscript can be right in the face of a number of others from which it differs, so a single family can be correct as against the other three. Indeed, motives that have nothing to do with critical standards

---

[5] L. VAGANAY, *Initiation à la critique textuelle néotestamentaire**, p. 96.

have at times facilitated the distribution of an inferior text in preference to a better one. The Byzantine influence has worked in favor of the Antiochene family, without thereby making its readings any more significant. It would also be imprudent to take the sheer antiquity of the witnesses as the criterion; a recent copy may have been made from a truly ancient text, since destroyed. Also, critics are diffident with respect to readings in the papyri; these are often " private copies, and of the bargain counter variety " (Collomp). A third unacceptable criterion would be that of the general dependability of a given witness; for a bad copyist may have had a good text in front of him.

With that, let us proceed to some positive principles. Those that most readily suggest themselves are those of what is known as " external " criticism, based on the characteristics of the manuscripts and not on the content of their texts as such. Seemingly the best such way of classifying readings is Lachmann's criterion of " common faults " in copies of the text, from which one can infer a common ancestry of the manuscripts. But this becomes difficult to apply because it presupposes, as Dom Quentin puts it, that the primitive reading can be attained by a fixed perspective. Dom Quentin would therefore prefer to disregard the common faults and establish as an " iron rule " a critical norm developed by rigorous statistical classification of the manuscript variants.

The fact of contamination makes it impossible for either of these methods to arrive at the true text without calling into play criteria which are not centered simply on the character of the witnesses, but rather on the text which they contain : without calling, that is, on principles of *internal* criticism. Not merely is it necessary to choose the variant from which the others have all arisen, but also " the reading which best squares with the special tendencies of the author, " that is, with the historical and psychological circumstances in which he wrote. As in many cases these circumstances and tendencies are difficult to reconstruct, the choice of a particular reading is often a matter for doubt.

For this reason, L. Vaganay opts for an eclectic procedure. The families of manuscripts are identified in the first instance by classification on the basis of " external " criticism. But good papyri, like the Pauline Epistles in the Chester Beatty collection, and worthwhile uncials, such as the Freer ms. (W), show us to what an extent the different families have become mutually contaminated. " Internal " criticism will then have the final say. It will not be subjective, in that it must always be based on observable data; but it will call for information and intelligence. The criticism which is most fully informed and most perspicacious will best know the author and, by comprehension of what he proposed to

say, will finally select the true reading obscured by the copyists. After
several centuries of textual criticism we can now affirm that the Vaticanus
(and in its absence the Sinaiticus) merits a presumption in its favor,
though it must not be forgotten that it too is sometimes at fault and
has a tendency to arrive at shorter readings by suppression. Thus the
favoring presumption will in many cases have to yield.

In Vaganay's short monograph there are given specific, concrete
examples as to how to proceed. Modern critical editions are less inclined
than Westcott and Hort to seeing the Alexandrian text as closely related
to the " neutral " text. They give greater scope to the ancient versions
and to patristic citations.

Among critical editions, that of H. Von Soden (1913) should be
cited for the very considerable work that went into its preparation. It
has been severely challenged, because it was based on the identification of
three supposedly distinct and independent recensions : H (Hesychius),
I (Jerusalem), and K (*Koine*, or Antiochene); where these differed, the
majority became the norm. Vogels' edition (4th ed., Freiburg im Breisgau,
1955) is clear and less systematic. Preference is currently given to two
manual editions that are more empirical in their choice of readings;
they offer a reduced but substantial textual apparatus which affords
a swift survey of the manuscript tradition.

A. Merk (8th ed., 1957) leaves the text itself free of any added symbol,
except for indicating the beginning of the numbered verse by a short
vertical line where there might be room for doubt. At the bottom of the
page, following the appropriate verse number there are to be found the
variants for that verse. The words of the text for which variants are to be
offered are cited again, with a list of the manuscripts that support the
approved reading. Then, following a square bracket the alternative is
given, followed again by the list of witnesses which support it. If words
are simply transposed, the text form is not repeated, but a looping sign (∞)
is used to note the fact, and the alternative order is cited with its witnesses.
The manuscripts are often grouped by families : K *(Koine)* for the
Antiochene, C for the Caesarean, and H for the Hesychian text (our second
family, above). Where the first hand of a subsequently revised
manuscript offers a special reading, the symbol for that witness is noted
with an asterisk. Additional words are preceded by a plus sign (+);
words omitted by certain witnesses are followed by the symbol (>)
and the citation of the witnesses. Readings known to the Fathers are
often indicated. [6] The list of manuscripts cited, with their symbols,

---

[6] On the importance of the patristic texts, see the studies of P. M. BOISMARD,
cf. *RB** (1948), pp. 5-34.

is given in the preface, along with a detailed key to all the signs and abbreviations employed.

E. Nestle (24th ed., Stuttgart, 1960) indicates in the text itself, by the symbol ⌐, the point at which a variant is to be alleged in his apparatus. If more than one word is involved, a closing bracket ⌐ is also employed. If a single word is simply missing from certain manuscripts, a small circle appears with it in the text; if more than one word, the symbols (□...\) enclose the words in question. After the verse number in the apparatus, the pertinent symbols are repeated. The symbol is followed by the variant and the witnesses that support it; after these again comes (: *txt*) followed by the witnesses for the approved reading. For a grouping of manuscripts by families, the Gothic forms of H and K denote respectively the Hesychian and Antiochene families; Greek λ and φ the families 1 and 13. The vaguer symbols *pc, al* and the like indicate " a few, " or " some other " codices besides those specified by their own individual designations.

These two editions, one Catholic, the other Protestant, agree to an astonishing degree in sheer quantity of text. Areas for divergence between their earlier editions were indicated in 1949 by G. D. Kilpatrick [7] as being limited to the following verses : Mt 9, 34; 12, 47; 16, 2-3; 17, 21; 18, 11; 21, 44; 23, 14. Mk 7, 16; 9, 44-46; 11, 26; 15, 28; 16, 9-20. Lk 9, 54-56; 17, 36; 22, 19b-20; 22, 43-44; 22, 62; 23, 17, 34a; 24, 12. 40. Jn 5, 4; 7, 53—8, 11. Acts 8, 37; 15, 34; 24, 6-8; 28, 29. Rm 16, 24, 25-27. 1 Jn 5, 7-8.

§ 3. Textual Criticism of the Old Testament

BIBLIOGRAPHY

J. COPPENS, *La critique du texte hébreu de l'Ancien Testament** (Bruges-Paris, 1950).

E. DHORME, " Le texte hébreu de l'Ancien Testament, " *La Bible et l'Orient* (Paris, 1955).

Because the nature of its manuscript tradition is different, the text-critical problem has to be formulated for the Old Testament in quite different terms. The accumulated Hebrew manuscripts do not yield upon examination a variety of families such as we have seen for the Greek manuscripts of the New Testament. Interesting though they may be, the differences of reading between the schools of Ben Nephthali and Ben

---

[7] *JTS* (1949), p. 155.

Asher are still relatively insignificant. Nor does the material from the Cairo Geniza, not yet adequately published, seem to offer a substantially different recension, though its variants in vocalization give evidence of a tradition less rigid in that regard than for the consonantal text as such. The same is true of the differences traditionally reported as between the consonantal text of the Book of Daniel and the pronunciation called for by the Massora.

The texts from Qumran have modified this situation somewhat; for they give us an actual glimpse of Hebrew recensions different from that in the consonantal text traditionally handed down. The problem is not properly posed in terms of the Book of Isaias, for which most evidence has been published. Its text tradition was fixed within very narrow limits prior to the two well-known manuscripts 1QIs^a and 1QIs^b; and the ten or more fragmentary copies represented in subsequent finds attest this same situation. It is usually said that the relation of 1QIs^b to the Massoretic tradition is a matter of minimal differences only; though this is an overevaluation of the manuscript in question, both for its orthography and for the faithfulness of the copy, the fact remains that there is no recensional difference to be discerned, and only a limited number of individual variants in the consonantal text that call for serious evaluation. The complete scroll, 1QIs^a, is quite different. It is commonly described as a " vulgar " text, replete with copyist's errors, some of which have been corrected by the first or by later hands. It is also a reworked text; and insofar as it may be called recensional, it is a conscious departure from the consonantal tradition represented in the Massora, which has priority over it even in most matters of minute detail. The " popular " character of the text is reflected in an expansion of the orthography on principles adapted from later Aramaic; this in turn reflects a mode of pronunciation important for the insight it affords into how Hebrew was read in the period in question, but not equally so for the forms or the wording of the text itself. The verb syntax of the original authors suffers at the hands of the Qumran scribe, or of his prototype, in the use of perfect and imperfect tenses especially. Irrelevant claims of a " Messianic " import have been made for a reading in Is 52, 14; like many another unique reading of this scroll, the explanation here is one of different form only. Few of the readings in 1QIs^a are genuinely in accord with Septuagintal evidence; and despite the light it sheds on an obscure period in the history of the Hebrew language, this scroll is more significant for its clues to the interpretation of the text than for the pristine state of the text itself. [8]

---

[8] J. T. MILIK, *Ten Years of Discovery in the Wilderness of Judea*, p. 24.

The mass of fragmentary evidence from Qumran for the rest of the Old Testament, described above, pp. 15 ff., is still in course of publication. It is clear that it has special significance for the support it lends in the Books of Samuel to a fuller and divergent Hebrew text related to the Septuagint; and for its witness to a shorter edition of Jeremias, also known to us from the Greek. For the rest, it shows three types of text in the Pentateuch (related severally to the Massoretic, the Samaritan, and the Septuagint forms), and in all books a much greater fluidity in matters of detail in their transmission than would be admissible in any subsequent period. [9]

In various ways, the Qumran discoveries have heightened the long-standing problem of Old Testament criticism as to how we are to evaluate the Septuagint, or rather, in the last analysis, the Hebrew text supposed by the Septuagint, when it differs from the Massoretic text. The Qumran Hebrew evidence for the shorter (by one-eighth) text of the Book of Jeremias, offered to us in the Greek, is slender but unmistakable. In such other books as Daniel and Esther it is clear the the Greek differences from the received Hebrew text amount to different editions of the Books. The crucial problem of the relationship between the Massoretic text and the Septuagint will in future be approached with added data; but it remains crucial.

The work of Old Testament textual criticism is complicated by the fact that the manuscript tradition of the Septuagint is far from displaying the approximate unity of the Massoretic tradition. The Vaticanus and Alexandrinus manuscripts contain quite different texts for the Book of Judges. In the Book of Tobias, there are really three texts; the Alexandrinus and Vaticanus have one same text, but the Sinaiticus represents (with the Old Latin) a notably different, much more fulsome, form of the Book which is matched by the Semitic fragments found at Qumran. [10] In the Book of Daniel, we have St. Jerome's witness for it that the received Greek text is actually that of " Theodotion, " while the Alexandrian Septuagint form in the Chigi manuscript has been set aside. Here, as in Judges, the question arises : one translation revised, or two distinct translations? Barthélemy's study of the Minor Prophets in Greek from the Wadi Khabra, taken with Cross' work on the relation between the Hebrew Samuel at Qumran and the Greek tradition give evidence of pre-Christian recensional activity in Greek, reflected in our actual LXX manuscripts.

---

[9] *RB* (1956), p. 60.
[10] *RB* (1953), pp. 18-29.

The variants in the Septuagint tradition scarcely make it possible, as of now, to identify manuscript families. Numerous as they are, they are of a different type from the work of the later translators Aquila and Symmachus (Theodotion is often a special case, and the label seems to cover quite early material at times). The field of Septuagint criticism has been thorny with controversy, represented most explicitly of late in the studies of P. Katz, H. Orlinsky and P. Kahle. As demonstrated already in the work of H. Swete, and more recently in the works of G. Gerleman on Job and Chronicles, J. Ziegler and, less successfully, I. Seeligman on Isaias, I. Soisalon-Soininen and Pretzl on Judges, the Septuagint reflects a Greek outlook, disconcerted by certain Semitic images and concepts. It echoes the religious preoccupations of the Alexandrian community, concerned to present God acceptably to Greek mentalities. It derives from the theology of its own day, for example in questions of Messianism : we shall see later on how it supplies precision to Is 7, 14 and Ps 109, 3. In other cases it forces the text to convey a meaning of resurrection. Of such circumstances, textual criticism must at all times take account. The men responsible for this translation had no little difficulty in recreating in their own minds the vital experience of the lawgivers and the prophets; they tended to orient towards Greek morality and Greek theodicy the divine command and the divine presence of the text to be translated. But if many a time they have badly understood and badly rendered, they are witnesses none the less, whose text in Samuel and in Ezechiel often takes actual priority over that contained in the Massora.

The Massora, indeed, is not without tendencies of its own. It carries with it unquestionable copyists' errors, of great antiquity. The extent to which it contains deliberate corrections, based on the development of the language, or of thought, is more difficult to estimate. If there is in the Septuagint a tendency to expand the number of the Messianic texts and that of allusions to the resurrection of the dead, it may be asked whether for its part the Massoretic text does not have a tendency to diminish the number of the Messianic texts and of the reproaches addressed to Israel (in the case that these indictments could call into question Israel's status as the Chosen People). It should also be noted that in the vocalization of proper names, the Septuagint represents an older, and in many cases a more satisfactory, stabilization of their orthography (cf. Salphaad, Nm 26, 33).

Arguments of this sort are already arguments of internal criticism. The reading to be rejected is the one accounted for by the mentality of a milieu subsequent to that of the composition of the text. Only rarely do the other Greek versions (more influenced by the parallel transmitted Hebrew), the Syriac, or the Samaritan Pentateuch provide readings of their own which are independent both of the Septuagint and the Massoretic text. Examples would be, for the Syriac, Ex 20, 24, " where thou wilt have my name invoked, " in place of " I shall have "; and for the Samaritan text, Dt 27, 4 (Garizim in place of Ebal). Usually their readings have support on one side or the other, as between the Hebrew and the Greek. Thus Ex 12, 40 in the Samaritan recension corresponds with an intentional correction in the Greek, over against the Massoretic text. Ordinarily, however, the correspondence of these witnesses will be on the side of the Massoretic Hebrew.

In practice, the Massoretic text is the necessary starting point. For comparison with this, one endeavors to reconstruct the text read by the versions, keeping in mind that there are often several Greek texts. The Samaritan and the Qumran texts must also be looked into, where they exist. What subsequent historical periods have to offer by way of explanation for the divergencies needs also to be studied. A text must be sought for which will be intelligible, not from our own standpoint, but from that of a contemporary of the original text. Sometimes, one is forced to argue to corruptions or transpositions. [11] We must face the fact that most conjectures not based on the Hebrew text or on one of the versions have proved untenable, especially since the Ras Shamra discoveries have restored to us pieces of ancient West Semitic literature and have enriched our knowledge of the Hebrew language. By contrast with the New Testament, which was published within a fifty year period, the elaboration of the Old Testament covered more than a millenium of time, in the course of which many changes took place in the script, in the syntax, and in the modalities of the Faith. It will often be obligatory rather to wait than to " correct. " Even when a correction is clearly called for, it must be shown for what reason the corrected text has come to be transformed into that which now exists; for the Ben Asher recension gives proof of being a conscientious and well-made recension, of unquestionable superiority to the Qumran Isaias, for example, which at one and the same time confirms the antiquity of the Massoretic tradition and shows itself textual, inferior from a critical standpoint. It is on these grounds that the Massora deserves a presumption in its favor.

---

[11] On the glosses, see G. R. Driver, *Glosses in the Hebrew Text of the Old Testament* (Louvain, 1957).

CHAPTER III

LITERARY CRITICISM

§ 1. The Problem of Biblical Languages

BIBLIOGRAPHY

F. M. ABEL, *Grammaire du grec biblique** (Paris, 1927).

J. NOUGAYROL—H. CAZELLES—G. RYCKMANS, " Langues et écritures sémitiques, " *SDB*, V, cols. 257-334.

A. SPERBER, " Hebrew Grammar : A New Approach, " *JBL*, 62 (1943), pp. 137-162.

F. BLASS,—A. DEBRUNNER, *A. Greek Grammar of the New Testament*, tr. and ed. by Robert W. Funk (University of Chicago Press, 1961; 3 rd impression, 1967).

J. H. MOULTON, *A Grammar of New Testament Greek* (Edinburgh : Clarke, 1949).

The study of textual criticism has shown us that in this matter we can hardly arrive at sound conclusions without making an appeal to proofs of internal criticism drawn from the content of the texts. But to establish the meaning of these latter, we must still take account of vocabulary and grammar. At the same time as it insists on the importance of textual criticism which, it says, " possesses rules so stable and assured that it has become a choice instrument for editing the divine Word with more purity and exactness, " the encyclical *Divino Afflante* underlines the necessity of " securing each day a greater mastery of biblical and oriental languages. " Language, this instrument which the hagiographer used, demands an attentive study and, in this domain, we know well enough that the rules of grammar are not mathematical rules! Morphology and syntax evolve; they also offer dialectical variations : one sound of the Hebrew language pronounced " *sh* " in the hill country of Ephraim was pronounced " *s* " in Transjordania (Jgs 12, 6), and in the time of Jesus the Galileans staying in Judea were recognized by their speech (Mt 26, 73).

The grammar of NT Greek is now much better known thanks to the papyri. Until the end of the last century, biblical Greek was spoken of as a separate dialect; we now know that it had as its basis the common language spoken in the whole of the Hellenized Mediterranean world, the

Koine. A. Deissmann has contributed a great deal to making the modalities of this language known. [1] G. H. Moulton and G. Milligan in England, W. Bauer in Germany, have published precise dictionaries of it, relying on the monumental " vocabulary of the papyri " arranged by Preisigke. [2] Finally, the grammar was drawn out and systematized by J. H. Moulton, F. Blass-A. Debrunner, Père Abel and several others, without counting more recent studies like those of M. Zerwick and of C. F. D. Moule. Thus tools are not lacking at the present time.

For Hebrew and Aramaic we have access to fewer documents, although the texts range over a much longer period. The classical grammar of the language of Isaias is not that of late texts; also the force of words changes with the preoccupations of the centuries, while preserving a certain general orientation. We must remember this when translating a text; we must cast a glance at the parallel passages, determine the field of vision of the author and establish in this way the real import of the passage while taking account of all the elements which condition it. In this domain as in that of Greek, our age has seen the tools perfected. We have grammars : Gesenius—Kautzch, Bauer—Leander, Joüon, Mayer—Lambert, Beer—Meyer for the Hebrew; Bauer—Leander for biblical Aramaic. We also have Hebrew-Aramaic dictionaries of the OT : Gesenius—Buhl, Brown—Driver—Briggs, and more recently Zorell and Köhler—Baumgartner. [3] There again, the most recent archeological discoveries and the studies of comparative linguistics have notably enriched our understanding of the languages of the OT; it suffices to mention the deciphering of the tablets of Ras-Shamra (Ugarit) for which C. H. Gordon has put out a grammar and lexicon useful to all biblical scholars. [4] In short, we are much better equipped now than 50 years ago to shed light upon the most puzzling passages of the holy books.

---

[1] A. DEISSMANN, *Light from the Ancient East*, tr. by L.R.M. Strachan (New York, 1927).

[2] J. H. MOULTON—G. MILLIGAN, *The Vocabulary of the Greek New Testament* (London, 1920); W. BAUER, *Worterbuch zum Neuen Testament*[4] (Berlin 1952); F. PREISIGKE, *Wörterbuch der grieschichen Papyrusurkunden* (Berlin, 1914-1927).

[3] And better yet *concordances* (MANDELKERN, LISSOWSKI), in which all the uses of a word are systematically put together.

[4] C. H. GORDON, *Ugaritic Manual* (Rome, 1955).

§ 2. Literary Criticism of the Old Testament

I. THE PROBLEM OF LITERARY GENRES [5]

BIBLIOGRAPHY

A ROBERT, " Littéraires (genres), " *SDB*, V, pp. 405-421.

A. ROBERT—L. VÉNARD, " Historique (genre), " *SDB*, IV, pp. 7-32.

R. BLOCH, " Midrash, " *SDB*, V, pp. 1263 ff.

C. JEAN, *Le Milieu biblique; II, La littérature** (Paris, 1923).

H. W. ROBINSON (ed.), *Record and Revelation* (Oxford : Clarendon, 1938).

" Questioni Bibliche alla Luce dell'Enciclica, " *Div. Affl. Spir.* (Rome, 1949).

E. NIELSEN, *Oral Tradition* (London : SCM, 1954).

A. GELIN—J. DELORME, " Genres littéraires, " *Catholicisme*, IV, 1836-1845 (Paris, 1958).

C. H. GORDON, *New Horizons in Old Testament Literature* (1960).

A. ROBERT—A. TRICOT, " The Literary Genres, " *Guide to the Bible*, I[2] (New York : Desclée, 1960), pp. 476 ff.

J. BRIGHT, " Modern Study of Old Testament Literature, " *The Bible and the Ancient Near East* (Garden City : Doubleday, 1961).

P. DUNCKER, " Biblical Criticism, " *CBQ*, 25 (1963), pp. 22-33.

FELDMAN, " Biblical Motives and Sources, " *JNES*, 22 (1963), pp. 73-103.

O. EISSFELDT, *The Old Testament, An Introduction* (New York : Harper, 1965).

To constitute a literature, it is not enough to have a vocabulary with its words, a morphology with its inflections, a syntax which lays down the order of words and their meaning according to this order. Each clause is written in a more general structure which allows the reader to discern in what sphere the thought of the writer is moving. This overall structure in which everything comes to be inserted so as to take on meaning is what we call literary genre. The 20th century reader well knows that he must not put himself in the same frame of mind to read a novel or to study a volume on history. His newspaper itself taxes its ingenuity to facilitate reading for him by putting its short story on the bottom of page 3, its political information on page 1, its scientific or literary reports on page 5. Each of these literary genres, if their laws are respected, communicates to the reader a certain *truth*, but in different orders : the one, in the psychological order; the other, in that of social life; and the third, in a more intellectual order. Assuredly, the incautious reader would expose himself to many pitfalls if he did not proceed, at the

---

[5] See p. 63 : the theology of inspiration and the literary genres.

moment he began reading, to adjust his state of mind in relation to his subject matter.

These pitfalls might be much more serious when one reads a text written a long time ago, when the intellectual, political and social conditions were not the same as today.   Here are the actual words of the encyclical *Divino Afflante* : " (What the ancient authors) wished to signify by their words cannot be determined by the laws of grammar or philology alone, no more than by the context alone.   It is absolutely necessary that the exegete go back wholly in spirit, as it were, to those remote centuries of the East and with the aid of history, archeology, ethnology and other sciences, accurately determine what modes of writing, so to speak, the authors of that ancient period meant to use, and in fact did use.   For the ancient peoples of the East, in order to express their ideas, did not always employ those forms or kinds of speech which we use today, but rather those used by the men of their times and countries.   The exegete cannot determine a priori what those were; he can only do so after a careful examination of the ancient literature of the East.   The investigation on this point, carried out with greater care and diligence during the past 40 or 50 years than ever before, has shown more clearly what forms of expression were used in those far-off times, whether in poetic description or in the formulation of laws and rules of life or in recording the facts and events of history. "

Every work of art intends to signify something to him who sees it or reads it; now the Bible is also a work of art.   From this standpoint, it is a library, rather than a book, in which are found joined together writings of diverse genres.   A. Robert compared literary genres to artistic styles : the Bible is like these composite cathedrals in which each epoch has contributed its share while placing its own mark on them.   To understand any great work, one must know how to take it all in with a single glance and at the same time to examine one by one the units which make it up, while keeping in mind the genre of each.   To confound the genres would lead to absurdity : the *Légende des siècles* is not history, nor is *Pauca meae* a courtly poem.   What holds for one author taken individually is all the more valid for the whole of a literature.   What variety there is in French literature, from *La Chanson de Roland* to *La condition humaine!* Without forgetting that from century to century some constants, some hidden connections and some permanent themes reappear, from the *Mysteries* of the Middle Ages to the *Eve* of Peguy, from *Tristan and Iseult* to the *Soulier de satin*.   The critic who must explain a French work cannot be content with analyzing it abstractly by isolating it from the wider tradition in which it is rooted.

Similarly the Bible is a human work whose composition ranges over 10 centuries and more. It is the Word of God, to be sure, as we have said above; but in human language, and in Hebrew and Greek language. Explaining it first demands a work of minute analysis : recognizing the authors who took part in its composition; isolating in the work of these authors the small units which make it up. Every well-done piece hands down a movement of thought which unites the different phrases into a single grouping. It is possible for this unit to appear at the first glance : such is the case, for example, in the canticle of Debora (Jgs 5); it also might be much less apparent, the text remaining in suspense and finding a harmonious sequence further on. Literary criticism then calls for bringing together what is apparently connected; but prudently, for the ancient mentality is not our own, and without fearing the risk of a hypothesis, for each author should be presumed to be intelligent, and an intelligible text is preferable to a text whose meaning is not apparent.

Once this preliminary work is done, we must bear in mind that the fragment thus put in evidence is not an isolated unit; eventually it takes its place in the whole of the literary work; at any rate, it can only be explained according to the actual personality of an author, and he, for his part, is rooted in a very precise milieu and epoch. The way in which the author expresses himself, and consequently the literary genre he uses, depends on the conditions of life in this milieu and this epoch, on the problems which occur, and the cultural canons in use. Every literary work is on the whole a dialogue between the author and the society of his time; because of this, the author must bow to the social exigencies of the dialogue. Literary genres are not arbitrary creations of the authors, but social phenomena; their variety echoes the variety of social life, and their evolution goes hand in hand with that of society. A thousand historical contingencies intervene to introduce nuances into the expression of human thought and to cause its modalities to vary. A biblical exegete who would not seek to explain the texts according to the social and historical conditions in which they were written would thus be ignorant of the nuances of the language employed in the holy books, and would thereby be prone to misunderstand their message. It is through the knowledge of an epoch, its modes of expression, its problems and its mentality, that we can determine exactly the literary genres then in use, employing the whole Bible itself to perform this labor; the immediate milieu of biblical works forms a living tradition which has its very distinct characteristics. But Israel was itself not isolated in history and geography; perhaps no other people was so swept along in the backwaters of history as it was, mixed into the immense stirrings of races and civilizations which occur in certain privileged regions, such as was from this point of view its native setting. Thrust into the eastern milieu, it has taken part in its culture.

II. LITERARY GENRES IN THE ANCIENT EAST

In studying Hebrew literature, for a long time Greek literature was the only means of comparison, but an insufficient one. Actually it was only quite late in its history that Israel came into contact with the Greek world, when its own thought patterns were already established. Since a century ago, the discovery of the great literatures of the ancient East, Mesopotamian and Hittite on one side, Egyptian on the other, and Chanaanite between the two, has put the Bible back into its real cultural context. In the course of its history, Israel actually found itself in contact with these diverse currents of civilization which cut across the very soil on which it was implanted. During the entire first half of the 2nd millennium, Chanaan was still culturally dependent on Mesopotamia; it is in cuneiform that letters are written there or that certain epic texts are copied (Epic of Gilgamesh). Then after 1580 the political preponderance of Egypt was established as far as the backcountry, and its cultural influence increased and persisted even after its political decline (12th). Thus it is that the Ugarit literature (north of the Syrian coast), gathered about the 15th century but produced much earlier, testifies to the Mesopotamian influence, although this does no harm its own originality. At the start of the monarchy the Israelite literature adds to this a certain influence of the Egyptian culture. In order to situate the literature of Israel, it is therefore useful to know what literary genres we find in Mesopotamia, in Egypt, and in Chanaan, the last being the most important for us, and the least known.

In *Mesopotamia*, the Sumerian [6] and Akkadian literatures differ in language but are closely intermingled, the latter owing much to the first. We recognize in them the following literary genres :

— Documents of everyday life : lists, receipts, quite numerous economic and administrative documents (censures, ceremonials).

— Juridical documents : contracts (rent, sale, adoption), court records, collections of laws.

— Letters of all kinds, letters of state and private letters.

— Collections for the use of scribes, such as lists of symbols and lists of words.

---

[6] Cf. S. N. KRAMER, *L'histoire commence à Sumer*, tr. Bottero (Paris, 1957).

— Astrological, astronomical, and mathematical lists.

— Divining lists and medical lists.

— Rituals for the various kinds of priests and magicians.

— Lamentations and hymns of a lyrical nature, distributed into different categories bearing technical names.

— Myths relative to the condition of man and to his relationships with divinity : thus the creation poem [7] (closely linked to a ritual), the Epic of Gilgamesh, the myths of Adapa and Etana.

— Inscriptions celebrating some foundation or great exploit of the king; when developed, thus genre gives birth to the Annals in which the king retells his campaigns.

— Royal lists and sometimes synchronous records of Ashur and Babylon.

— Dialogues or reflections on the human condition, which fall into the general category of wisdom literature, also represented by fables and proverbs. [8]

Actually, not all those genres have a rigid structure. Although several among them relate to history, we do not find in them disinterested historiography. A good survey of these texts approximately grouped by genre and epoch will be found in *La littérature des Babyloniens et des Assyriens* by C. F. Jean; but documentation has accumulated considerably since the appearance of this book (1923). *Choix de textes religieux assyro-babyloniens* by P. Dhorme gives fewer selections, but gives their text and translation (1907).

Egyptian literature has its own divisions which do not cover the preceding ones, even though one is led to call them by similar names. Here is how the Egyptian texts are classified in the collective work published by Kees and other German Egyptologists :

— Literature of the dead, subdivided into : texts of the pyramids, texts of the sarcophagi (Middle Empire) and Book of the Dead (New Empire); guides for the afterlife (books of Amdouat, book of Doors, book to pass into eternity).

— Theological teachings (documents of Memphite theology), and especially hymns, rituals, myths and a mass of religious pieces done on the walls of the temples (Edfou, Dendera...), and finally magic texts.

— Wisdom texts : teachings attributed to some king or vizier; writings of a political nature; divine histories, stories and fables.

---

[7] R. LABAT, *Le Poème babylonien de la création* (Paris, 1935).

[8] VAN DIJK, *La sagesse sumérienne* (Leyden, 1957).

— In the category of historical writings can be listed : Annals celebrating the conquests of the Pharaos, the " novellen " relative to some event of a reign (consecration of a temple), and lastly the biographies and autobiographies. These genres obey certain set procedures or conventions.

— Texts of love poetry (Papyrus, Chester-Beatty, Harris 500. . .).

— Satires aimed at an ignorant scribe, for example, or at the professions.

— These can be considered as scientific genres : astronomical and mathematical texts, medical literature (Lefebvre), catalogues and word-lists (*Onomastica* published by Gardiner).

Documentation in regard to *Syria*, *Phoenecia*, and *Palestine* is much less available; it shows noteworthy affinities with the preceding two.

Aside from Ras-Shamra (Ugarit), we know only of inscriptions (in the Phoenician or Aramaic language) : tomb inscriptions, dedicatory or triumphal; these latter tend toward the historical genre when they relate in detail the exploits of the king (Mesha of Moab, Zakir of Hamath, Kilamuwa and Panammu of Sam'al, Azitawadda, king of the Danounians). However, we have a text (mutilated) of a treatise (Mati'ilu of Arpad with a certain Bar-Ga'ya of KTK) and two political letters (the ostracon of Ashur and the papyrus of Saqqara).

Ugarit has yielded :

— A great mythological epic, probably divided into several cycles : Baal and Anat.

— The *libretto* (still very obscure) of a ritual linked with a cosmogonical myth (the birth of the " amiable gods ") and another similar religious document for the " marriage of Nikkal and the moon-goddess " (probably translated from Hurrite).

— Two legendary sagas, the first closer to mythology (Aqhat), the second perhaps comprising some historical traditions (Keret).

— Lists of divinities and of sacrifices to offer.

— Letters, diplomatic and administrative documents, inventories and even fragments of a hippiatric treatise. [9]

This is enough to have some idea of the literary canons in current use in the little kingdoms near Israel; far from enough, however, to have terms of comparison with the whole of biblical literature; very often one must seek them out in Mesopotamia or Egypt, without forgetting the Hittite documentation found in Asia Minor.

---

[9] Almost all the texts were published by C. VIROLLEAUD in the Review *Syria*. The main texts are found in C. H. GORDON, *op. cit.*, p. 122 and G. R. DRIVER, *Canaanite Myths and Legends* (Edinburgh, 1956).

III. ISRAEL AND THE ANCIENT EAST

But if we must cast a glance on the other literatures of the ancient Near
East in order to shed light on the literary genres of the biblical texts, it
would be a mistake to try to reduce the literature of Israel purely and
simply to that of its neighbors. Israel had to solve its own problems;
its cultural development was worked out within an ideological framework
unparalleled elsewhere; a whole conglomeration of facts has thus led it
to procure an original literature. Doubtless one might think a priori
that by penetrating into Chanaan the Israelites began by employing the
genres in current use in the country whose language they borrowed
(according to Is 19, 18 Hebrew is the "language of Chanaan "). But as
regards the period that may be called classical (10th-7th), one is quite
compelled to affirm that some of their creations have specific characteristics. If the Israelite " novelle, " for example, can be compared with the
Egyptian " novelle, " [10] we find since the era of Solomon, in the account
of the succession of David, a historiography whose equivalent in Egypt
or Assyria would be sought in vain. Similarly, however interesting
are the meager specimens of the prophetic genre (in the broad sense)
provided by the texts of Mari, the Egyptian literature (voyage of Wen-
Amon and " prophecy " of Ipuwer), and the stele of Zakir, [11] we must
admit that biblical prophecy develops along lines far different and much
richer, even from a literary standpoint. Finally, we must not deny the
contacts between the Israelite wisdom and that of Egypt (unfortunately,
Chanaan's is unknown). Similarly, the poet of Job develops with a very
personal art the theme of the suffering Just Man, which is also familiar
in Mesopotamia.

In order to clarify all, it is not enough to project contacts between
the Bible and the neighboring literatures; we must still take account of
the evolution of the genres within the biblical literature itself. And what
is more, even the imitation of the foreign models is not always a sign
that a selection is ancient or lacks originality; this may be due to a passing
fad or an exercise of a learned writer who renews in this way his artistic
resources. Thus can be explained the contacts with Phoenecian culture in
Ezechiel (14, 14; 28) who is certainly not the least personal of the Israelite
writers (cf. also Is 14); likewise a stylistic Phoenecian influence has been
sought in Ecclesiastes (Dahood). [12] In fact, the problem of foreign

---

[10] S. HERRMANN, " Die Königsnovelle in Aegypten und in Israel, " *Wiss. Zeit.*
(Leipzig), III, pp. 51-62; " Untersuchungen zur überlieferunggestalt mittelag, "
Literaturwerke (Berlin, 1957).

[11] Texts of Mari and stele of Zakir, pp. 469 ff.

[12] The Language of Qohelet, " *CBQ* (1952), pp. 127-232.

influences on biblical literature is set in new terms at each turning point of Israel history. Once its individuality was formed and well-affirmed, the creative genius of Israel found itself successively confronting the most diverse cultures : Assyrian (8th-7th), Babylonian (6th, and still later for the Jewish communities of Mesopotamia), Persian (6th-4th, and beyond for the same communities), Greek (5th and later), without counting the constant proximity of the Phoenecian and Aramaic world, and even of Egypt. Its great faculty of assimilation allowed Israel to make the best of everything; that is a factor which must be considered when we study the evolution of the genres. Thus, the Apocalypse springs from prophecy and its images, but it springs from within a given cultural context, which has not entirely been made clear, but in which the Persian element is not foreign.

Let us note one last fact. The literature of Israel must not be handled as a purely written literature. It is rooted in a very living oral tradition, especially at its high point or in works which in all times draw their essential materials from there. Now the products of oral cultures have their proper laws, concerning which the writers of the ancient East do not teach us much, being witnesses of more advanced cultural stages. We must have recourse to ethnology to learn the forms of primitive literatures such as they are still now being worked out in societies scarcely evolved, analogous to the Israel of the patriarchal epoch, of the time of the conquest, and of that of the Judges. While allowing for the difference in mentalities, we find among certain peoples living at the same cultural stage, notably the nomadic shepherds, [13] story forms, proverbs, " sayings, " and poetic genres which may allow us to shed light on certain primitive sketches of the sacred literature of Israel. That this comparison is difficult to handle, we can understand; it is nonetheless necessary.

IV. The literary genres of the old testament

The analysis of the literary forms of the biblical texts has always been a preoccupation of the exegetes, but it is only the modern discoveries of archeology and ethnology which have enabled them to work it out systematically. [14] The most advanced attempts have been carried out, not without some excess at times, in the so-called " Formgeschichte " School (" history of forms "). [15] Once the necessary distinctions are

---

[13] Card. E. Tisserant, " Notes sur l'histoire des Patriarches " *Studia Anselmiana*, 27-28 (= *Miscellanea biblica* A. Miller *oblata*) (Rome, 1951), pp. 9-14.

[14] *Los generos literarios de la Sagrada Escritura** (Barcelona-Madrid, 1957).

[15] Cf. our *Introduction to the Old Testament*, pp. 111ff.

worked out between the purely literary task of analysis of forms and the value judgment on the essence of the work, which necessarily appeals to other criteria, it remains that the classification of the literary genres represented in the Bible is an indispensable aspect of criticism. Unfortunately, it is difficult to establish, and the very number of classifications proposed shows that none of them musters unanimity of agreement. Then too, the judgment on the essence is often intermingled with the appreciation of the form, since no classification of the genres can stick to purely " formal " criteria, especially in matters of history. By way of example, here is a classification based largely on the one which the Protestant A. Bentzen [16] proposes.

Bentzen strives first of all to separate in the Bible oral tradition from written literature, a much discussed problem, for we do not know when the biblical books, particularly the oldest ones, were set down in writing. We actually know that, in many civilizations of old, the epics and the religious texts (hymns, rituals) were transmitted from mouth to mouth for a long time; the classical case is that of the Vedas of India, the most archaic fragments of which may go back to the end of the 2nd millennium B.C., while their consignment to writing is only partially attested to in the 11th century A.D. [17] Similarly, it is estimated that the mythical epics of Ugarit may go back as far as the beginning of the 2nd millennium, though transcribed about the 15th century. The south of Chanaan invaded by Israel had known writing for a long time [18] and it can be admitted that history unfolded there in an atmosphere of a written culture, but only to a certain extent; for many centuries, the influence of the oral tradition must be taken into account. Moreover it would be a mistake to completely separate oral forms and written forms : the second stem from the first through an imperceptible transition and, after all, " an entirely stereotyped narration in the oral tradition does not differ at all, in respect to form, from a written document. " [19] It is fairer to distinguish, on the one hand, all of the simple elementary forms and, on the other hand, the composite works which gather materials from diverse forms, and this in poetry as well as in prose.

---

[16] *Introduction to the Old Testament*, I, pp. 102-264.

[17] L. RENOU and J. FILLIOZAT, *L'Inde classique*, I, nos. 515 and 535. But according to P. MASSONOURSEL (*L'Inde antique*, Paris, 1933, p. 261), " the Vedas were only written quite late, at the end of the 18th and at the beginning of the 19th, under the influence of Europeans, and through the ' treason ' of some Brahmans. "

[18] Cf. *above* p. 71.

[19] J. LINDBLOM, cited by BENTZEN, *op. laud.*, p. 105.

The poetic forms

As *elementary* poetic forms, Bentzen cites the chants of the workers (Neh 4, 4), which often turn into an incantation for the purpose of hastening and accomplishing the work (Nm 21, 17 f.); the satires (cf. Is 47); drinking songs (Is 22, 13); the love songs so popular in Egypt (Is 23, 16); funeral chants (2 Sm 1, 17; 3, 33; cf. the ironical imitations of Is 14, 4 f. and Ez 27, 32); war chants (1 Sm 17, 7), which can turn into incantation (4 Kgs 13, 17). It will also be noted that the Bible has preserved only very rare traces of genres that can be called " profane, " while remarking, however, that war belonged to the domain of the sacred, as did the nuptial ceremonies whose form must be compared, at least in essence, with the Canticle of Canticles. We might further note the " maternal sayings " (Gn 4, 1; 21, 7; 33, 31 f.) and the paternal blessings (Gn 9, 26-27; 27, 28-29 and 39-40; 49) often matched by parallel curses (Gn 9, 25).

Selections which belong to these genres are often very short; when they are developed (notably the wedding and funeral chants), they already recall the *psalms*. In primitive times these latter draw essentially from the lyric style of worship : hymns to the glory of divinity, thanksgivings after a success, lamentation after a defeat or a catastrophe... in practice, however, it happens more than once that the genres intermingle (as in proper, for example, in complex " liturgies "), and above all, that the psalm genre is imitated outside of the liturgical setting. Aside from these imitations, we generally observe a constant harmony between the genres and their settings : an entire pattern of phraseology imposes itself in a given circumstance and finds itself taken up again without great changes from century to century.

The *wisdom* literature comprises popular genres and scholarly genres which remain profoundly interconnected. Its nucleus is the popular proverb which arises from the observation of a situation or of a character (1 Sm 10, 12). Then it is elaborated into a maxim; but this is a carefully sculptured work of art, whose distinctive mark is the parallelism in which words and phrases correspond in pairs (Prv 10 f.). This fundamental genre finds more complex developments : the riddle (Jgs 14, 12), the parable (2 Sm 12, 1-4; Is 28, 23-29), the fable (Jgs 9, 7-15), the dialogue which treats of a problem of life (Jb), and the allegory (Prv 9).

It is difficult to distinguish formally the *priestly* genres from the *prophetic* genres, for if these latter experienced an abundant and varied efflorescence in Israel, they developed, according to the theory of S. Mowinckel, from set forms in cult prophecy. Basically, it is, above all, a question of a divine word addressed to men. From the beginning this assumes a rhythmic pace (cf. e. g. Gn 25, 23 or Jgs 13, 3-5) and takes on a

certain profusion in the promises made to the patriarchs. It is rather
in the priestly sphere that the oracles given in the sanctuaries are situated,
the *torôt* (*torah* = law; cf. Ag 2, 11 f.); likewise the oaths of purification,
the blessings and curses, liturgical or not, and even the juridical solutions.
For their part, the prophetic oracles develop into promises and threats,
reproaches and admonishments, admonitions and discourses; [20] but there
they relinquish the rhythm of poetry to adopt that of prose; the same
happens with the priestly sermons. The oracles of warnings and of
promises are themselves subdivided into different categories, less according
to their *form* than to their *object*—but often rather fixed literary conventions correspond to their different objects; we should mention especially
the "oracles against the Gentiles" and the eschatological oracles.
Naturally the prophets might have recourse to all the other genres not
especially prophetic (lamentation, hymns, parable, etc.), while the
prophetic genres can also be imitated in all other contexts (for example,
in certain psalms). Finally, the mixing of genres is not too uncommon.

The forms of prose

First of all we find, as always, some forms barely elaborated literarily
but all the more stable from age to age : contracts (Jer 32), agreements
and treaties (1 Mc 8, 22-32), genealogical lists, lists of functionaries
(3 Kgs 4), letters (Nm 20, 14-19; Jer 29), inventories and architectural
plans (3 Kgs, 6—7). Still better arranged and closer to the poetic rhythm
are the prayers in prose form (3 Kgs 8) and the discourses; these may be
political, religious (notably among the prophets and in Deuteronomy)
or sapiential (Prv 5; Tb 4).

The *laws* must be divided up among several genres because of the
different redactions of their articles. Alongside the *torah*, to which one
might be led to attribute a religious origin (as we have just seen), there is
custom, which is the fundamental principle of the judgments *(mispât)*;
the commandment *(miswah)* which implies an act of authority; the
hôq, in which Père Van den Ploeg sees an idea of "determination,
settlement," and which may have been originally something like an
inscribed decree; finally the "words" *(dâbâr)* which comprise divine
judgments, juridical cases, or sapiential exhortations. Collections of
similar articles were formed very quickly.

In addition to the laws, there are the *narratives*. "The classing
of the different types of narratives is difficult," Bentzen thinks. In
principle, it would be a mistake to make the classification according
to the credibility of the accounts. To speak of legends, tales, or histories

---

[20] See our *Introduction to the Old Testament*, pp. 263 ff.

would lead to adopting a terminology far different from the point of view of the ancient authors, without understanding either their conditions of life and thought or the ends which they pursued. For this reason, the exact designation of the narrative genres is one of the most arduous tasks of modern criticism. Besides, ethnologists are in the process of giving new meanings to old words formerly rather pejorative : among primitive people, the *legend* is practically the first form of what has become history to us (the " conservatory of memories "), and the *myth* is not so much a fictive creation of the human imagination as an imagistic and often dramatized expression of rich and profound views concerning the human condition—all at once a " wisdom " and a metaphysics, in some way; in a somewhat different sense, M. Eliade has written some interesting pages on " the truth of the myth. " [21] In this sense, myth and legend in ancient civilizations often constitute the " sacred narrative " read within a sanctuary, on the occasion of a religious feast whose meaning or origin they express. [22] Nevertheless, the words *myth, legend,* and *tale* have an unfortunate connotation in everyday language, in the sense that they seem to deny any relationship between the narrated events and historical or religious reality; so it would be best to avoid using them in regard to the Bible, lest anything equivocal be introduced into literary criticism. But we must take into account the technical meaning which they tend to actually take on when we encounter them from the pen of certain exegetes; it is a question of a terminology in the process of stabilization. Until this is defined in strict fashion, we may cling to more general designations : *accounts, narrations,* with the understanding that the same formal traits may be encountered in compositions of quite different orders : historical episodes, didactic accounts, narratives of a mixed type.

We must avoid ranking all accounts of miracles [23] in a single literary genre. The exegete should not have any preconceived notion of the historical reality or the fictive character of a narrative which includes an account of this kind; it may pertain to areas quite different. The aim of the author may be to emphasize by way of a miraculous episode the supernatural character of a teaching or of a law, in the course of an essentially didactic narrative (Jonas); in other cases it may be a question

---

[21] See also, although more disputable, R. PETTAZONI, *Essays in the History of Religion* (Leyden, 1954), pp. 11-23.

[22] J. SCHILDENBERGER, " Mythus-Wunder-Mysterium, "* *Der christliche Erzieher* (1955), 3/4, pp. 2-25.

[23] Cf. A. LEFEVRE, " Miracles..., " *SDB*, V, cols. 1295-1308; E. GALBIATI and A. PIAZZA, *Mieux comprendre la Bible,** Fr. tr. (Paris, 1956), pp. 224-241; J. DE FRAINE, *Secoli sul Mondo,** pp. 177-179.

of a historical episode reported as such.   Even in this case literary criticism
remains difficult.   For, on the one hand, the supernatural aspect of the
deed does not exclude its other components, natural, physical or sociological; on the other hand, the narrator may appeal to emphasis, hyperbole,
or poetics of the miraculous, in order to make the readers feel the
enchanting character of the event, as happens in epic narratives.   In
short, the study of the texts demands constant attention to all the
elements which play a part in them.

Among such accounts, especially when they report ancient traditions,
we must set aside those which are called *etiological*.   These always have
some connection with geography, history or sociology.   They are attached
to places, to customs, to ways of life, whose origin, worth, or sacred
character they intend to explain.   They do so for the ancient sanctuaries,
for example, whose foundation they recall (Gn 12, 8) or whose name they
explain (Gn 28, 11-19).   Others deal with an ancient personage, often the
ancestor of a tribe (eponym) or a hero whose memory is preserved.   Their
connection with history is not always what one might imagine in the
first reading : Gn 18 establishes a link between Abraham and the holy
place of Mambre, but that does not imply that all the details of the
religious meal offered to the mysterious visitors took place thus, for we find
certain features of them in the Ugaritic " legend " of Danel; the historical
element of the account is not necessarily the most prominent.   Still
other accounts aim at recalling the legal ties existing among the tribes
and the peoples; for example, the treaty between Laban and Jacob
(Gn 33) sets the boundaries of pasture rights recognized in Transjordania
for the " children of Jacob " and for the Arameans, while the " table of the
peoples " (Gn 11) attempts a historico-geographical synthesis which
must not be considered exactly as a record of vital statistics.   The
etiological accounts are a mine of information, but interpretation of them
is generally delicate and one must weigh all the elements in order to
grasp their exact import.

The Israelite genius excelled in the composition of little tableaux
comprising an introduction, presentation of characters, dialogue or drama,
and conclusion.   Each scene of this genre has its point and its rhythm.
Even when several are united to form a collection, one can recognize in
each a distinct literary unit which allows separate treatment : thus,
in the history of Joseph, the episode of the wife of Putiphar.   In this
latter case, the preoccupation with *moral* teaching is obvious; moreover,
the narrative is handled in a more *epic* style (the crossing of the Red Sea,
climax of the struggle of Yahweh against Egypt) or, when epic elements
are set aside, it gives rise to the *historical* account (campaign of Gedeon

against Zebah and Salmunna, according to H. Gressmann). It also develops into the most diverse strains, according to our modern categories. In this area, as in Egypt, we have " novellen " touching upon some important event in the life of a hero (Joseph, Ruth) or of a king (Solomon in the high place of Gabaon, 3 Kgs 3).

Finally, through stages and work of synthesis, elementary compositions find themselves reset in complex works demanding more inspiration and broader outlooks. Then the scenes are linked with one another by a connecting thread, and give way to a continuous narrative; such is the case in certain sequences of the Pentateuch and in the history of the succession of David (2 Sm 9—3 Kgs 2). Each synthesis of this kind has its own literary genre, its procedures of composition, its manner of employing documents or traditions (which, taken individually, preserve their original character), and finally its problems. Therefore it is important for the interpretation of the Bible that literary criticism first determine the milieux and the sociological conditions in which the basic literary genres were developed then the complex literary genres which are not without relationship to the preceding, but often modify their original state. In Israel history is not a simple genre.

V. Evolution of the genres

In the era of Israelite classicism (royal era), works tend to group themselves into quite differentiated strains : legislation, historical works, prophetic collections, religious lyricism, and books of wisdom. But in practice, these strains intermingle : some narrative incorporated into a historical book has as its purpose to justify a custom or a rite (Ex 12, 21-28); another gives a theological interpretation of events which likens it to prophetic literature (Jgs 2); another borders on the teaching of the wise men (Joseph). In time, the situation changes with respect to genres and new genres arise.

We must especially note the appearance of *midrash*, that is, religious reflection on the ancient traditions and on the Scriptures already established. [24] Sometimes this *midrash* draws from Scripture, witness of the divine will, rules of conduct (this is what Judaism will call *halakha*), sometimes simply edifies the reader (this is the purpose of the *haggada*), or else gives support to a theological proposition (it is for this purpose that the chronicler resumes some accounts from Kings). *Midrash* realizes the greatest variety in its literary expression : from thesis history

---

[24] On *Midrash*, see pp. 174 ff.

(Chronicles) to didactic narrative (Tobias). In each case, therefore, it is essential to establish what genre of teaching the writer wishes to inculcate, for very different outlooks may be hidden under identical external forms. When *midrash* is applied to prophetic oracles, in which it seeks some light on the meaning of contemporary events or their future outcome, it gives way to what is called *pesher* : such is the case when Dn 9 reinterprets Jer 25, 11-12.

In the Persian and Greek epochs, while history is evolving towards forms nearer to the Hellenic ideas (classical historiography of 1 Mc or the moving history of 2 Mc), wisdom teaching is expressed more and more spontaneously in the form of the *haggada* (Tb; Dn 1—6) and encompasses what was once the prophetic discourse. In return, the eschatological oracle gives rise to the *apocalypse*, in which the revelation of divine secrets essentially takes on the aspect of strange dreams and visions, whose explanation crops up under the text or is even given in plain language (thus Dn 2 and 7—12). This new genre has its own conventions, its symbolic material, often recurrent, its characteristic atmosphere, strained, mysterious, sometimes strange.

Finally, Judaism of the late era frequently resorts to pseudepigraphy by placing recent works under the guise of ancient authors long since dead. This is the case in more than one sapiential work fictively placed under the patronage of Solomon, the initiator of wisdom literature : so it is for Proverbs, Ecclesiastes, Canticles and Wisdom. In the apocalyptic era, this becomes a law of the genre : so it is with the numerous apocrypha which revolve around Enoch, Moses, Esdras, Baruch; thus we can understand that it may be the same in Daniel and in the canonical Baruch. Likewise we see the flowering of the genre of apocryphal " testaments, " haggadas with a sapiential demeanor : Testaments of the Twelve Patriarchs and, in the Bible itself, Tobias (in the first person singular in the Sinaiticus version).

In short, the history of the literary genres in the OT is even more complex than in our modern literatures. It is all the more necessary to study it closely if we wish to know the meaning and the import of the books. Without such a study, the exegete would face many false problems which would render his task impossible.

VI. NOTE ON BIBLICAL POETRY (by P. AUVRAY)

To avoid any ambiguity we will distinguish poetry properly so called, poetic processes, and prosody.

Poetry

Poetry properly so called cannot be reduced to formulae. Furthermore, it transcends languages and civilizations. It is a matter of *esthetics*, in which we can only refer to the general features. All we can say here is that it aims at creating a kind of *verbal music*, formed all at once out of auditory sonorities and affective evocations (the " talismans " of which Abbé Bremond speaks [25]).

The poetic processes

They are easier to analyze. Among eastern peoples, they mainly break down to the use of parallelism. [26] We distinguish three kinds of parallelism :

    1) synonymic parallelism : simple repetition of the same idea under a slightly different form :

> Try me, O Lord, and test me;
> Examine my mind and my heart (Ps 26, 2).

Sometimes the repetition is made in a negative form :

> Thou hast given him the desire of his heart;
> And the petition of his lips thou hast not withheld (Ps 21, 3).

    2) antithetical parallelism : partial correspondence of the two expressions in order to emphasize an opposition or a contrast :

> For the Lord knows the way of the righteous.
> But the way of the wicked will perish (Ps 1, 6).

    3) synthetical parallelism is more delicate to characterize. It resides in the form, not in the essence; it is the effect produced by a period of two (or three) members, the first of which announces and waits upon the following. As Lowth remarks, " in this class all parallels not included in the other two come to be listed. " He gives Ps 18, 8-9 as an example :

> The law of the Lord is perfect,
>   renewing the life;
> The decree of the Lord is trustworthy,
>   making wise the simple;
> The precepts of the Lord are right,
>   rejoicing the heart;
> The command of the Lord is pure,
>   enlightening the eyes.

---

[25] Cf., for example : H. BREMOND, *Prière et Poésie.**

[26] On the parallelism in the texts of Ras-Shamra, cf. C. H. GORDON, *Ugaritic Manual* (Rome, 1955), n. 13, 99-161.

As we see here, a synonymic parallelism (by verses) is superimposed on a synthetical parallelism (by hemistichs). As we also see by this last example, the parallelism may be in three terms, in four terms, or more.

Aside from parallelism, we know of other processes which sometimes have the aim of emphasizing : *alliterations, rhymes,* [27] etc. But their usage does not seem subject to precise rules.

Lastly, the *alphabetic* process, used mostly but not exclusively in the didactic sections, seems to have a mnemonic purpose (Ps 9—10; 119, etc. Cf. aside from the Psalter : Lam; Pv 31, 10 ff. etc.).

Hebraic prosody

Today no one attempts to reduce Hebraic prosody to the use of *feet* (ordering of longs and shorts) in the manner of the Greeks and Latins, nor to discover in it verses composed of a fixed number of *syllables*, as in French. By almost common consent, in Hebraic poetry, only counts the number of accented syllables, the unaccentuated syllables being undetermined in number.

Given the law of parallelism, the verse generally is composed of two hemistichs (sometimes of three stichs) corresponding to each other and, in principle, bearing an equal number of accents. Thus we have verses of 2 + 2 or 3 + 3 or 4 + 4 accents. But often there is a certain caprice in the ordering and succession of rhythms. We will likewise note the rhythm (very precise) of the dissymmetrical *qînâ* (elegy or lamentation), that is to say, in verses composed of two unequal stichs : either 3 + 2 or 4 + 3 accents (Ps 25; 27 etc.).

Often enough there are strophes, that is, groupings of verses recurring with a certain regularity, as in Ps 5 (strophes of two verses). These strophes are sometimes emphasized by the use of a refrain (Ps 42, 6. 12; 43, 5) or by an alphabetic process (Ps 9—10; 119). Sometimes we observe parallelisms between the strophes (whence the notion of antistrophe). But in the use of all these processes there is some uncertainty which is not always due to the bad state of the text. Caprice is the law of all living poetries, and the first duty of the exegete, in the study of the texts, is compliance with the facts.

For an intensive study, one should refer to the classic, though quite old, work of R. Lowth, *De Sacra poesi Hebraeorum Praelectiones Academicae*, Oxford, 1753 (Fr. tr. : *Leçons sur la poésie sacrée des Hébreux*, 2 Vols., Lyons, 1812). More recent and very complete, E. König, *Die*

---

[27] See also J. MAGNE, " Répétitions de mots et exégèse dans quelques psaumes et le Pater, " *Bi* (1958), pp. 97-197.

Poesie des Alten Testaments, Leipzig, 1907. Much more accessible and helpful : E. Dhorme, *La poésie biblique, Introduction... et trente chants de circonstance*, Paris, 1931.

Music

It has been said that the Psalms were habitually (if not always) sung with a musical accompaniment. We are rather poorly informed on Israelite music, as we are on that of almost all ancient peoples. Nevertheless, the cross-checking of archeology and ethnology helps us to recover little by little its circumstances of performance and its diverse forms. Concerning musical instruments and melodies, we might consult the manuals of archeology, such as : A. Barrois, *Manuel d'Archéologie biblique*, II, pp. 193-205, and especially the well-documented article of E. Gerson-Kiwi, " Musique (dans la Bible), " *SDB*, V, cols. 1411-1468. This last treatment distinguishes " priestly " instruments (horn and trumpets); the " levitical " instruments (*kinnor;* Greek : κιθαρα or κινυρα, that is, the lyre; *nèbèl*, that is, the harp or lute; *'asôr*, that is, probably a six-cord harp); finally the " lay " instruments (*'ugab, halil, abub*, which appear to be different varieties of flutes). As for the melodies used, it is difficult to assert anything certain in the present state of investigations.

§ 3. The Literary Criticism of the New Testament

(by A. FEUILLET and P. GRELOT)

BIBLIOGRAPHY

C. F. BURNEY, *The Poetry of Our Lord* (Oxford, 1925).

P. BENOIT, " Réflexions sur la Formgeschichtliche Methode, " *RB* (1946), pp. 481-512.

L. CERFAUX, *La voix vivante de l'Évangile** (Paris-Tournai, 1946).

M. ALBERTZ, *Botschaft des Neuen Testaments*, 3 Vols. (Zürich, 1947-1954).

A. M. HUNTER, *Interpreting the New Testament, 1900-1950* (1951).

S. NEIL, *The Interpretation of the New Testament, 1861-1961* (New York : Oxford, 1964).

The NT is also expressed in diverse literary genres, and we can make here the same distinction between the elementary genres (words of Christ, typical deeds of Christ or of the apostles, summaries of catechesis, hymns, etc.) and the syntheses (such as the Gospels and the Acts of the Apostles). The problems are not the same from one part to another : the elementary genres are deeply rooted in the Christian oral tradition, while the syntheses suppose an overall reflection and are finally works thought out, composed by authors, obeying the rules of written composition. Alongside these books, we also find the Epistles, letters of doctrinal content, whose forms vary from one author to another (James is closer to the Jewish wisdom genres; Paul sometimes resorts to the processes of the Hellenistic diatribe); lastly, an Apocalypse.

I. The materials of the synoptic tradition

In regard to the diverse elements which the synoptic tradition makes use of, the partisans of *Formgeschichte* have strived to connect them less to the life of Jesus than to the needs of the early Christian community : missionary preaching, liturgy, catechetical instruction, apologetics, polemics, internal discipline of the community. We will return to this subject in the chapters dedicated to the Synoptics. Let us say for now that, if the classification of materials for the Synoptics according to distinct literary genres often proves to be extremely difficult, something can be retained from what Albertz, Dibelius and Bultmann have proposed. [28]

The words of Jesus

The task is the easiest for the words of Jesus. In these it is a question of literary forms which for a long time had been in common use in the Jewish world : sapiential maxims, prophetic discourses, laws, parables often combined with allegorizing features. The classifications of Bultmann and Albertz can doubtless be accepted along general lines. It is thus interesting to note that the diverse literary traditions of the OT have their prolongation in the preaching of Jesus. He speaks in turn as a lawgiver who corrects and enriches the Torah; as a Wise Man who crowns Jewish Wisdom; as a prophet who castigates the sins of His time, repeats the ancient announcements of the Judgment and the Kingdom by interpreting them in a new perspective, and, in formulating them, does not disdain to resort, on occasion, to the style of the apocalypses. Doubtless we will find these genres put into use in the early Church; but there is no reason to deny any of them to Jesus Himself, and their rules become clear when we reset them into the framework of Palestinian Judaism of this epoch. Similarly, the parables have their counterpart, not in the rules formulated in the Hellenistic milieu, but rather in the canons of the rabbinical *mashal*. [29]

---

[28] R. Bultmann, *Die Geschichte der synoptischen Tradition*[2] (Göttingen, 1931).

[29] R. Pautrel, " Les canons du maschal rabbinique, "* *RSR* (1936), pp. 5-49; (1937), pp. 264-281.

The Gospel accounts

The classification of the Gospel accounts proves to be more arduous. A knowledge of the exact aims to which they corresponded at the time of their literary crystallization, and of the social structure in which they took form, would be capable of shedding light on their structure. But it is sometimes difficult to link them thus to the diverse activities of the early Church. In principle, we can say that the different modes of preaching on the one hand, and the needs of the liturgy on the other hand, played an important role in the elaboration of the apostolic recollections which gave birth to the evangelical pericopes. Thus, many brief accounts could have served to illustrate preaching, apologetics, or polemics.

Once this principle is admitted, we can still clarify the problem of their literary redaction by determining what forms were in use in the milieu in which they took on their form. But on this point, the pioneers of *Formgeschichte* made the double mistake of appealing, in too one-sided a fashion, to the analogies taken from the Hellenistic world, and of unduly passing from literary criticism to historical criticism. Dibelius and Bultmann compared the miracle accounts, preserved in the Gospels, to the accounts of cures worked by Aesculapius in the sanctuary of Epidaurus. Surely there are some analogies, but these are restricted to the common theme of the cure and to the popular character of the accounts, adapted here and there to the intellectual level of a simple public. Not only the climate, but also the point, the outlook and the aim of the Hellenistic accounts and the Gospel episodes differ profoundly; here are legendary traits meant to satisfy the curiosity of the public and its taste for the supernatural; there, traits meant to be historical because they give the key to the personality of Christ according to criteria worked in the prophetic Scriptures : Jesus " fulfills the Scriptures " by triumphing over sickness, death, and Satan.

Without wishing, however, to deny all influence of the Greco-Roman milieu on the literary formation of the pericopes born in the Christian communities of the Greek Language, it is better to look for their counterparts in the heart of Judaism itself. For example, we must bear in mind the narrative forms which were developed in the synagogical commentaries on the Scriptures : they offered themselves as such for nascent Christianity to pour forth its message of the Gospel, just as the Jewish liturgy supplied ready-made patterns, easily adaptable to Christian prayer. Again we must not push the analogies too far, since what the Apostolic Church wished to establish was, above all, a *testimony* concerning essential *facts* of the faith, and not simply material of relatively secondary importance, destined to illustrate the Scriptures. The originality of the content could not but react even on the forms in which it was handed over to the public.

But all in all, we can shed light, to a large extent, on the Gospel accounts, through Jewish analogies, and secondarily through Hellenistic ones. We can admit the existence of certain clearly characterized types, such as miracle accounts and accounts which culminate in a saying of Jesus from which they derive all their value (" *pronouncement-stories* " of Taylor, the first group of " *Apophthegms* " of Bultmann); but in designating these types, it is preferable to avoid Hellenistic terminology. We must further remark that, alongside these pure types, contaminations exist among bordering groups. Finally, this literary analysis leaves untouched the question of the substantial historical authenticity of the accounts under discussion : in order to determine this, we must have recourse to other criteria.

II. THE SYNTHESES OF THE GOSPELS AND THE ACTS

The Synoptics [30]

Taken in their entirety, the syntheses which the Synoptics represent belong to a very special literary genre. They hardly resemble biographies, in the modern sense of the word. They are not meant to satisfy the curiosity of the faithful while also edifying them (this is generally the case in the apocryphal gospels), but to nourish their faith. For this reason, they strengthen, with the aid of materials drawn from the apostolic tradition, the various aspects of the evangelical preaching : the message of salvation, instruction of the faithful, foundations of Christian liturgy. This explains their poverty, not only in chronological, topographical or geographical facts (they often speak of a mountain, house, desert, sea, without any precision), but also in psychological data, whether in regard to Jesus, His enemies, His disciples, or the close circle of the Twelve (only Peter is an exception, up to a certain point).

On the whole, these are catecheses, with a minimum of literary elaboration in Mark, some historiographical viewpoints in Luke (who consciously imitates, in the chapters on the infancy, the style of certain OT pages), and with a rather apparent apologetical intent in Matthew (whose parallel chapters seem to emerge from a synagogical commentary on the Scriptures, carried out in a Christian perspective).

---

[30] M. DIBELIUS, *Die Formgeschichte des Evangeliums*[2] (Tübingen, 1933).

The fourth Gospel

Like the Synoptics, the fourth Gospel is also connected in some way to early Christian preaching; but despite its greater richness in chronological and topographical facts, it is even less a biography of Jesus than the other three. A detailed study of this very personal work will be taken up piecemeal in the chapters to be especially set aside for it; here we will note only two points. In John, the narratives are often presented in a more elaborated literary form than in the other evangelists. They are no longer simple and popular sketches, but so many little dramas arranged by an author very aware of his didactic purposes. Hence they are handled with consummate skill, and the meaning which the evangelist attaches to them unfolds little by little through the particular features he has chosen for this purpose. As for the style of the discourses, it is essentially a style of revelation which well corresponds to their purpose : Jesus reveals in them the essence of His person and of His mission.

This special language has given rise to many studies. Its prototype has been sought in Hellenism or in eastern religions. All influence of this kind is not to be excluded : wishing to show that Jesus gives the true knowledge of the divine mystery, the evangelist could have had recourse to a style related to the " mystery " style known to the recipients of the work. However, the Johannine style has antecedents in certain passages of the Synoptics (notably the Johannine " logion " : Mt 11, 25-30) and finally, in spite of its profound originality, it is not without some relationships to several literary trends proper to the OT and to Judaism : the apocalyptical, in so far as it is a " revelation " of divine secrets, and especially the great developments relative to divine Wisdom (Prv 8 and Sir 24).

The Acts of the Apostles

The Book of Acts belongs more to the classical historical genre. However, it offers a great variety of aspects according to its different parts. The first chapters recall the style of composition of the Synoptics; there Luke presents a mosaic of episodes of every kind, intended to throw in relief one fundamental idea : the progression of the Gospels. The very forms of these episodes often recall those of the evangelical pericopes (for example, the miracle accounts); but we also find materials which show the variety of genres in common use in the Apostolic Church : sketches of discourses, fragments of hymns, liturgical prayers, confessions of faith. The Semitic style of several of the narratives, and the archaizing doctrine of the discourses, have suggested to certain exegetes that the first fifteen chapters could be making use of a particularly ancient Aramaic source.

On the contrary, in the second part of the book, the narrative takes on quite a different aspect. The Hellenistic mentality causes the influence of its literary canons to be felt there, notably in the passages borrowed from the " logbook " of the narrator (for example, in the shipwreck account). Preceded by a prologue in classical form, the whole of the book thus brings to mind the works of the Greek historians; but this comparison should not be exaggerated, for it leaves untouched the question of the sources used by the author.

III. The epistolary literature

The epistolary genre in the Hellenistic milieu

The epistolary literature of the NT is quite varied. The bulk of it is made up of the Pauline Epistles. A brief comparison with the secular letters which antiquity has bequeathed to us will be helpful. The private letters, like the ones preserved by numerous papyri, were most of the time redacted by the author of the letter himself. [31] The same held true for the private correspondance of the great personages (Pompey, Caesar). But it was not always easy for a very busy person to take time out to write letters. Thus, most of the time a secretary was employed to whom letters were dictated. This was a tedious job for the secretary. In order to avoid errors, one usually dictated, not phrase by phrase, nor even word by word, but syllable by syllable. Thus practiced, dictation would have soon been unbearable unless the one making it was devoted to other activities at the time; for example, he dictated while having dinner, or while walking. But the important figures who wrote a great deal had still another manner of going about it : they contented themselves with making known orally or in writing the general outlines of their thought, leaving the trouble of developing it to the secretary. They thus ran the risk of seeing their thought rendered unfaithfully. Nevertheless, it is a fact that this method was used, especially by persons of a certain class. Quite naturally the question comes up as to whether certain Epistles of the NT were not composed according to the same method.

Among the numerous letters of antiquity which have been preserved, about 4,500 (according to Roller) have a complete preamble of unchangeable structure, composed of three elements : the *intitulatio* or *superscriptio* mentioning the name of the sender; the *adscriptio* or inside address designating the name of the recipient, and the *salutatio* or formula of greeting.

---

[31] A. Deissmann, *Light from the Ancient East.* S. Lyonnet, " De arte litteras exarandi apud antiquos, " *Verbum Domini*, 34 (Rome, 1956), 3-11.

The Epistles in the New Testament

In two letters of the NT that we can consider earlier than those of Paul (letter of the Assembly of Jerusalem : Acts 15, 23 ff.; letter of James), we find this classic preamble with its three elements. St. Paul followed it also, while profoundly modifying it, however. [32] He developed the *intitulatio* considerably, for he wanted to emphasize the authority he held from his apostolic dignity : he wrote to the communities, not as an ordinary man, but as an apostle delegated by God. In the same way, he transformed the *adscriptio* : addressing himself not to ordinary men, but to Christians forming part of the new world inaugurated by Christ, he stated the true titles of nobility of his addressees, their Christian character. There is the same transformation in regard to the salutation : no more the common " rejoice " of the Greeks (χαιρε), corresponding to our hello, but " grace " (χάρις) and " peace, " with the indication of the source of these Messianic benefits immediately following : " grace and peace from God and from the Lord Jesus Christ. " So the simple study of the preamble of the Pauline Epistles testifies to the wonderful newness brought into the world by Christianity.

Deissmann has strongly contrasted, on the one hand, the letter, an occasional writing without literary characteristics, not destined for publication, and, on the other hand, the epistle treating of general topics, having literary pretensions, and destined for a more or less numerous group of individuals. But in reality there is no absolute contrast between letter and epistle, and it often happens that a letter borders on an epistle. Deissmann also exaggerates the assimilation of the Pauline writings to the private and popular letters preserved by the papyri. These are certainly true letters, but they distinguish themselves from ordinary letters by their spiritual and intellectual elevation, and by their predominant didactic feature; for Paul excels in placing himself in the most universal and the most elevated viewpoint in order to discuss the particular questions submitted to him. Then too, except for the note to Philemon, the Pauline Epistles are all aimed at churches or even groups of churches; furthermore, even during the lifetime of the Apostle, they were read in public and were circulated (1 Thes 5, 7; Col 4, 16). But it is true that in sometimes resuming the same topic under a more elaborate form, Paul tended to transform into an epistle (in the sense of Deissmann) what at first had more the spontaneity of a letter; so in the Epistle to the Romans, which expands the Epistle to the Galatians. He did the same with certain preaching themes entrusted to the living word before being set down in writing.

---

[32] O. ROLLER, *Das Formular der paulinischen Briefe* (Stuttgart, 1953).

The other epistles of the NT are of varied forms. The Epistle to the Hebrews constitutes a veritable treatise on theology, intimately linked to an exhortation of a homiletic bent. The two Epistles of Peter and Jude bring to mind at once homilies and encyclicals. Devoid of all personal comment and of all circumstantial detail, filled more than any other writing of the NT with reminiscences of the OT, especially of the sapiential books, the Epistle of James could be " an example of the Jewish homiletics of the synagogue, adapted by a Christian author " (Chaine). Beginning without a name of an author and without any personal greeting, but not deprived of personal traits in the course of its developments, the First Epistle of John seems to represent a mixed genre, both a letter and a doctrinal treatise. As for the other two Johannine Epistles, they are true letters, very brief. Finally, the " letters to the seven Churches " form a junction between the epistolary genre and the apocalyptic genre.

IV. THE APOCALYPTIC GENRE

The apocalyptic genre is represented in the NT by fragments inserted into the most diverse frameworks : apocalyptic logia of the Synoptics (notably the great collection gathered together in the " eschatological discourse, " whether or not one admits its original unity); fragments gathered up in the Acts (vision of Stephen, vision of Peter before the visit to Cornelius); occasional passages of the Pauline Epistles (notably in 1 and 2 Thes and 1 Cor).

But it presents itself in almost the pure state in the Johannine Apocalypse, which employs all of its literary processes, well-developed in non-canonical literature, Jewish and Christian : fantastic symbols, constant intervention of the angels, statement of doctrinal thought under the form of symbolic visions, constant intercommunication between the things of earth and the things of heaven, a very peculiar concept of history in which the events here below appear, up to a certain point, predetermined by God in heaven. Nevertheless, the book is signed and it is addressed to the contemporaries of the author, without any reference to a hero of the more distant past (Enoch, Esdras, etc.). Moreover, it is largely inspired by ancient prophecy whose texts it constantly puts to use to explain how the eschatological oracles of the OT take their definitive meaning within the historical perspective of the Church reaching towards the " consummation of things. " There are no cosmological speculations like the ones we find in Enoch; no fancy inquiries concerning the date at which " these things will take place; " but above all it is a message of encouragement and hope : the immolated Christ, enthroned in heaven by His Resurrection, assures in time the triumph of

His Church in spite of the persecutions which assail it.   In a strange form, disconcerting for us but not for its contemporaries, it is lastly a theological treatise on Christian eschatology which is outlined in this mysterious book.

V.   IMPORTANCE OF THE LITERARY GENRES IN THE NEW TESTAMENT

The study of the NT could not therefore be understood without an inquiry of literary criticism which takes account of the milieux and of their languages, of the personality of the authors, of the genres admitted by the public to whom the books were first directed.   A priori, we cannot discard as unworthy of the word of God any of the literary conventions then in use so long as they corresponded to the end which the authors pursued and did not give offense to the readers.   Even the process of pseudepigraphy, classic in the Jewish milieu, cannot be rejected on principle, provided that solid reasons lead to considering it and that for its use we find honest motives capable of warranting it (something else than a " pious fraud ").   It is not a question of right, but of fact. Doubtless it would be senseless to call in question a priori the traditional attributions of the books of the NT : the data preserved by tradition have a point of departure, a *raison d'être*, and thus a value.   But the fact remains that the notion of *author* has not always been understood in the strict sense in which we intend it today.   Still on this point, a prudent inquiry is capable of shedding much light on the enigmas by showing *in what manner* each writing is connected with the personality under the guise of which it has been preserved : directly, as in the great Pauline Epistles; by giving a rather large share to a secretary, as one might think for the First Epistle of Peter or even the pastoral Epistles; or in still less immediate fashion, as might be the case for our Greek Matthew or the Second Epistle of Peter.

Such an effort is full of nuances; it is important to carry it out in serene fashion by clearing it of apologetic concerns—either to see in it only a way of resolving troublesome questions, or to reject without investigation suggestions which do not absolutely fall in line with the ready-made solutions accepted by the old exegesis.   The examination of the author and of the literary genre of a given work has as its purpose the exact understanding of the message which this work comprises. If at times certain critics have misused this examination by putting it to the service of a " reverse apologetic " which eliminated the supernatural or emptied biblical history of its contents, it is important not to yield to the contrary prejudice.   Criticism must remain altogether open to the supernatural and aim at the most complete objectivity; thus it will enable faith to reach the authentic meaning of the Bible.

CHAPTER IV

HISTORICAL CRITICISM

§ 1. The Problems

I. The importance of the milieu

By establishing the literary genre of a work, we achieve only a first idea of its author's psychology. By this one perceives, for example, if he intended to narrate real events, commemorate the glory of a king or a god, or give his readers advice about how to succeed in life. But there are diversities in literary genre as in all artistic styles : they lend themselves to very different concrete realizations. The Greek tragedies are all in the same dramatic category, but they differ in spirit, and the message of Oedipus to Colone is not the same as that of Bacchus' priestesses. The understanding of a work in depth demands that it be placed in its exact historical situation. An author who intended to write only for himself would still be influenced by the time and society in which he lived. He must be put into these circumstances again to understand the problems that he considered and the way he expressed them. This general norm becomes more apparent when we deal with a literature which, like the Bible, is social, addressed to a well-determined public to treat of life's problems. We are not dealing with an esoteric book, but with one deeply rooted in the milieu in which it was born, which speaks its language, follows its literary conventions, respects its mentality. For example, the apocalyptic genre is very puzzling for us precisely because of the gulf that separates us from the age and place which created that means of expression, the key to whose interpretation we have partly lost.

The exegete must consider the circumstances in which the work being studied was composed. The better he knows them, the better he is able to grasp the view of the author. These circumstances are the place, date, social milieu in which the work appeared. An exegetical study, wehenit handles difficult passages of a work, will take different directions according to the solutions given to each problem thus posed. It would matter little if the author of Job lived in Egypt or Palestine if these countries did not imply different spiritual climates and ways of life. It would make little difference if the author of Qôheleth were Solomon or a Jew of the Greek period, if that fact did not entail great differences in the psychology of the author, a deeper understanding of his thought, of the problems he faced and the positions he took. It would be ideal to go further yet and to know even the name, the personality, the life of the author, and the precise time of his life in which he composed one or the other of his works. Thus it is not a matter of pure curiosity to try to determine whether the Epistle to the Galatians preceded or followed the Epistle of St. James : our understanding of the text would be changed by this information.

But it must be admitted that in the present state of our information, we must often be content with approximations. The development of historical knowledge pertaining to the ancient Orient, however, permits us progressively to examine the problems more closely. Now not only the Greek world from the 6th or 5th century is accessible to us. The art of deciphering hieroglyphs and cuneiforms permits us to trace in general (and sometimes in detail) the history of the Orient from the third millennium. In spite of enormous gaps, the entire Bible is now situated within an historical halo. The Bible continually shows us the people of Israel in relation with its neighbors; it thus obliges us to appeal to all the documents of the Near East to illustrate all its details.

II. The components of the milieu

Because it is essential in exegesis to know the conditions of life in which each work was composed, the following points must be determined :

The economic situation

" *Primum vivere deinde philosophari* " : this well-known proverb does not rise out of a materialistic philosophy, but rather expresses a clear view of what conditions the life of every human group, of all thought, of all literature. The Bible itself is not addressed to an unincarnate humanity; although the message it bears is transcendent, its expressions depends on a host of concrete circumstances, among which must be included economic realities : the means of production and the needs of the population. In poetry, for example, the imagery reflects the circumstances in which the author lives : city or country dweller or nomad. His perceptiveness is as it were impregnated with whatever constitutes his habitual way of life. That influence is even greater in legislation, because juridical texts are a part of the economic and social structure in which live the men whose conduct they intend to regulate. Laws are an echo of eternal principles which they adapt to well-determined temporal circumstances, and they must develop with them in order to play the role of regulators of society.

The political situation

Except for some texts of nomadic origin, biblical literature developed in the context of a politically structured society, a nation, though not always independent and unified, in relation with other states, its neighbors, its rivals and its overlords. Moreover, in the revelation of the Old Testament, Yahweh is presented as the national God of Israel. The picture given of Him is still tied to the events of the nation's life. It is through these events that His actions are understood, and through them His plan and His mysterious being. From this flows the importance of the history of Israel for understanding the books of the Bible. Through internal political events the Israelites learned to discern the structure that God willed for His people; through the happenings of foreign politics, they gradually understood the place God intended to give His people in the midst of other powers—in other words, the profound sense of their own national existence. This fact explains why history occupies so important a place in works which profess to be essentially religious. Hence the exegete must determine as precisely as possible the elements involved in the events cited in them, and within which they were composed.

The mentality of the times and currents of thought

In every age a common mentality can be found among any given human group, according to their level of konwledge, the general problems they sought to solve, the world view they held, etc. Thus it was in Israel. [1] For example, nowhere in the Bible is the question whether the earth moves around the sun raised. The idea of creation is always expressed in an antiquated cosmology. Economic and social evolution presents new problems : while the question of weekly rest is hardly raised in the desert, one must think of " letting the servant and slave breathe " when Israel becomes agricultural. From 735 on, Juda and Israel could not ignore the Assyrian threat; the danger was not only political, because subjection ran the risk of religious consequences. But from 610 this danger disappeared, and finally the practical attitude of Jeremias toward Babylon differed profoundly from that of Isaias toward Assyria. Contact with new cultures brought about a development of mentality. From the time that the Orient was Hellenized, certain minds were affected by the problems of Greek philosophy. In the face of ancient questions there were different reactions; accordingly we find in the Bible itself

---

[1] On the Israelite mentality consult J. PEDERSEN, *Israel, its Life and Culture* (Copenhagen, 1926) (I-II) and 1940 (III-IV).

currents of thought which differ considerably. After the Exile a more nationalistic tendency insisted especially on the divine election of Israel, while a more universalist tendency insisted more on Israel's missionary task directed to the salvation of the nations. Like tendencies exist in the New Testament, and one must not be hasty to declare them contradictory. One was more Judaizing, the other was more open to Hellenization.

All of these facts help illuminate the viewpoint of each author, the meaning of his language, and even the literary genres he used, because it is quite impossible to determine genres a priori, independently of the milieu. Historical criticism and literary criticism mutually aid and complement each other.

§ 2. Useful Sources

I. BIBLICAL ARCHEOLOGY

The exegete uses first of all the Bible itself to comprehend the historical component of biblical thought. For a long time one had to be content with the information it furnished. Older works, such as the *Biblische Archäologie* of Benzinger, are for the most part a reconstruction of the Israelite milieu founded on biblical data. More recent works, such as that of A. G. Barrois, [2] still rely heavily on this data, and rightly so.

The discoveries of the last decades have, however, considerably increased our information. Inaugurated in 1890 by Flinders Petrie after some previous attempts due especially to E. Warren, Palestinian archeology has uncovered the remains of numerous cities which permit the historian to retrace the general lines of civilization's development in that region. One must not think that what is dug up from the Palestinian soil confirms or weakens the truth of the Bible. The new data, interesting in itself, at best presents elements which allow us to discern the literary genres used by the sacred authors. Through a better knowledge of the milieu, the events, the literature of the time, and even from the ancient copies of the sacred text, the form in which religious truth was recorded can better be discerned. For a certain book it is question of history, established by texts and facts discovered. For other works, on the contrary, discoveries will show another didactic form. On another level, archeology provides information about the religion of Chanaan before and after the arrival of the Israelites. It reveals a certain number

---

[2] A. G. BARROIS, *Manuel d'archéologie biblique* (Paris, 1939 and 1953).

of historical facts mentioned (or omitted) by the biblical text.   It gives us the background of the civilization and customs from which these texts sprang.

Here we will not recount the history of the excavations.   The work continues and should continue for some time yet.   The most important excavations are those of Megiddo (Schumacher 1903-1905, Fisher and Guy 1925-1939), Beth-shan (FitzGerald, Rowe 1921-1934), Samaria (Reisner 1908-1911, Crowfoot 1931-1935), Gezer (Macalister 1902-1909), Beth-shemesh (Mackenzie 1911-1912, E. Grant 1928-1933), Tell ed-Duweir (Starkey 1933-1938), Tell Beit Mirsim (W. F. Albright 1926-1932), Jericho (Sellin and Watzinger 1907-1909, Garstang 1930-1936, Miss Kenyon 1951-1956), Jerusalem itself, despite the difficulties of the site, and many other less known sites.   In 1907 Father H. Vincent presented an early summary of the excavations (Chanaan); in 1939 A. G. Barrois published another, and more recently a very competent résumé was published by W. F. Albright. [3]   Publications like *Revue Biblique*, *Biblica*, *Studii Biblici Franciscani Liber Annuus*, *Bulletin* of the *American School of Oriental Research*, the *Palestine Exploration Quarterly Statement*, the *Archiv für Orientforschung*, the *Zeitschrift der deutschen Palestina-Vereins*, the *Israel Exploration Quarterly*, and a number of others keep their readers informed of the successive discoveries that an exegete cannot ignore.

The excavations in Palestine have uncovered especially walls and ceramics.   Simple and usually plain pottery made its appearance in the neolithic age, at the same time as agriculture.   It is found alongside ancient stone tools, and remained in use even after the discovery of metal.   Its worth consists not so much in furnishing examples of pots to which the Bible alludes, but rather in furnishing a means of dating, thanks to differences in composition, methods of baking, and especially form and decoration, which vary from age to age.   In the well-stratified debris resulting from the successive ruins of the ancient villages (truncated cones called *tells*), it is possible to determine the sequence of ceramic types and date them in relation to the use of metal.   After the poorly baked and porous pottery of the neolithic period, the brilliant gray ceramics or the horn-shaped vases of the chalcolithic period appear (4th millennium B.C.).   The Bronze Age started about 3000.   It is subdivided into three grand periods.   The Early Bronze covers the 3rd millennium and is characterized by flat bottomed jars.   Within this period four phases can be distinguished.   In the first " the jars are covered with parallel or criss-cross (lattice) patterns made by bands of slip,

---

[3] W. F. ALBRIGHT, *The Archaeology of Palestine* (Pelican Books, 1949). Reprinted several times, most recent, 1963 (?).

usually on the smoothed natural surface of the vessel. " [4]   Towards the
29th century " pattern-combining and burnishing, sometimes in quite
intricate designs, become very popular. " [5]   The following period is
contemporaneous with the Age of the Pyramids (26th-23rd centuries)
and produced the magnificent pottery called " Khirbet Kerak " with its
fluting, spirals, curves, and especially its lustrous red and black burnish. [6]
Early Bronze IV witnesses the disappearance of the old forms, and its
characteristic is the " envelope ledge-handle. " [7]

Middle Bronze begins in the 21st century with an intermediate phase
of brown or cream-gray pottery which still has a flat bottom.   But this
type disappeared.   Between 1900 and 1750 the site of Ras-el-Ain furnishes
beautiful ovoid jars which show better use of the potter's wheel.   Afterwards we have the period called " Hyksos, " clearly characterized bsy it
little pear-shaped jars called Tell el-Yahudiyeh jugs, its small water jugs,
keeled bowls with trumpet shaped stems, and its vases in the form of
animals (1750-1550).   Foreign influences then began to make themselves
felt.   Less original than the preceding period, the Late Bronze Age is
one of the most beautiful from the point of view of ceramics.   In the
15th century there are beautiful bicolored vases ornamented with birds
and fish, as well as jugs with circular bases and long necks often curiously
bent.   After the Cypriot and then the Mycenean influence, evolved types
are found; the lamp lips become progressively turned inward.   About
1200 the Iron Age begins.   In Iron I the clay was well baked; bichrome
gave way to a sub-Mycenean ceramic called " Philistine. "   The jugs
become squat and tend toward the cylindrical; heavy and complicated
forms appear.   From about 800 (Iron II) ceramics degenerate.   With the
Hellenistic Age ceramics cease to be a chronological criterion.

In the context of this approximative framework other archeological
remains can be dated.   Walls are unknown at Teleilat el-Ghassul
(chalcolithic), but appear very early in Jericho.   The walls are massive,
sometimes nine yards thick, but they are poor examples of masonry, no
more than heaps of stones between two facings of stone.   By contrast,
during the Hyksos period are found beautiful sloping glacis and fortress
gates with double or triple enclosures.   Good masonry with carved stone
appears in Megiddo and afterward in Samaria under the monarchy.
City walls are not the only ones to be considered.   There are also walls
of houses and palaces from the early mud structures and apsed houses

---

[4] *Ibid.*, p. 72.

[5] *Ibid.*, p. 74.

[6] Cf. *ibid.*, p. 76.

[7] *Ibid.*, p. 78.

to the magnificent Herodian constructions of which there are remains at
the fortress of Jerusalem, the Temple, and at Hebron. Excavations
have unearthed metal utensils, weapons, ovens, dying vats, silos, etc.
They have also supplied works of art, ivory carvings and statues, but few
written documents. From the 2nd millennium we have no more than a
few inscriptions in archaic characters, some letters in cuneiform (Taanach,
Gezer, Shechem), some Egyptian stelae of Beth-shan (which are important,
especially that of Sethos I, which mentions a tribe called '*Apiru*). There
exists then from the 10th century an agricultural calendar, besides the
documents discussed above when we considered writing. [8] We can also
mention some small finds such as inscriptions on amphorae, seals and
jewels, but these hardly make history.

II. ORIENTAL ARCHEOLOGY

We must turn to the great peoples near Israel who left us more numerous
texts. Strange to say, it is not the nearest neighbor, Egypt, that furnishes
more documents which illuminate the history of Palestine. Egyptian
documentation is more copious for Chanaan than for Israel. Extremely
valuable are the Execration Texts of the Middle Empire (1900-1700), the
Annals of Amenophis II and Tuthmosis III who fought in the region, the
Turin papyrus with all its allusions to the geography of Asia, the travels
of Wen-amun in Phoenicia about 1100. For Israel we have only the
Stele of Menephtah, the first text which mentions Israel (about 1225) [9]
and the list engraved on a column at Karnak of cities taken by Pharao
Sheshonq during his campaign about 930. The Bible more often refers
to Egypt than Egypt alludes to its smaller neighbor. But the biblicist
would do well to know in detail Egyptian history. J. Breasted has
collected the relevant documents and translated them into English
(*Ancient Records of Egypt*, 5 Vols.). The index of this work is very useful.

The historian of Israel will discover more direct information in the
cuneiform tablets. Salmanasar III not only passed through Syria and
Lebanon, but in 853 (give or take a year) he engaged a Syrian coalition
in battle at Qarqar. In his Annals he lists among his allied enemies
" Achab of Israel. " Afterwards Israel and Juda are mentioned often,
so that thanks to their chronological lists the Assyrian documents furnish
a basis for an absolute dating of biblical history. Necessary guidelines
are found in the *Babylonian Chronology* of Parker and Dubberstein. The
biblical historian must pay great attention to Assyrian testimony,

---

[8] Cf. p. 72.

[9] Cf. our *Introduction to the Old Testament*, p. 15.

although it needs critical study to be interpreted. Sometimes there are several editions of the same Annals, several reports about the same event, and these parallel texts are not lacking in differences and exaggerations. There is, nevertheless, a collection of invaluable information assembled in *Records of Assyria* by Luckenbill, who has likewise provided a useful index.

The other inscriptions found in Syria should not be overlooked. Some of them furnish very interesting insights, such as those of Karatepe and Zendjirli, the Stelae of Neirab, the victory inscription of Zakir, king of Hamat. They complement the above cited texts of Ras Shamra and Byblos (Phoenicia) by enlightening us about the life of the minor peoples of Syria who were in many respects like those of the Palestinian kingdoms. In an indirect way, that is, by revealing facts about customs, beliefs, geography and place names, the Punic, Hittite, and Aegean documents (which are being deciphered) are a great aid for research on the history of Palestine.

There have been efforts to place all this information at the disposition of biblical scholars by publishing collections in which these texts, written in very different languages, are translated and presented by specialists. Schrader did this in 1880 for the cuneiform texts, and his work has been reedited with additions several times. In 1906 H. Gressmann presented a collection of Oriental texts and monuments in his *Altorientalische Texte und Bilder zum alten Testament*. This well-done work had a second enlarged edition in 1926. Americans under the direction of J. B. Pritchard produced a similar work in 1950 with more texts and notes, *Ancient Near Eastern Texts Relating to the Old Testament* (second edition, 1955). This was followed in 1954 by a volume of photographic reproductions, *The Ancient Near East in Pictures*. In French there is *Archéologie mésopotamienne* of A. Parrot (2 Vols. 1946-1953), the *Manuel d'archéologie orientale* of G. Contenau (4 Vols. 1927-1947), and the incomplete *Manuel d'archéologie égyptienne* of J. Vandier (4 Vols. had appeared by 1955).

Good though these works are, they are incomplete. A good historian who is familiar with the life and events of the ancient Near East can find unexpected pertinent information in documents which seem at first sight to have nothing to say about the Bible. Not everything is included in such works. They would be quite enormous if they included the Greco-Roman period. From that time a mass of documents which did not have to be excavated have come down to us. Fortunately, the three-volume classic of E. Schürer on the history of the Jewish people at the time of Jesus admirably collects all the historical facts needed for the interpretation of texts relating to Judaism and primitive Christianity. The

162 THE RULES OF RATIONAL CRITICISM

Historia aetatis novi Testamenti of U. Holzmeister (Rome, 1938) and the *Histoire de la Palestine* of P. Abel (Paris, 1952) might be added here. Meanwhile the discoveries continue. If there were only that of Qumran, the historian would still have to rework his material in the light of the new facts.

§ 3. The results

I. HISTORICAL CRITICISM

The historian does not understand the full import of the text unless he has a sense of the life and law that rule human societies. History is not just a collection of documents, nor a collection of old stones. It is a participation in the life of men of the past. The life of men of antiquity was at the same time very different from, and very similar to our own. Economic trends were not the same in their day as in ours; neither were the means of production the same. They did not have the same social problems to solve. They were not in possession of the same historical and geographical facts. They were, nevertheless, men like us with a body, senses, and intelligence to live in the midst of other men, and of a nature " one conquers only by obeying. " (Bacon) The good historian is one who knows well the permanent laws of human life, and who at the same time can overlook all that happened to man between the period that he is studying and the one in which he lives, in order to put himself in spirit in the life situation of the age and the author he is studying. In history a twofold intellectual effort is required : 1) through study and experience to draw the immutable laws applicable to the past as well as to the present, and 2) to have sufficient imagination directed by objective facts to enter into the problems of life in the past.

This double movement seems sometimes so difficult to our contemporaries that they doubt the possibility of an objective history. A. Piganiol, H. Marrou, P. Ricœur, and J. Hours have recently discussed the problem. A biblical archeologist, W. F. Albright, in presenting his *From the Stone Age to Christianity : Monotheism and the Historical Process*, dedicated two chapters to the problems of historical criticism and the philosophy of history, discussing in passing the positions of Toynbee, Sorokin and O. Weber. Such discussions are important because they help to form a clear realization of what conditions historical objectivity. Without adopting a conclusion, we can state that points once obscure are now admitted by all. Just as moving is a proof of motion, the worth of history is proved by what it has already produced of value. Evidently every historian has his strong and weak points.   One, a good economist, can best determine the conditions of production and distribution in antiquity.   Another, a sociologist, can tell if a given law pertains to a patriarchal or to a sedentary society.   A third develops a history of ideas; a fourth is occupied with religious life and cult.   The best historian would be the one who could master all of these disciplines, allowing each to enrich the others, since life is a whole and it consists of all the different facts that science must separate in order to analyze them.

II.   The historical method in exegesis

This is the procedure when the historical method is applied to biblical exegesis.   Every text must be situated in its historical milieu in order to be correctly explained.   The task is the more difficult when the text is very short or displays a genre that is less directly dependent on contingent events.   Thus there are difficulties in exactly dating a psalm, and even more a proverb.   In practice the processes of literary criticism and historical criticism do not follow one another either logically or chronologically.   They work together, they support each other.   The study of literary genres and the modes and expression used by biblical authors requires a knowledge of the milieu in which they lived.   On the other hand, the knowledge of that milieu depends largely on the study of the texts themselves.   This does not create a vicious circle, but it is a necessity of scientific procedure when one is studying the past.   Its different aspects, history, sociology, literature, thought, clarify themselves together and progressively.

Before the ancient Orient was rediscovered after many centuries of oblivion, it seemed comparatively easy to trace biblical history from the Bible itself.   Now the Bible has been placed in a milieu of which the Church Fathers and the Jews of the Hellenistic Age had only vague ideas.   It now appears as an unparalleled but complex source of documentation.   The texts stand out better, but their relation to history is not always exactly what it seems to be at first sight.   Neighboring literatures furnish us many examples of customary ways that our modern mentality finds difficult to accept : the Pharaos list among the villages they have conquered those conquered by their predecessors, because in their age they would have been highly embarrassed if they did not include them among their own victories.   In a somewhat similar fashion, a sense of continuity in certain biblical literary veins sometimes expressed itself by placing under the name of great authors of the past works which claimed their patronage : Moses remained the legislator par excellence even though his legislation was developed over the years; David was the type of the psalmist, and Solomon the wise man. Consequently, the mere presence of these proper names in the text does not suffice to settle the question of date or author. It might be a question of ancient works having literary authenticity in the modern sense of the term. It might also be a question of more recent compositions in which the venerated name represents for the reader something entirely different than an indication of authorship.

This simple example shows how the secret of the works is pierced only at the price of long study after groping attempts with only a certain measure of success. History is a science of successive approximations, not in the sense that it arrives at only hypothetical conclusions, but in the sense that ancient life and thought become clear only little by little as they emerge from the shadows which hid them. The study of evidence of the past is yielding more and more certain facts. It is still true that around the solid core of these facts areas of shade can still be found. The historical method applied to the Bible does not diminish its worth; on the contrary, it enables us to know more exactly what was really the divine revelation granted to one people among many in the framework of its history. That revelation was thrust deeply into a train of events that is important for understanding the word of God itself. The text certainly contains that word, but in the context of the ages, milieux, and mentalities that conditioned its expression. [10]

---

[10] On modern methods in archeology, one may profitably consult the collective work entitled *La découverte du passé* edited and presented by A. LAMING (Paris, 1952). (Add or substitute ALBRIGHT and KENYON).

FROM BIBLICAL CRITICISM
TO THE MEANING OF THE BIBLE

Textual criticism establishes the precise text of the books of the Bible;
literary criticism determines the genre and mode of expression; historical
criticism determines the social milieu. Is that all? Are the books then
entirely intelligible? No, because given the understanding of what a
given milieu would expect of an author who addresses himself to it in
a determined literary form, plus the geographic, economic and political
conditions along with the philosophical and religious climate in which
the author moved, we still must enter into the mind of the author himself,
in order to discern what he intended to say when he wrote his text in
this form and in these circumstances. Here ultimately lies the meaning
of the biblical books—not in the words themselves considered in an
abstract way, but in the living thought of a man. Of this latter his
words are only a translation.

This final task of exegesis is an art. It demands first of all sympathy
with the author being studied. Beyond pure criticism we must reach
the man who speaks to us, whatever the difficulties or apparent contra-
dictions in what he wrote : these could be the result of faulty transmission,
but they could also be the result of a mentality that differs from our
own, or a puzzling literary genius. The exegete must not dissimulate or
minimize them. He must grasp them to discover what an intelligent
man who wanted to transmit a message could have wanted to express.
A strange expression might have seemed necessary for him to convey,
not an everyday thought, but a truth rarely perceived. A typical case
is the Books of Chronicles. A simple comparison with the Books of
Samuel and Kings shows that the Chronicler's presentation of the history
of Israel and Juda does not agree with these books. Some have tried
to minimize these differences; others have emphasized them, and find in
this a proof that the work of the Chronicler is worthless because he did
not hesitate to revise his sources. Today it is recognized that his message
demanded both allusion to past events and revision of the sources in
order to make his contemporaries understand his view on the exact
nature of " the kingdom of God " expected by men. The first difficulty
that arises when one begins to explain the Book is resolved through a

better understanding of its purpose, content and meaning. Behind the
dead letter is the psychology of a man anxious to transmit a religious
message important in his day.

That is often the case with the Bible. The exegete, equipped with
all of his scientific knowledge, must realize that beyond the facts of
philology and history there is a person to person encounter between the
author and his reader. Thus it is not a matter of mere science, but of
a personal relationship that demands sympathy. One might not find
the art of Rimbaud or the style of Valéry to his taste, or not savor a
symphony by Beethoven or Vincent d'Indy. In that case he should not
occupy himself with these geniuses. One should not judge what he
does not understand. Biblical criticism is like art criticism : it must seek
that which is most personal in the artist's expression. Any study
of a written work demands a certain type of intellectual gymnastics.
The critic must share with the author the latter's knowledge of the
language and mentality of his contemporaries, those whom he addresses.
It is not enough to be familiar with the 19th century in general to
understand Balzac. Through careful readings of his works and study of
his characters one must acquire an intimacy with the world of Balzac,
a certain familiarity with the author and his characters. All of this is
even more true for biblical authors. They cannot be explained by their
historical circumstances alone. A knowledge of such circumstances might
indicate the possible problems with which they were faced, but to arrive
at their particular message and to grasp the full range of their writings,
attentive and repeated reading is necessary to penetrate their innermost
thought and feelings. The reader must not be sidetracked by vocabulary
or peculiar flights of imagination. He must artfully discern the personal
way in which each author employed the methods and literary genres
current in his day.

Exegesis is then a search of the most concrete sort imaginable, that
of living thought within its fixed expression. All the auxiliary sciences
only help to clear the way, to exclude false solutions, and to open positive
perspectives. Ultimately the exegete must apply his sympathy as the
only way to discover behind the signs of the text he is studying the light
in which the obscure becomes clear.

Can he go further to discover in the thought of one man a greater
meaning for the whole of humanity? Modern studies seem to affirm this
possibility. They lean toward a history of literatures and a history of
religions considered in a total perspective. Plato and Confucius are
interesting not only for their own thought ; they are fully understandable
only in the context of the entire current of Greek and Chinese thought,

and these currents in turn take their place in the general current of human civilization.

This is also true of the books of the Bible. For a long time Jews as well as Christians have considered the Bible as a collection of texts that could be explained only in relation to each other. The exegete, then, cannot fulfill his task satisfactorily unless he places the thought of Isaias, Jeremias, or Ezechiel in the general context of biblical thought. He must even try to place all of this in the development of thought of the ancient Orient, which is but a division of human civilization and culture. This is not to say that the task has already been accomplished, nor that it is easy to accomplish. But it is imperative for biblicists to undertake it with all their critical sense.

Within what sort of framework is this critical work to be done? It certainly pertains to the history of civilizations, and it must be noted that the Bible belongs to the most complex, ancient and dynamic civilization of the world, [11] and for the individual at once the most stimulating and the most formidable. But this critical study depends also on a judgment concerning human life. A critical study that is beguiled by a superman ideal can hardly appreciate the prophetic movement, which takes up and amplifies the humanitarian demands of the Mosaic law. A Pharasee, for whom the law is an absolute, would tend to emphasize the value of the legalistic mentality. A Christian, for whom the law is an absolute but still inadequate (because it is only too mocked in this world) and for whom the key to this life lies in love and pardon, discerns the perfection of this trend in the gospel message that the Church carries to the four corners of this world. It is clear that such a judgment concerning the most profound value of a biblical text brings into play much more than merely critical principles.

Judgment on the value of a text depends finally on a judgment of faith, which is certainly not independent of rational considerations. Scripture itself plays a role in that judgment, but the latter remains in another domain. Exegesis is then a mixed terrain in which the understanding of reason and of faith meet. To arrive at certitude in this matter other criteria than simple critical examination are necessary. The following chapters will take as their viewpoint the perspective of faith within the Roman Catholic Church.

---

[11] The renowned Chinese civilization enters history only with the Chang dynasty (18th or 16th century B.C. according to R. GROUSSET in *Histoire générale, Moyen Age*, Vol. X [Paris, 1941], p. 163 ff.; about 1500 according to W. EBERHARD in *Historia Mundi*, II [Munich, 1953], p. 573), while writings appeared in Mesopotamia and Egypt around 3000. The Hindu and Mexican-Inca civilizations are still more recent.

THE CATHOLIC INTERPRETATION OF SACRED SCRIPTURE

by P. Grelot

F. X. PATRIZI, *De interpretatione scripturarum*[4]* (Rome, 1876).

P. G. DUNCKER, " De vera et genuina Sacrae Scripturae Interpretatione, " *Angelicum*, XX (1943), pp. 53-62.

C. SPICQ, A. ROBERT, L. VAGANAY, " Interprétation, "* *SDB*, IV, pp. 561-646.

P. CRUVEILHER, " Herméneutique sacrée, "* *SDB*, III, cols. 1482-1523.

J. DANIÉLOU, *The Bible and the Liturgy** (Notre Dame, 1956).

L. BOUYER, *Meaning of Sacred Scripture** (Notre Dame, 1958).

C. CHARLIER, *The Christian Approach to the Bible** (Westminster : Newman, 1958).

C. GIBLIN, " As it is written. . . " *CBQ* (1958), pp. 327-353.

J. D. McKENZIE, " Problems of Hermeneutic in Roman Catholic Exegesis, "* *JBL*, (1958), pp. 197-204.

A. ROBERT, A. TRICOT, *Guide to the Bible** (New York : Desclée, 1960).

A. JONES, *God's Living Word** (New York : Sheed and Ward, 1961).

Preliminary Remarks

I. THE LIMITATIONS OF BIBLICAL CRITICISM

The various steps of biblical criticism have just been sketched. But these steps do not constitute all of exegesis. They represent the point of view of the scientist who wants to elucidate as much as possible all the human problems which are presented by Sacred Scripture, such as establishing exactly the original texts by means of their versions and their manuscript tradition; seeking for each book or fragment thereof its origin, its date, its geographical area, its author and the circumstances of its composition; a literary study of the work itself, clarifying its aim, its *genre* and finally the slightest idiosyncracies of its vocabulary and style. In fact, such a method of scientific investigation is not peculiar only to the Bible; it applies to all the documents of the past. If the study of the Bible requires that it be used, it is because this is a fully human book where the Word of God has in some way become incarnate in human speech, thereby subjecting itself to all the controls to which human speech is susceptible, with a humility analogous to that of the Son of God who " took the form of a slave and acted in all things like a man " (Phil 2, 7).

It remains that this biblical criticism has some limitations. On the one hand, on the scientific level to which it strictly adheres, it runs into problems that it cannot fully explore, for lack of indispensable data or because the data that it does possess are themselves obscure or complex : will it ever be possible some day to completely restore, for example, the historical details of the era of the patriarchs? On the other hand, even when the results obtained are based on solid data, criticism advances only step by step toward indisputable certitudes. Its restoration of the past ends only little by little in syntheses closer and closer to reality. Such is the first limitation of biblical criticism. It poses a serious question for the Christian, who seeks above all in Scripture the food for his faith : if he must wait for criticism to establish by its own means the meaning of each passage of Scripture before knowing what God says to him in these difficult texts, how is it possible to reconcile this delay with the immediate needs of the life of faith? How can it be admitted that faith depends, so to speak, on the results of a study undertaken with purely human means, or that it is subject to the fluctuations of a science which gropes in the midst of the most diverse hypotheses before arriving at undisputed certitudes?

But biblical criticism has a second limitation, more fundamental still, which its very method prevents it from overcoming. Having put itself deliberately in the flow of historical science, it places its inquiry on the level of objective facts, ascertainable by human means; it seeks to establish their reality, to find their link in the order of secondary causes, to make their meaning apparent, but without going outside the field into which it has placed itself. However, when these facts belong to the supernatural order (history of salvation, unfolding of the divine plan or God's revelation to men) must it not stop at the threshold of the Mystery which it will never see clearly, for lack of means to sound its depths?

To recognize these limitations of human science in the matter of historical research, to realize that they affect biblical criticism since the latter applies to the holy books the methods of human sciences, is not to minimize its value; it is simply to appreciate this value for its true merits, which are great but remain without a common measure with an order of things where faith alone can gain access.

II. Biblical criticism and the Christian reading of the Bible

Just so, biblical criticism cannot in any case be sufficient unto itself, Historical research in general is not assimilatable in all points to the sciences of nature, especially in what concerns the objectivity of its results. When a man attempts to retrace human history, he does not propose only to notice the existence of certain facts and to establish certain laws which govern the train of events. Beyond what he calls facts, he is also primarily interested in man : he studies man's behavior and his historical becoming in order to better know his nature, to clarify his destiny and to arrive at practical norms capable of orienting the behavior of individuals and of societies. It is very impossible, then, to abandon oneself to history or science without mixing therein preoccupations of another order, be it philosophical or religious, which guide the scientific steps and especially which interpret their results.

And this is much more the case when one deals with the Bible. The global religious fact of which it is the witness cannot be coldly studied, as one could study the evolution of reptiles during the secondary era. There is a vital question which must be asked and which no scientist could avoid : What is the place of the Bible in the universal religious phenomenon? What is its value for modern man and for the scientist himself who is striving to retrace its history? Does there exist in it, yes or no, the revelation of God, and the way of salvation, as the Bible itself pretends? In face of such a problem no man can remain neutral; it is in fact the principal problem around which all the others revolve, the one which dominates human existence. To pretend to ignore it, is still to answer it, negatively, that is.

According to the personal answer that the critic gives to this question, all his scientific research changes meaning. Let us understand that in all probability, it can, on its own level, be conducted with the same intellectual honesty and with the same care for objective fact. But it is integrated into the whole idea of a living thought whose orientation is radically different in the man who believes in biblical revelation and in the man who studies the Bible from the outside, even if he is sympathetic to it. Once this fact is recognized, it is not difficult to understand how two exegetes, one a believer and the other not, can react so differently to the same facts, can propose at times different interpretations, and can even be led to reconstruct quite differently the face of events, when they seek in their general concept of man and of history a supplementary illumination capable of filling the gaps of their information.

These general considerations are not superfluous. They enable us to understand how biblical criticism becomes integrated, for the Catholic exegete, into a study of Scripture which surpasses the immediate possibilities. These two things are not at odds : they are not developed independently in a parallel fashion; even more so, their respective requirements are not contradictory. Simply speaking, all the steps of criticism are informed (in the scholastic sense of the term) by a spirit of faith which, because it puts the spirit in direct contact with divine Truth, enables all together to apply with precision to the word of God the properly scientific methods of investigation and of analysis and to correctly interpret the results obtained in this way.

This is why we must now study the conditions of this Christian reading of the Bible without which biblical criticism would remain a dead science. In order to do so, it is useful to first of all question past centuries. How has the people of God constantly read the Scriptures? To what end, in what spirit, by which ways? In the framework of Jewish exegesis, the New Testament has laid the basis for a new interpretation; then the Church, in the course of its history, has elaborated on this a rational methodology. At the end of such an inquiry, it will be easier to see how, at the present time, in a cultural context where the methods of biblical criticism have been made precise in the manner indicated, the question of Catholic exegesis is asked.

CHAPTER I

THE FOUNDATIONS OF CHRISTIAN EXEGESIS

BIBLIOGRAPHY

J. BONSIRVEN, *Exégèse rabbinique, exégèse paulinienne** (Paris, 1939).

P. LESTRINGANT, *Essai sur l'unité de la révélation biblique* (Paris, 1942).

J. VAN DEN PLOEG, " Les exégèses de l'Ancien Testament dans l'Épître aux Hébreux, " *RB* (1947), pp. 199-228.

H. J. SCHOEPS, " Paulus als rabbinischer Exeget, " *Aus Frühchristlicher Zeit* (Tübingen, 1950), pp. 221-238.

C. H. DODD, *According to the Scriptures* (London, 1952).

J. W. DOEVE, *Jewish Hermeneutics in the Synoptic Gospels and Acts* (Assen, 1954).

R. BLOCH, " Midrash, " *SDB*, V, cols. 1263 ff.

J. DANIÉLOU, *From Shadows to Reality** (London : Burns and Oates, 1960).

E. ELLIS, *Paul's Use of the Old Testament* (Edinburgh : Oliver and Boyd, 1961).

M. BARTH, " The Old Testament in Hebrews, " *Current Issues in New Testament Interpretation*, eds. W. Klassen, G. F. Snyder (New York : Harper, 1962) ; *Conversation with the Bible* (New York : Holt, Rinehart, Winston, 1964).

§ 1. Biblical Exegesis in Judaism

I. ORIGIN OF JEWISH EXEGESIS : MIDRASH

Even in the Old Testament, the people of God scrutinized the Scriptures, which were the rule of its faith and of its conduct. The problem of exegesis is therefore one that occurs very early, not in terms of *scientific knowledge* (toward which its culture hardly tends), but in terms of *life*. God spoke through His emissaries, His Word was collected in books; later events placed the seal of God on this Word by inscribing in history signs capable of proving it. Immediately, a certain attitude toward the books is taken : it is faith in what they say, and obedience to what they prescribe. But what exactly do they teach? This must be carefully rooted out. That is why, from the moment when Judaism is organized, dispersed communities (which only have in common between them the link of one same faith, of one same Law and of one same worship) are seen attaching themselves to the Scriptures, where this faith, this Law and this worship find their norm, and striving to rate their value even before the list is closed.

How are these Scriptures to be read? What does one look for in them? How does one bring out the permanent value in them? On these points we have direct information from only a relatively late period (toward the 2nd century B.C.); but the Old Testament itself contains some traces of a very old exegesis, the forerunner to what has been later called *midrash*. Midrash : what does this mean? The verb *aarash* suggests the idea of search : the Scriptures are scrutinized, not for the curiosity of knowing who wrote them or in what circumstances they were written, but to establish what they mean at the present time. This research is born in the schools where priests, cantors and literate laymen, the intellectual elite of the nation, are trained; also, in the pietist circles, more or less tied to the former, who attempt to build upon the meditation of the Scriptures a more fervent spiritual life (the *Anawim* of the Psalms and the Assideans of the Machabean period); finally the synagogues, where the liturgical reading of the texts and the singing of Psalms is accomplished by explanations and homilies, in order to maintain the crowd in faithfulness to the faith and traditions of Israel. Naturally, there are among these places considerable overlappings; it is not our duty here to trace their obscure and complicated history; it is sufficient to note that results are achieved by their search into the meaning of the Scriptures.

These can be judged by analyzing different materials. In the inspired books themselves—and very early—the intentional re-use of expressions borrowed from the most ancient books indirectly attest to the interpretations that were given to them. Secondly, a whole series of writings, inspired or not, are grafted so sensitively on this exegesis that they tend to be called *midrash*. Finally, some extrabiblical works are explicitly devoted to the interpretation of texts, more and more numerous, beginning with the 2nd century B.C. They emanate either from official circles (such as the rabbinical works) or from sects (such as the Qumran writings). Their purpose is always the same : to make the Scriptures *meaningful*. But this effort takes on different forms. They are largely divided into three groups.

II. THE FORMS OF MIDRASH

The first form of midrash, the one whose object is best defined, is the *halaka*. It has as its purpose to seek in the Scriptures, especially in the Torah, rules of conduct, especially of a juridical nature. Although it is not out of place in the synagogue sermons, it is easy to understand that it is mostly developed in the literate circles : among the priests and scribes, as sort of a commentary on the Torah, and also in the pietist groups when they want to prescribe for themselves precise rules (for example the various rules of Qumran).

The second form of midrash is the *haggada*. Jewish doctors called by this name any commentary on Scripture which had as an aim the spiritual training of listeners according to vastly different points of view (moral exhortation, explanation of liturgical feasts, doctrinal commentary) and by the most diverse means (from simple exposition with a view to clarifying a text to a free narrative grafted on the text to illustrate it). It is normal that this form of exegesis was particularly flourishing in synagogal preaching, but not exclusively there.

A third form of midrash, with a definite objective, is also noticed. This is what is known as the *pesher*, a name found in a number of Qumran texts. In these, the prophetic writings are brought up to date, along with others, by showing their fulfilment in the events of the recent past and in the present, in order to induce " what will happen afterwards. " Dn 9 is a characteristic example of this; but its presence is already sensed in the background of quite a few later prophetic passages, where ancient writings are reinterpreted in the light of a new historical perspective (for example in Za 9—14).

III. SPIRIT AND METHOD OF MIDRASH

In all probability, midrash seeks in the texts only their life-value. To bring it to light, the interpreter illuminates the Scriptures with the help of all the means at his disposal, in order to bring forth beyond the words a meaning relative to the problems of his time. The concept of inspired book, which dominates such an exegesis, emphasizes its divine origin : coming from God, Scripture contains all His secrets and has an absolute value—it contains lessons adaptable for all times. To grasp this divine idea enclosed in the texts, the interpreter hardly bothers to return to the inspired author's thought, in which the supernatural Truth could be grasped. The very personality of the author is of relatively no importance to him and he is satisfied with rather summary generalizations : Moses is the Law, David is the Psalms, Solomon is Wisdom. Likewise his critical requirements do not extend very far when it is a question of knowing in what historical circumstances the sacred books were written. On the other hand, he has an acute feeling for the unity and continuity of Scripture. That is why he methodically confronts each text with the totality of divine revelation which he knows by the collection of sacred books and by the living tradition of Judaism; he casts this light on each text, sometimes to raise it to this level in the case of an archaic text, sometimes to adapt its message to contemporary circumstances, even if he must, in order to do so, tear it away from a clearly indicated historical framework which conditions its expressions.

By this means, the Bible fulfills in Judaism an essential function : it crystallizes around itself all the life of faith which finds food in each of its pages. To do this, exegesis does not approach it in a piecemeal fashion, nor with any respect for pure objectivity. It is by tying each text to the whole of Scripture and to the totality of faith that a teaching relevant to the vital needs of men emerges. If it succeeds, it is not because it has at its disposal a perfected scientific critical apparatus; it is because it possesses this teaching from another source before finding it in any individual text. In short, then, it starts from faith to find its content in Scripture rather than starting from the texts to reconstruct methodically the content of faith.

In the meantime, the exegete has recourse to practical means in use and regulated by usage before the rabbinical schools attempt to codify them. There is first of all the confrontation of the text which is explained with other biblical passages likely to shed light on it. The bringing together of these texts is normally based upon verbal coincidences which establish between the texts a materially verifiable relation. With this as his starting point, the exegete uses his reason, comparing the data present with all his faith but also with all his ingenuity. For example, he adapts a text to the situation of another, or again he attempts a precise analysis of the meaning of the words. Let us not imagine here recourse to scientific philology and semantics : the meaning of the words in his eyes comes from their usage in common parlance and especially in the Bible, and by a completely subtle game of comparing roots of related consonance. In short, the exegete uses for his interpretation everything that he can know of biblical language.

In order to illustrate the texts and show their scope, he also has recourse to elements made available to him by the living tradition : customs (especially in matters of law and worship), the oral development of popular narratives which have more or less come from the Bible or have been grafted upon it, and beliefs already received but not as yet inscribed in the texts. All this, which is a part of the legacy of the people of God, the exegete reads retrospectively into the biblical passages which he is commenting upon, and ties them together in ways already mentioned. He shows thereby that, through these customs, these stories, and these beliefs, the Scripture are confirmed.

Finally, discovering in the events lived by Israel the fulfilment of a divine plan which he feels has been totally predicted in the Scriptures under the aspect of a secret hidden behind the words, the exegete strives from this point of view to bring the mystery to light, deciphering the texts as one would decipher a premonitory dream sent by God Himself. Whence come explanations which show the Scriptures as partially fulfilled in the destiny of Israel, and this initial fulfilment makes him hope that the promises not as yet fulfilled will be fulfilled at a time determined by the Master of centuries.

IV. EXEGESIS AND FAITH

Such is Jewish exegesis, luxuriant, going in all directions, but first of all, a work of faith. In this faith, it possesses a sense of the Scriptures which is global, even if it experiences some difficulty in connecting this meaning to specific passages of the holy books, even if these passages resist analysis. This very difficulty stimulates it and pushes it to the point of sublety. Careful to flow into life, it no less uses the resources offered by the science of the day : knowledge of history, as much as it is available, knowledge of traditions preserved by Judaism in a parallel fashion to the Scriptures and even a philology in line with its ability.

When Judaism becomes implanted in Alexandria, it attempts even to use for a similar purpose the means offered by Hellenistic culture, for example recourse to allegory. This is especially the case of Philo, who thus finds the means of connecting to the Bible his philosophical concepts integrated into his view of the world, of man and of history which remains intentionally, if not always actually, Jewish. But a danger is obvious in this : namely, that Hellenistic culture will supersede the data of the Jewish faith, when exegesis thus practiced abandons its vital objective to tend toward intellectual speculation. In truth, Scripture was otherwise oriented; the objective to which it was constantly associated was the Mystery of the relations between God and man, not the philosophical knowledge of man and the universe.

§ 2. Exegesis of the New Testament

I. GENERAL PERSPECTIVE

The exegesis of the New Testament was born in Jewish circles. That is why it was necessary to analyze at some length Jewish exegesis, in order to situate it in its historical framework and understand some aspects troublesome for modern minds. The revelation of the New Testament carries with it the essentials of Jewish faith, with the difference that it introduces some discriminations and centers all the materials that it preserves on an absolute novelty : the revelation of the Son of God. However, to make itself intelligible, the very expression of the novelty borrows a language from the Scriptures. Thus is seen how prestigious these latter appeared in the eyes of Christians. They are still read and explained both by Christ and by the apostles, and according to a method conforming to Jewish tradition. But they are read by new eyes, put back into a perspective which, even though it remains in line with that of the Old Testament, nonetheless differs from it in a radical manner; eschatology, which is the key because it is also the result, is no longer to be situated in the future; it has already been inaugurated.

In the preaching of Christ, the kingdom of God toward which the whole Old Testament tended is proclaimed to be present, in His person, in His message, in His work and in His life. That is why Scripture is not *abolished*, but its " fulfilment " (Mt 5, 17) is the equivalent of a veritable reinterpretation : not that the new meaning eliminates the old, but it causes unsuspected depths to appear. In the same manner, in the apostolic preaching, Jesus is presented as the Messias of Israel announced in the Scriptures " put to death and buried in conformity with the Scriptures, resurrected on the third day in conformity with the Scriptures " (1 Cor 15, 3-4). All the Scriptures are thus *reread in the light of the resurrection :* their definitive scope is sharpened as anticipated traces of the Mystery of Christ are found in them. It is in this general climate that the Christian midrash of the Old Testament is developed.

II. CHRISTIAN MIDRASH OF THE OLD TESTAMENT

For Christ and for the primitive Church, the Scriptures are composed exclusively of the Old Testament and even in the Greek-language Church the sacred text which serves as a basis for reading and commenting is the Septuagint. The exegesis of these books finds in the life of the Church thousands of occasions to express itself, in order to answer the most essential needs : announcing the arrived kingdom, then the arrival of Jesus the Messias and Son of God, is done by means of the Scriptures which are witnesses of it (Lk 4, 16-22; sermon in Acts); the moral teaching of the faithful seeks in the Scriptures rules of conduct by interpreting them in the light of the teachings of Jesus; controversy must justify to the eyes of the Jews the attitudes and beliefs which are opposed to the traditions of the doctors or apparently contradict certain data of Scripture (Mt 21, 12-13; 22, 41-45; Rom 4); finally, in the liturgy, Jewish prayers, woven

from biblical expressions, take on a new meaning because of the Mystery
of the Kingdom, then of the Mystery of Jesus (Acts 4, 24-30).   Thus,
Scripture occupies everywhere an essential place, immediately relative
to the central object of faith; the practical ends to which its explanation
corresponds are fundamentally the same as those of Jewish midrash.

This is why all the forms of the latter are also found in the Christian
context.   If the *halaka* is disappearing, it is because Jesus has put an
end to the *tradition of the Ancients* and substituted for its juridicism a new
Torah where the best of the old Torah, of prophetism and of Jewish
Wisdom emerge as " being fulfilled. "   Christian *halaka*, essentially
of a religious and moral order, is therefore met by the preoccupations
of the Jewish *haggada*.   On the other hand, preaching and controversy
make use of the *pesher*.   This is clearly seen in the sermons of Acts or in
certain characteristic passages of the first Gospel; also, to explain the
meaning of events where the destiny of Jesus and the Church is found,
and to evoke in advance the consummation, at the end of time, of the
already inaugurated Kingdom, Christian eschatology has recourse to
similar means, from the synoptic apocalypse to that of John.   Finally,
the Christian *haggada* experiences a vigorous development.   It constitutes, on the one hand, the framework within which the Gospel traditions
take their literary form : in the Epistles, numerous traces of this are to
be found, even certain narrative materials from the Jewish *haggada*
(Acts 7, 22; I Cor 10, 4; Jude 9; 2 Tm 3, 8).

However, Christian midrash often shows itself to be more attentive
than Jewish midrash to the first purpose of the texts which it explains.
Undoubtedly, most of these practical means used in Judaism are found
in its Christian counterpart, including certain subtleties of reasoning
(I Cor 9, 9), etymological explanations (Heb 7, 2), even considerations
on the silence of Scripture (Heb 7, 3), etc .... There remains that, in
this regard, it is more discrete, in the same proportion as it is more
simple, more detached from the arguments of schools, since the Mystery
of the Kingdom is revealed to the simple and to the small, rather than to
the erudite (Mt 11, 25).

III.   THE FULFILMENT OF THE SCRIPTURES

If the exegesis of the Old Testament, at the beginnings of Christianity,
thus prolongs Jewish exegesis, its original characteristics do not fail to be
quickly noticed.   In the books of the apostolic generation, a language
which attempts to define them is developed.   And first of all, there is
the principle of the " fulfilment of the Scriptures. "   The idea, translated

by the two verbs *pléro-ô* and *teleio-ô* was not unknown in rabbinical circles; but it takes on now an entirely new shade of meaning. In fact, it no longer is limited only to the Torah and to the prophets (Mt 5, 17-19; Lk 4, 21; Acts 1, 16; Mt 2, 22; Jn 19, 28, etc...). " The times " are also fulfilled (Mk 1, 15) and this " fullness of time " (Gal 4, 4) marks at the same time the end, the crowning and the perfection of a whole preparatory economy (Rom 10, 4; Heb 10, 1, 14). In Christ everything is fulfilled (Jn 19, 30), eschatologically fulfilled; the *telos* is there, in relation to which previous history and all of Scripture was ordained. This is to say that the true import of the texts is perceptible only through this *telos*, which defines its perfection and its plenitude. Such is the perspective from which the idea of a *sensus plenior* attributed in Christianity to the Scriptures of the Old Testament is best understood : not only is it an essential requirement of faith, but the very expression which designates it is authorized by its use in the New Testament and not only by an altogether modern approach. We will see, however, that this approach does allow us to make the notion more exact.

IV. PAULINE PRINCIPLES

In order to say the same thing, St. Paul was led to distinguish in Scripture between the *letter* and the *spirit* (2 Cor 3, 4 ff.; Rom 2, 29; 7, 6). By *letter*, he does not mean the literal meaning of the biblical books in the modern sense of the word, but rather the result of a reading which would not go beyond Jewish perspectives, surpassed since Christ's arrival. The *spirit*, on the other hand, is the understanding of the Scriptures which flows from their reference to Christ; it is only accessible in faith and with the moving power of the divine Spirit, the same Spirit who inspired the sacred authors and deposited in the letter of these texts this profound meaning linked to the terminal development of revelation. In fact, in their *letter* the Scriptures are conditioned by all the elements of the preparatory " pedagogical " economy (Gal 3, 24) which Paul includes under the name of Law. But how can one overcome these fragile elements without mistaking their own value? How can one explain that they can be abolished as institutions while preserving a meaning for the Christian reader, to whom they speak in their own way about the things of the New Covenant?

This is where the principle of typology enters into Pauline exegesis. Scripture contains *typoi* which interest us. Let us understand by this not only examples (as could be thought from 1 Cor 10, 11) but prophetic figures which even in the past obscurely announced what was going to

happen " at the end of time " (I Cor 10, 11); this comes from the treatment
to which Paul subjects the events of the Exodus (I Cor 10, 6) and from
the parallel that he draws between Adam and Christ (Rom 5, 14).   God
has therefore sketched from the beginning the plan which He proposed
to finally realize in Christ; He has also modeled the facts, the characters
and the institutions of Israelitic history on this plan; these first imperfect
sketches, however, were only the " shadow of things to come " (Col 2, 17).
It does not follow that the *spirit* of Scripture must be the exact equivalent
of the *typoi* which it contains : the two notions are connex, but they are
not equivalent.   The *spirit* is attainable sometimes thanks to a simple
deepening of the meaning of scriptural terms.   But insofar as the lessons
included in the Bible and even the language in which they are formulated
are related to the preparatory economy, the principle of typology is the
only one which allows us to grasp its present-day import, which is the
sensus plenior we spoke of previously.

The Christian reading of Scripture thus leads in St. Paul to certain
applications which seem at first sight without any direct relation to ist
original meaning.   But transfers of this sort are justified when, because
of providential relations between the two Covenants, the texts related
to the first suggest something other than what they designate at first.
This is why St. Paul has no scruples when it comes to *allegorizing* (Gal 4,
21-31).   The allegory does not designate for him a doctrinal principle
like the spirit and the letter or typology; it is essentially a practical
means used by the exegete to bring out the Christian value of a text.
Only in the case where he expressly uses this term is he from the start
inspired by an authentic typology to finally transform the passage he is
commenting into a series of metaphors tied together, and of which he
proposes a coherent application.   This process was not unknown to the
rabbis; but it was even more widespread in Alexandria.   When Paul
uses it (as he sometimes uses other rabbinical procedures : etymology,
a fortiori reasonings, etc. . .) he makes it a part of the general perspective
of his exegesis : it is typology that suggests to him the way in which to
use his allegorization.   Whether there be afterwards some artificiality in
the applications of detail that he proposes is a matter of relatively
secondary detail; it is sufficient for his purposes that by this means he
may enunciate, starting from Scripture, a datum of faith contained in
the general object of Scripture, in its *spirit*.

V.   THE EPISTLE TO THE HEBREWS

The Epistle to the Hebrews frequently uses the same technique, which
is not surprising, when one realizes its relations with Alexandrine culture;

but it fails to define it. In fact, in 9, 9 and 11, 19 the word *parabolè* is not only a synonym; the author finds only in the sacrifices of the Ancient Law and the sacrifice of Isaac *symbols* of the sacrifice of Christ, center of the Mystery of faith. But on what in his eyes is based such a symbolism? It is indispensable to see it clearly in order not to attribute to it too quickly a method of exegesis copied on that of Philo.

The foundation of this symbolism is a typology which is expressed here in a more precise and more methodical manner than in the other Pauline epistles. The word *typos* only appears once (8, 5), no longer in the meaning of prefiguring or of example (as in 1 Cor 10), but in the sense of archetype. Interpreting Ex 25, 40, the author induces that the things of the Old Covenant had in heaven a pre-existing archetype; from this heavenly reality, they were only the earthly image : *hypodeigma* (reproduction : 4, 11; 8, 5; 9, 23) *antitypos* (replica : 9, 24) or *skia* (shadow : 8, 5; 10, 1). This heavenly archetype, existing in God from the very beginning as the heavenly Jerusalem of the apocalypses was nothing other than the Mystery reached at the " consummation of the centuries " (9, 26) : that of the sacrifice of Christ, which introduces here below the true goods (8, 2; 9, 24), the eternal goods (5, 9; 9, 12; 13, 20), the goods " to come " (2, 5; 9, 11; 10, 1; 11, 20; 13, 14).

There is thus an identity between two orders of things : that of eternity and that of the " century to come " (6, 5), an eschatological consummation toward which the history of Israel tended, and which had arrived with Christ. The archetype of the things of the Old Covenant was therefore Christ and all the economy that he had inaugurated, that in which everything is consummated and attains its perfection (2, 10; 7, 19; 10, 14). At present, this archetype is represented here below by its eikon (10, 1) an image which is not any longer only the shadow but contains its presence under sacramental signs. Such is the principle of understanding of all of Scripture. It already concerned the entire Mystery of Christ, the end of God's plan; but the manner in which it spoke of it was veiled. That is why the real import of it is measured only in terms of the now-revealed archetype, the facts, characters and institutions which were its antitypes. In this light, there can be referred to Christ texts which, according to their initial objective, concerned Melchisedech or the Expiation ceremonies, Moses or the patriarchs. This transfer, which is sometimes developed in a detailed allegory, is not arbitrary exegesis; even if it does not care for exact biblical criticism, even if it denotes certain traits characteristic of the Alexandrine culture, it is founded upon a theology of history essential to Christian thought, since all of history is now integrated into the mystery of Christ.

It is obvious that the meaning of the word *typos* is opposite in the Epistle to the Hebrews and in the Pauline epistles; so is the meaning of *antitypos* in Heb 9, 24 and 1 Pt 3, 21.   But the concept of typology is, with some appreciable nuances, fundamentally identical and in both cases it allows one to bring out the Christian sense of the Old Testament

VI.   THE CHARACTERISTICS OF CHRISTIAN EXEGESIS

The New Testament has established once and for all the directing prin. ciples of Christian exegesis.   On the level of human reasoning, it brings nothing new : the practical means of rabbinical exegesis are still used, sometimes raised by a note borrowed from Alexandrianism, to make the meaning enclosed within the text emerge.   But these means are subordinated to an understanding of faith which marks a new stage in the reading of the holy books.   Christ is the key to Scripture : Scripture is entirely oriented to him.   His Mystery is its only object; he is its spirit; he is its fulfilment, its consummation, and its fulness.

This certitude, reached by higher and surer ways than the purely rational analysis of the texts, orients this very analysis, allows it to become an exegesis faithful to the profound thought of God, and indicates the way in which it can surpass the perspectives of the Old Testament where these are found to be limited and outdated (this is the meaning of typology).   The method which emerges from this integrates the data of a reasoning whose imperfections can be brought to light, if it is so desired : it is the method of a time, of a milieu and of a culture which have not yet perfected a scientific criticism.   But this aspect of the problem is secondary, because when scientific criticism is developed, it will also have to become integrated into a method which will continue to be ruled by the principles of the New Testament in order to remain Christian.

THE PRACTICE OF CHRISTIAN EXEGESIS

BIBLIOGRAPHY

G. BARDY, " La littérature patristique des Questiones et Responsiones, "
RB, XLI (1932), pp. 210 f., 341 f., 515 f.; XLII (1933), pp. 14 f.,
211 f., 328.

C. SPICQ, *Esquisse d'une histoire de l'exégèse latine au Moyen-Age** (Paris,
1944).

G. BARDY, " Commentaires patristiques de la Bible, " *SDB*, II, cols. 73-
103.

J. DANIÉLOU, *Sacramentum futuri** (Paris, 1950).

W. BURGHARDT, " On Early Exegesis, " *TS* 11 (1950), pp. 78-116.

R. E. McNALLY, *The Bible in the Early Middle Ages** (Westminster :
Newman, 1959).

J. N. D. KELLY, *Early Christian Doctrines* (New York : Harper, 1960).

J. D. SMART, *The Interpretation of Scripture* (Philadelphia : Westminster,
1961).

R. M. GRANT, *A Short History of the Interpretation of the Bible* (New
York : Macmillan, 1963), rev. ed.

B. SMALLEY, *The Study of the Bible in the Middle Ages* (Notre Dame :
1964).

In the history of Christian exegesis, three stages are to be distinguished :
the patristic age, the Middle Ages, and modern times, inaugurated by
the Renaissance. This history does not have to be sketched in detail;
only its constant traits and its principal turning points are important,
and these can clarify the present position of the exegetical problem.

§ 1. The Patristic Age

I. THE PROBLEMS

In order to correctly understand patristic exegesis, it must be placed into
its general framework. It is obvious, then, that its essential coordinates
are not concerns of a *cultural* nature, even if these sometime become
incidentally manifest; rather, they are the *vital* needs of the Church, as
in Judaism and during the apostolic age. The Bible no longer includes

only the books of the Old Testament; those of the New Testament have joined them, and the latter are the key to the former. With the help of these writings, which are an integrating part of its living tradition whose essence they fix under " canonical " form, the Church announces the Gospel to the infidels, teaches and exhorts the faithful, and celebrates a worship centered on the Mystery of Christ, to which Christians are united by sacramental participation.

But new problems are raised, which affect exegesis. First of all, there is the question of *controversy*. The apostolic times had already experienced it : an apologetic founded on Scripture in the preaching to the Jews; defense of the true faith against incipient deviations, thanks to faithfulness to the traditional deposit and to the holy letters (2 Tm 3, 14). The same methods are to be found now, either in controversy with the Jews (thus in the *Dialogue with Trypho* of Justin), or in the struggle against heresies. It is sometimes necessary to insure the triumph of the *spirit* over the *letter*, or to defend entire parts of Scripture whose value is contested (Marcion), at other times it is necessary to maintain in balance the exegesis received from the apostles when a heterodox thought (gnosis), using the techniques of Alexandrine allegorism, perverts the authentic meaning of the sacred books. Naturally, these operations raise a problem : How can one incontestably establish the juridical value of the texts and the meaning which is imposed to faith? Let us add to this the need to defend the Bible against attacks of pagans such as Celsius or Porphyrus, by following them onto their own field; the apologists are then led into the field of criticism and philosophy.

At the same time as they maintain the faith, and to better maintain it, the Fathers develop little by little the orthodox expression of *dogmas ;* by systematic *theology* they even attempt to synthesize revelation and human learning, using rational speculation as a tool in the service of faith. In these two tasks, however, their thought continues to be expressed starting from Scripture. They seek in it not only a support (which is also given to them by the liturgical texts and the works of their forebears), but also a standard and a vocabulary. However, the greater the requirements which they owe to their culture or which are imposed by the problems to be solved, the more necessary becomes the development of an exegetical method adapted to its object.

II. THE ELEMENTS OF THE EXEGETICAL METHOD

Here again, the essence of the method conforms to the exegetical tradition of the New Testament. When the Old Testament is explained, it is the same search for the *spirit* hidden under the *letter*, the same projection of the Mystery of Christ in its religious vocabulary, which sketched only its first outlines, the same eventual recourse to typology, establishing thereby an allegory which is developed with more or less freedom. For the texts of the New Testament, the problem is presented differently. Ideally, there is no longer any need to allegorize, since here the Mystery is clearly expressed, and there is no need to seek by any means whatsoever any more profound meaning than the letter. But when there is a desire to define the action of Christ in souls or the eschatological consummation of His Mystery, it is still possible to start from the facts of His life on earth by looking for what they symbolize. This exegesis, in its principle, is in keeping with the tradition of the fourth Gospel; but allegory will oblige that it be given a considerable extension.

In fact, under the pressure of controversy or in the framework of theological elaboration, a new way of approaching the texts is gradually integrated into the search for the meaning of Scripture. This is because the cultural milieu, in which the people of God thinks its faith, has changed. It is now the milieu of the Hellenist civilization which is imposed on minds even where the common language is Latin or Syriac. Recourse to the resources of culture to help the exegete is first noticed in the school of Alexandria, whose best exegete is Origen. [1] Imbued with the principles of the New Testament, the latter is also led by the habits of his environment when he develops in a systematic manner the Pauline procedure of *allegory*. He finds in it the possibility of expressing dogma and the Christian mystique, by starting from any text of the Old Testament, for the spiritual profit of some faithful who are not dismayed by such a method. Not that he thus evacuates the *letter* or the *history* brought out by a first reading; but he uses it as a springboard to reach greater depths, capable of acting as food for faith. When the natural pitch of the text does not lead in this direction, allegory nonetheless allows him a practical means of attaining the Mystery. It also helps him to rebuke the attacks of Celsius, by showing that the scope of Scriptures is not reduced to its *corporal* meaning, too gross to interest a Greek philosopher : it is of the order of the *spirit*. Such a distinction owes something to Platonic vocabulary; but the spirit, as Origen sees it, remains nonetheless in keeping with Pauline theology. As has been seen previously, [2] Origen is also concerned with textual criticism. The undertaking of the *Hexapla* has for its purpose to establish as exactly as possible the text which juridically is a matter of faith. At about this time,

---

[1] H. DE LUBAC, *Histoire et Esprit; l'intelligence de l'Écriture d'après Origène** (Paris, 1950). Cf. C. MONDÉSERT, *Clément d'Alexandrie** (Paris, 1944).

[2] Cf. pp. 91 f.

efforts are made (especially in Alexandria) to improve the text of the New Testament; these efforts will produce " recensions " which, in the light of the times, are already scientific works. In short, in several fields the Christian interpretation of Scripture resorts to a *tool* of a rational order, drawn from the culture of the times. It is no more a sign of decadence than is the development of theology itself.

With various orientations, the patristic schools continue the work inaugurated by Origen. If on the level of rational criticism the school of Antioch pays more attention than that of Alexandria to the literal and historical meaning of the holy books (that which flows from the words themselves), its *theoria* is a sequel to the *allegory* of Origen. [3] In St. Augustine, [4] we see different concerns, according to the circumstances. For example, the method of allegorical interpretation helped him to overcome the repugnance which his cultivated mind felt with respect to the Bible; but subsequently he nonetheless writes a literal commentary of Genesis against the Manicheans. In the *Enarrationes super Psalmos*, a constant use of typology allows a Christian reading of the Psalter; but the *De consensu Evangelistorum* approaches problems of literary and historical criticism. In St. Jerome, [5] the demands of criticism become clearer insofar as the means of times allow. The one who wants to bring the Latin translation back to *veritas hebraica* reacts vigorously against the allegorism of Origen, on whom he nonetheless depends from several points of view.

In a general way, exegesis is developed with methods more flexible and more varied in the works of the pastoral order (preaching, liturgy), with more rigorous methods in controversy and theology. In the first case, the allegorism of Origen remains in vogue; let us think for instance of *Moralia on Job* of St. Gregory the Great. In the second case, the obvious meaning of the text is upheld, by interpreting however those of the Old Testament in the light of the New Testament, for the Bible is entirely the book of the Church and the Mystery of Christ is its only object.

III. The problem of scriptural meanings

In the patristic age, exegetical methodology begins to be crystallized in a problem which will become classical : that of the meanings of Scripture. Two types of data are joined here : those of the New Testament (letter

---

[3] J. GUILLET, " Les exégèses d'Alexandrie et d'Antioche : conflit ou malentendu*, " *RSR* (1947), pp. 257f.

[4] M. PONTET, *L'exégèse de saint Augustin prédicateur** (Paris, 1945).

[5] A. PENNA, *Principi e caratteri dell'esegesi di S. Gerolamo**, (Rome, 1950).

and spirit, typology and allegory); those of a cultural milieu, linked first of all to the Alexandrine culture, but which after some time evolves in the last centuries of the decadent Roman Empire. This double source is revealable in the vocabulary where the problem is expressed. On the one hand (and this is the essential part), Christians are seen as reacting with a spirit of faith in the face of the Word of God; on the other hand, these men, belonging to a determined civilization, approach the texts by applying to them their mental categories. There results from this a certain lack of precision in the terms used, which does not help to clarify the problem.

The Pauline opposition between *letter* and *spirit* remains fundamental. But sometimes the *spiritual* meaning is confused with the meaning that issues from the allegory and this latter, whose value is overestimated, tends to be generalized to the detriment of an objective reading; at other times, as a reaction against these excesses, the *literal* meaning is revalued, by which is meant the one which results from the very words of Scripture. This superimposition of the vocabulary of literary analysis on the Pauline vocabulary is not only a cultural fact : the Pauline principles, developed in terms of the Old Testament, do not furnish an adequate vocabulary for the exegesis of the New Testament.

The same lack of precision applies for the expression *figurative* meaning, which is at times the equivalent of *typical* meaning (type-figure), at times designates *figures of speech*, especially in decadent Rome. To designate the hidden meaning of Scripture, its *spirit* (in the Pauline sense) or its fullness, the words *mysterium* or *sacramentum* are also used : whence the idea of a *mystical* meaning. It would be excellent if they were not more or less confused with the results of the allegorical method, even when they find their source in the ingeniousness of the interpreters more than authentic typology. Origen equates *literal* meaning with *historical* meaning, with *corporal* meaning, to which he opposes the *spirit* of Scripture. But this position is not without pitfalls : has not the Holy Spirit wished to teach us a sacred history? Finally, according to the objectives aimed at by the exegete in his practical applications of the texts, the expressions *tropological* (moral) meaning and *anagogical* meaning (relating to heavenly realities or eschatology) are used. But at this point we do not see clearly whether this vocabulary aims only at the allegorical applications (based or not on solid typology) or whether it concerns the meaning which flows from the words, when this meaning approaches the same areas.

Despite these difficulties, the whole of exegetical methodology tends little by little to build itself around the problem of the scriptural meanings.

That is why it becomes indispensable for the exegete to know how to distinguish them clearly, how to correctly appreciate the value of each, how to use them wisely. This operation appeals in part to the data of literary criticism. It is however situated on an essentially theological plane, for it intends to actualize an interpretation in keeping with the tradition of the New Testament. It is in order to reach it that it attempts to integrate, in the manner of useful instruments, certain rules of rhetoric or of the allegorical method. These are undoubtedly imperfect instruments but they correspond to the cultural level of the period and in any case do not act as a barrier between faith and the reading of the Bible. Possessing through his faith the global meaning of the sacred texts, the exegete strives to get back to it on the level of each text taken by itself. The very variety of the proposed interpretations for a good number of texts during the patristic period suffices to show that the objective meaning of each was not at that time defined by a standardizing tradition.

§ 2.   The Middle Ages

I.   Problems and methods

The problems which the exegete must face during the Middle Ages are first of all of a pastoral nature; in this perspective, the Middle Ages continue the efforts of patristic exegesis, both with the compilers, such as Venerable Bede and with the creators, such as St. Bernard. However, especially from the 12th century onward, a double concern is brought to light in the Latin West : that of a systematic theology which starting from the commentary on the *sacra pagina* gives birth to the *Summae;* and that of an apologetic aimed specifically at the Jews and Moslems. From both sides an appeal is made to rational reflection; its light is brought into a synthesis of the sacred sciences which seeks in Christian faith its principles and strives to justify its conclusions by the authority of the Bible. Beginning with the 13th century, in a whole current of ideas whose importance is considerable, the Aristotelian dialectic furnishes to dogmatics an instrument of elaboration which is judged to be adequate.

This evolution of thought has profound repercussions on the method of exegesis. If the high Middle Ages were in the field especially influenced by St. Augustine and the practices of St. Gregory, little by little the authority of St. Jerome gains ground. This is because in theology reasoning can hardly be founded in a firm manner upon unauthorized allegorizations of certain clear passages of Scripture. What is important is the meaning resulting from the words themselves. On this point, the critical mind of St. Jerome renders an immeasurable service : by its search for the original text; by its effort to translate it properly; by its literary analysis, pursued as far as his knowledge allowed; and by its attention paid to the historical references of the texts, as far as he can know them. Such is the state of mind which dominates the work of Hugh of St. Victor and Albert the Great.

From this fact, the problem of the scriptural meanings evolves also. For example, for the Venerable Bede allegorical exegesis erected into a system showed the strong influence of the rhetors of the Low Empire. Having learned from them to seek the *figurative* meaning behind the figures of style, he would transpose this operation into the exegetical field; the *spiritual* interpretation became for him a search for the meaning hidden behind the *tropi* and *schemata* of Scripture. In St. Thomas, this position of the problem will be surpassed.

II. THE PROBLEM OF THE SCRIPTURAL MEANINGS IN ST. THOMAS

St. Thomas (*STh* Iᵃ, Q. I, art. 10; Quodl, 7, art. 14, 15, 16) establishes a clear distinction between two orders of facts which, despite their close connection, have nonetheless different values.   On the one hand, the Holy Spirit speaks to us clearly in some texts; His message comes from the very words used there, taking into account the figures of speech.   This is the *literal* meaning.   This is the only one on which the theologian can base his work.   On the other hand, it is also true that the things of the Bible can have a symbolic meaning, and this for two reasons : things here below can be the symbols of things from on high; the things that the history of Israel bring about during its course could have been disposed by God, the master of this history, with a view to signifying ahead of time the things of the New Covenant.   This is the *spiritual* meaning, which can also be called *typical, mystical* or *figurative*.   The theologian cannot base himself on it to demonstrate truths to be believed; further-more, there is nothing in this spiritual meaning which is not clearly said somewhere in Scripture in the literal meaning.   Pushing this analysis further, St. Thomas notices that the literal meaning can be called *proper* when it designates its object without resorting to figures of speech; in the contrary case (comparison, metaphor, parable) it will be called *figurative*.   As for the spiritual meaning, it can have various applications : the economy of the New Covenant (*allegorical* meaning), the heavenly consummation of things (*anagogical* meaning), the conduct of human life (*tropological* meaning).

The advantage of this distinction is clarity.   It is the study of the literal meaning which, properly speaking, constitutes exegesis; because the latter is an analysis of the text performed in the light of faith, and thereby furnishes to theology the matter of its work.   The study of the spiritual meaning is rather an aspect of biblical theology, an important aspect, since it allows for justifying and evaluating in a Christian perpective the things of the Old Testament; St. Thomas resorts to it, for example, in his treatise on the ceremonial precepts contained in the Mosaic law (*STh* 1ª, 2ªᵉ, Q. 101).

However, by contrasting this systematic exposition with its New Testament foundations, one feels uneasy.   In fact, the essential distinction between the *literal* meaning and the *spiritual* meaning restates the Pauline principle of *spirit* and *letter*, while giving to the words a very different meaning.   On the one hand, the literal meaning of St. Thomas supposes a Christian understanding of the texts of the Old Testament, therefore an interpretation of Scripture carried out " according to the spirit. " On the other hand, the spiritual meaning is identified with typology, which is the foundation for an allegorical transposition of Scripture : the terminology and practice of St. Paul entailed more nuances, and a certain influence of Origen is felt here.   Thus the classification by St. Thomas of the meanings of Scripture discloses an exegetical methodology fundamentally in keeping with the spirit and rule imposed by the New Testament and followed by the patristic tradition; but it is rethought in the light of the human problematic of the 13th century.   Compared to the classifications which preceded it, it shows a great progress.   It clarifies once and for all the notion of literal meaning, a meaning which results from the words and can be proper or figurative.   Thereby, it leads to the principle of literary genres, which modern criticism will more accurately formulate.

Its technical vocabulary was not however always respected by later authors.   We will see that the *literal* meaning of contemporary biblical criticism is not exactly synonymous with that of St. Thomas.   Furthermore, the use of the expression " spiritual meaning " has never ceased to be extremely varied; people have understood by this expression either typology (St. Thomas), or any recourse to allegorization (in line with Origen), or " what the Spirit tells us in Scripture " or *spirit* in the Pauline sense of the term, or any meaning giving food for spiritual life.   It is not astonishing that there often follows a great confusion when the respective value of literal exegesis and spiritual exegesis is discussed, without defining the words used and without casting a glance on the history of the problem of scriptural meanings.

§ 3. The Modern Period

I. EVOLUTION OF THE CULTURAL FACTOR

From the Renaissance onward, the manner in which the Bible is approached as a human document is profoundly changed. The rationalist spirit is not to blame here, only a certain scientific technique, which allows us to delineate with greater accuracy the problems raised by the sacred books. In short, it is a problem of criticism—textual, literary, and historical—the rules and methods of which are perfected little by little. Not that Christian antiquity was ignorant of them; but the progress of science in all fields allows them now to be rigorously formulated. Let us think, for instance, of what represents for the literary and historical criticism of the Bible the discovery of ancient Eastern literatures and the offerings of archeology. Exegetical methodology very early strives to assimilate this effort of the human mind to put it to the service of Christian interpretation. But then, the difficulties begin. They bear especially on certain aspects of literary criticism (the genres and their truth value) and of historical criticism (the exact historical import of the biblical narratives). The climate of struggle between rationalism and faith, where this effort of adjustment takes place, does not make its rapid success an easy matter.

At the same time, as the practice of exegesis thus faces difficult problems, it is noticed that the theoretical presentation of its methodology does not change. The best treatise on the question in the 19th century, the *De interpretatione scripturarum* of Patrizi is an excellent commentary on the Thomist positions. But we can say that the essential questions raised by literary and historical criticism are neither faced head on in it nor are they integrated into the traditional approach. On this point, in order for the problem to be rethought (as it was in the time of Origen, of St. Augustine, of St. Jerome, of the Venerable Bede or of St. Thomas) a long elaboration will be needed, and at the present time, it has not yet been altogether achieved. Before examining its result, we must now make a quick sketch of our historical inquiry.

II. SKETCH OF A HISTORICAL INQUIRY

In the people of God, the recipient of the Holy Scriptures (Judaism, then the Church), exegesis is never considered as an operation of disinterested science. Its purpose is related to life : it is a question of establishing a link between the faith having reached a certain level of development and the Word of God on which it is founded. To succeed in this, they do not limit themselves to analyzing each text separately; they seek in the whole of Scripture and in the totality of revelation a light which will allow them to see its import.   This is already visible in Jewish *midrash;* it is found again in the New Testament even though the latter marks a radical change of perspective when compared to *midrash.*

For this purpose, exegesis constantly resorts to all the human means furnished by the culture of the period.   But culture changes and with it the way of approaching the texts and bringing its contents up to date. The procedures used in the rabbinical circles are little by little supplanted in the patristic period by procedures furnished by the Hellenistic culture. These procedures are developed in two different directions : that of an embryonic criticism, which must allow the texts to be linked to the faith, by starting from the meaning which flows from the words; and that of allegory, which transfers the texts to other objects than those spoken about in the words, by basing itself on the symbolic meaning of those words.   The practical character of the second method, which explains its abundant use in preaching up until the modern period, does not however hide its limitations and dangers.   The concerns of controversy and of systematic theology lead one to give priority to the former, whose rules, however, are clarified only little by little, in step with the other human sciences.   In all probability, allegory and criticism remain subordinated to the standards of faith.

PRESENT STATE OF THE PROBLEM

BIBLIOGRAPHY

L. PIROT, " Commission biblique, " *SDB*, II, cols. 103-113.

L. BOUYER, " Liturgie et exégèse spirituelle, " *Maison-Dieu*, 7 (1945).

A. M. DUBARLE, " Le sens spirituel de l'Écriture, "* *RSPT* (1947), p. 413.

P. BENOIT, in *La Prophétie** (Somme théologique, éd. Revue des Jeunes) (Paris, 1947), pp. 353-376.

C. CHARLIER, " La lecture sapientielle de la Bible, "* *Maison-Dieu*, 12 (1948).

A. G. HEBERT, *The Authority of the Old Testament* (London : Faber, 1947).

J. COPPENS, *Les harmonies des deux Testaments*[2]* (Tournai-Paris, 1949). This work contains an exhaustive bibliography. " Nouvelles réflexions sur les divers sens des saintes Écritures, " *NRT* (1952), pp. 1-20.

R. E. BROWN, " History and Development of the Theory of a Sensus Plenior, "* *CBQ*, 15 (1953), pp. 141-162; *The Sensus Plenior of Sacred Scripture* (Baltimore : St. Mary's, 1955).

P. SYNAVE, P. BENOIT, *Prophecy and Inspiration** (New York : Desclée, 1961).

R. E. BROWN, " Sensus Plenior in the Last Ten Years, " *CBQ*, 25 (1963), pp. 262-285.

§ 1. The Requirements of Theology

The books of the Bible are not books resembling any others. They constitute a unique case : they fix divine revelations, they are inspired and they are confided to the Church by God who has founded it. Consequently, their interpretation is not a matter of science alone; the method which is proper to it is subjected to higher rules, which come from theology. If it assumes criticism, it is only as an instrument, not as an end in itself. The meaning of Scripture can only be achieved in faith. That is why it is not true to say that " if the exegete wants to take up biblical studies in a useful way, he must first of all do away with any preconceived opinion with regard to the supernatural origin of Sacred Scripture and, consequently, interpret it like any other purely human document " (modernist proposition condemned by the decree *Lamentabili*). [1]   We must say here what are the requirements of theology with respect to the methodology of exegesis.

I. THE THEOLOGY OF REVELATION

The Bibles fixes Revelation.   But this revelation is one, homogeneous and continuous.   It culminates in the Mystery of Christ, totally revealed at the moment when it is actualized in human history; but this mystery is already present in a certain manner at the very moment when it starts. The religion of the Old Testament is already centered on it; and the Christian religion will be less its undoing than its fullness.

The Mystery of Christ is therefore the only object of Scripture; the Christian interpretation of the Bible has for its purpose to show it, even if it can do so in several ways.   In this respect, the work of exegesis is not the same according as it is located in a context of apologetics or one of theology.   In the first case, it is indispensable to follow rigorously the ways of criticism to establish the reality and the true figure of the facts where will be uncovered the signs of divine intervention in history; otherwise, the demonstration would go around in a vicious circle.   In the second case the problem of faith having been supposed as resolved, it is a question only of rereading all the texts in its light and to clarify thereby the different aspects of the Mystery of Christ.   Without neglecting the indications of criticism, the problems which it is not yet capable of resolving can however be held as secondary : the imperfections of criticism in Christian antiquity or in the Middle Ages do not render useless all the theology of previous centuries.

However, revelation has not been given to men all at once.   It was developed with the times.   In the Old Testament, the presence of the Mystery of Christ remains veiled.   It informs the structures which are only preparatory to Christian structures.   This is where biblical *typology* enters.   In fact, recognizing that these Christian realities are already underlying the events of the Old Testament is to affirm that these things are the *signs* of the former, still enigmatic but already full of meaning, sufficiently related to future realities to allow the people of God to participate in them secretely.   In the framework of a provisory economy, our fathers in the faith already believed in Christ, and received from Him the supernatural goods which He alone brings into the world (Heb 11—13).   The Christian interpretation of the Old Testament, in order to be complete and to surpass the more or less satisfying results of a purely

---

[1] *EB,* 196.

scientific study, must make evident this universal presence of Christ in Scripture. It must therefore pay constant attention to the profound meaning of the things of the Old Testament, since it is on their basis that the texts which concern them take on their definitive import.

There is more than that, however. Since revelation forms a whole, all its parts are coherent. To clarify each biblical text, it must not be isolated. To relate it to the other texts, and more generally, to all the content of faith such as the living tradition preserves it (just as exegesis has always done in Judaism and in the Church), is to replace it into its vital milieu, and to put it into its exact perspective. The *analogy of faith* can thus allow the removal of certain interpretations which, founded upon badly understood appearances, would put this text in disagreement with the whole of divine revelation. From the simple point of view of historical criticism, there is a valuable element in this and it would be wrong to ignore it : how can one explain the texts correctly without taking into account their roots in a current of thought which surpasses them and dominates them? For example, the manner in which the Jewish and then the Christian faith understood and commented upon Gn 3, 15 helps us to orient the general meaning of the passage, even if its obvious meaning is related to an archaic stage of revelation. It is not a matter of wanting to artificially project a dogmatic content which was only affirmed later on; but it is important to underline that this dogmatic content is already sketched therein, however rudimentary the sketch.

II. THE THEOLOGY OF INSPIRATION

The doctrine of inspiration also influences exegesis. It prevents one from attributing to the sacred authors erroneous affirmations. At the same time, it accurately establishes in what order of things their teachings are to be looked for : this is where are situated revelation, the Mystery of Christ and of the salvation of the human race, and not the satisfaction of human curiosity in scientific matters, for example. It is important, therefore, not to consider as teachings certain data of the cultural order, which are to be considered more as secondary elements of the thought of the sacred authors, but which do not constitute the purpose of positive affirmations. Such is the case, for instance, of their representation of the world which is the representation of their time and is only a secondary concern in their doctrine of creation. Certainly, it can happen that it is difficult to distinguish between two elements so narrowly mixed; but in principle, the distinction is essential.

To do it justice, it is indispensable to examine all the coordinates of biblical language : the social and cultural milieu of the authors, the literary genres in use in their times, and the personality of each one. On this point, the doctrine of inspiration, by recalling that God respects the proper nature of the human instruments which He uses, invites us to resort in a systematic manner to historical and literary criticism. The progress made during our times by these sciences, as well by their method as by their documentation, can only be joyfully received; it is known however how much the encyclical *Divino afflante spiritu* urges exegetes to become resolutely engaged in this direction in order to know what God tells us in the Bible. [2] It is important, in fact, not to attribute to the Holy Spirit, in one or another passage, what the interpreter's ingeniousness could succeed in inserting into it. Many of the allegorizations due to ecclesiastical writers, while being perfectly orthodox and obeying the analogy of faith could not be regarded as the authentic meaning of the texts to which they are attached. There is more to do than to hold to them : it is to start from the meaning which flows from the words, only later to make precise how it must eventually be prolonged in order to keep account of all of revelation.

In effect, the fact of inspiration does not have as a consequence to remove from the sacred authors all human limitations—those of their personalities and also those of their times. They transmit the message which God entrusts to them, but this message is incorporated into the general current of a revelation which is progressive (this remark is valid essentially for the Old Testament). There can thus be a difference between the meaning which the biblical authors have consciously attached to their texts and the import acquired by these texts since then, in the light of a later revelation. It is not possible to say that this import is, as it were, outside the texts : God foresaw it from the very beginning and, by inspiring the writers, He has henceforth enclosed it in their work. Criticism could never, by its own lights alone, reach more than the obvious meaning of the texts, the one which corresponds to the horizon of the inspired authors; such a result must be completed in order to really answer the norms of Christian interpretation. Thus the problem of the *sensus plenior* of Scripture.

III. THE THEOLOGY OF THE CHURCH

Finally, it is important not to separate the Bible from the Church, as if each Christian could discover in it divine revelation by himself, independently from the society instituted by God Himself to lead men to salvation. Scripture is entrusted to the Church. Not that the Church can interpret

---

[2] *EB*, 550-551, 556-564.

it as it likes, independently of its objective meaning; but the same Spirit which inspired the sacred authors also helps the Church to understand their works. Thanks to the Spirit, the Church has instinctively the meaning of Scripture. That is why the exact meaning of Scripture must be regarded as " the one which Mother Church has considered and considers such, to whom it belongs to judge the meaning and the interpretation of the sacred books " (the encyclical *Providentissimus*, recalling the teachings of the Councils of Trent and of Vatican I).

In fact, the Church itself has been careful to recall that its right to authentically interpret Scripture is exercised exclusively in the framework of its divine mission, to safeguard the deposit confided to it; it concerns therefore only " the things which touch the faith and human conduct " *(in rebus fidei et morum)*. When the texts touch this object directly, the Church has a *positive* right of interpretation; but it does not seem that it claims it for those matters only indirectly touched upon (for example the date of Joel or the itinerary of the Hebrews as they came out of Egypt). It maintains however a right of negative interpretation, for it can reject any interpretation which would lead to a contradiction on any point of the doctrine of which it is the guardian.

§ 2. The Directives of the Church

I. The authentic interpretation of Scripture

The Church has intervened by *solemn judgment*, in order to define the authentic interpretation of certain biblical passages, only in rather rare cases. It made use of this to reject certain errors bearing upon dogmatic texts : thus for Rom 5, 12, which concerns the transmission of original sin *(DB, 791)*; for Mt 26, 26, where the words of the institution of the Eucharist must be taken in their literal meaning *(DB, 874)*; for Lk 22, 19, which concerns the institution of the priesthood *(DB, 949)*; for Mt 16, 18 and Jn 21, 16 where proof is found for the primacy of the papacy *(DB, 1822 ff.)*. Sometimes the intervention of the Church has only had as its purpose to reject an erroneous interpretation without, however, imposing a choice between other possible explanations : when Pius VI condemned the interpretation of Is 7, 14 proposed by Isembiehl, he left open the problem of literal or typical Messianism of this passage;[3] the same was the case for the allegorical interpretation of Jn 20, 22, proposed by Theodore of Mopsuestia.[4]

---

[3] *EB*, 74 (59).
[4] *DB*, 224.

However, must we not look also in the *ordinary and universal magisterium* of the Church for authentic interpretations binding on all exegetes? The problem is raised especially in those cases where the Church, defining a truth of faith, has brought as proof of this truth a scriptural text : has not the meaning of this text then been indirectly defined? It is in fact possible; but this conclusion must not be too hastily reached, by attributing to the Church certain intentions which it did not carefully make definite. It is are that an alleged text in an official document of the magisterium is the only one on which the faith of the Church is based. Generally the documents of the magisterium accumulate several texts, which can have very different probative values; some play an explanatory or an illustrative role for the doctrine rather than one of apodictic proof. The same prudence is required when an authentic interpretation of the scriptural texts is looked for in the patristic tradition or in the liturgy. The same text often received several interpretations; it is therefore wise to recognize as authentic only that which enlists the moral unanimity of the tradition and which, furthermore, would be put into immediate contact with a doctrinal affirmation.

It is important not to confuse all the opinions adopted in past centuries on essentially critical problems with the doctrinal tradition of the Church. The history of exegesis during the course of the past century shows that a transfer has progressively taken place between the *dogmatic interpretation* of Scripture which finds its criteria in tradition, and *critical opinions* which can always be revised and which seek in the perfecting of scientific methods the means of always circumscribing more narrowly the obvious meaning of the texts. There remains that the narrow link between dogma and criticism, in matters of exegesis, must incite one to prudence. Even in the purely critical field, the Church can intervene to encourage exegetes to expose in public only really mature opinions, which are solidly supported and directed toward the benefit of the faith, especially if they modify points of view currently accepted up until then in Catholic circles.

II. The Interventions of the Church in the Contemporary Period

In the contemporary period, the Church has solemnly intervened in the problems of exegesis by three encyclicals : *Providentissimus* (1893), *Spiritus Paraclitus* (1917), *Divino afflante Spiritu* (1943), and most recently the Constitution *Dei Verbum* which is dealt with at the end of this book (pp. 212 ff). We must add certain indications of the encyclical *Humani Generis* (1950). It is in the light of these texts that we have here tried to define the Christian interpretation of Scripture. The encyclical of 1943 is in this regard the most complete. Insisting on the necessity of integrating into exegesis the progress of biblical criticism, it orients it resolutely toward the study of the literal meaning and denounces the dangers of a subjective or fanciful interpretation which would be unduly called spiritual exegesis. We will again run into these important rules later on.

Furthermore two Roman organisms have the charge of supervising the work of Catholic exegetes, either to prevent them from going off into dangerous directions, or to positively orient them. These are the Holy Office (now the Congregation for the Doctrine of the Faith, since Vatican II) and the Pontifical Commission for Biblical Studies. As Pius X recalled, the decisions of these organisms, approved by the Sovereign Pontiff, oblige in conscience with respect to the faith when they bear upon points which concern doctrine. The decrees of the Biblical Commission have sometimes borne upon questions of another order : authors of the biblical books, modes of composition, literary genres, or the authenticity of a pericope. In these questions, the Commission has not always wished to positively resolve the problems at hand; it has sometimes been a question of a prudential directive; in the present state of the problem and until further information is available, it is better to adhere to commonly received opinions in the Church. This is what is clearly meant by the answer given to the question of the *Comma johanneum* (1 Jn 5, 7) where the consultation of 1927 enlarges the directives of the Holy Office given in 1897.[5] Such answers do not prevent the study of the problems; on the contrary, they invite scholars to pursue them assiduously; but they require a serious examination of new theories before they are proposed in public, with a full consciousness of the importance of matters treated and of a spirit of full submission to the decrees published by this Commission. This important text [6] is due to Rev. Fr. Miller, its secretary. He underlines that to understand the import of the decrees, it is always necessary to replace them into their historical context; it seems clear then that thanks to them, the Church has defended " the purity and the truth of the Word of God, " at a time " when the flow of liberal and rationalist criticism threatened to remove all the barriers of the traditions which had up until that time been regarded as sacred. "

In the past few years, the work done since the encyclical *Divino afflante Spiritu* has noticeably changed the outlook of those official documents. This is especially apparent in the Instruction from the

---

[5] *EB*, 135-136 (120-121).
[6] Cf. *RB*, 62 (1955), pp. 416-419.

Biblical Commission on the Historical Truth of the Gospels (May 14, 1964) in which the critical approach is positively encouraged, provided that it be employed with the required prudence. This view was finally confirmed in the Constitution on Divine Revelation *(Dei Verbum)* whose textand commentary appear in an appendix to this book (pp. 212 ff.).

§ 3. The Problem of Scriptural Meanings and Biblical Criticism

Since in theological tradition, exegetical methodology is crystallized around the problem of scriptural meanings, it is necessary to reexamine the latter in the light of present culture, where biblical criticism has taken on a fullness and an accuracy unknown in past centuries.

I. THE PROBLEM OF LITERAL MEANING

We have seen that St. Thomas, by establishing a classification of scriptural meanings, had clearly brought out the idea of a *literal* meaning flowing from the very words of Scripture. This was not only a theological principle borrowed from the doctrinal tradition of the Church; it was also a judicious use of the rules of human speech, which are the bailiwick of literary criticism. By perfecting its methods, literary criticism has made obvious the importance of *genres* in literature. They considerably determine the nature of the teachings which can be enclosed in the texts; it is within their general rules that the activity of authors is exercised and that their didactic aim is made clear. It is this aim or purpose which gives to literary works their meaning and their importance. The literal meaning, in the eyes of the critic, is that which corresponds to the *intention* of the author. A word, a phrase, or a series of propositions have meaning only in relation to a broader context; that of the living thought of a man who, in such or such determined circumstances, strives to transmit to his contemporaries a message which he conceives of as clear, by resorting liberally to a given particular form of speech to express himself.

The theology of inspiration, far from contradicting this notion of literal meaning, assumes it fully. The sacred authors are not passive instruments in the hands of God. God respects their nature of free and intelligent beings. What He tells us through them, He makes them personally conceive it and knowingly say it with all the resources of their genius. That is why the encyclical *Divino afflante spiritu* gives the following rule to exegetes : " Let them apply themselves to discerning and determining this meaning of the biblical words which is called the literal meaning " (§ 27); and further : " Let the professors expose the

literal meaning and especially the theological meaning in a solid manner "
(§ 45). Not that it is necessary to distinguish between the literal and the
theological meaning; the literal meaning itself is by its very nature of
a religious order; it always aims at "teaching, refutation (of error),
correction (of morals), and training to justice," in sum, at all the tasks
of edification which "train the accomplished man of God, equipped for
every good work" (1 Tm 3, 6); it is weighted with divine mysteries and
a good number of other realities hidden therein." It undoubtedly also
raises many questions of all orders, especially of the historical order.
We must attempt to clarify them. But this part of the study only plays
a preparatory role : it allows the exegete to better appreciate the doctrinal
affirmations of the sacred authors; in short, it necessarily leads to biblical
theology.

II. The development of revelation and the problem of the *SENSUS PLENIOR* [7]

It is nonetheless true, however, that the literal meaning, grasped at the
level of biblical criticism, does not go beyond the horizon of each sacred
author. Now, divine revelation developed. Later on, the notions put
to work in the Bible underwent from one book to another and especially
from the Old to the New Testament, a deepening process; in a parallel
manner, the terms which express them received a richer meaning. Thus,
the idea of the *Kingdom* designates a certain supernatural reality whose
content has been made precise and has emerged, from the work of the
royal annalists to the prophets, to the psalmists, to the book of Daniel
and to the Gospel preaching. To have on this point a clear idea of the
development of revelation, it is important to circumscribe the import
of the term at each of the different stages; but when the end is reached,
it is equally legitimate to project on the former stages the light of the
present ones. The Christian who reads the history of the kingdom of
David can give the texts a doctrinal content more important than
that resulting from pure criticism : in the kingdom of David, the anointed
of Yahweh, the "kingdom of Christ and of God" (Eph 5, 5) is already
secretly present, and that is why its history interests us.

Is this to go outside the literal meaning? Some contemporary
theologians such as G. Courtade think so. It is repugnant to them to

[7] J. Courtade, "Les Écritures ont-elles un sens plénier?*" *RSR*, 37 (1950),
pp. 481-499; F. M. Braun, "Le sens plénier et les encycliques," *Revue thomiste*
(1951), pp. 294-304; R. E. Brown, *The Sensus Plenior of Sacred Scripture** (Baltimore,
1945).

think that the Scriptures should be attributed a literal meaning of which the sacred author was not aware : God affirms no more than what the author affirms himself.   But it must be remembered that the sacred author can act with regard to God who inspires him " *tamquam instru-mentum deficiens,* " according to an expression of St. Thomas.   He can only see in a confused manner what God says to men through his mouth. When he designates in the language of his time realities which will only be fully revealed at a later time, the expressions which he uses are them-selves left open to a richer content; the meaning that they assume in the Christian perspective is not heterogeneous to their obvious meaning : it only makes explicit a virtual content, still veiled by the historical conditionings to which the word of God has subjected itself.   The Christian value of the biblical texts, although only perceptible in the light of total revelation truly then belongs to the literal meaning of Scripture, but to a meaning " *plenior et profundior* " which constitutes its *fulfilment* (to repeat here an expression familiar to the New Testament).   The message of God to men, contained on each page of the Bible, is that meaning.   And it is just in this manner that the Thomistic classification understands it when it defines the literal meaning : the meaning which God, its principal author, signifies to us by the words of Scripture.   The literal meaning thus conceived goes beyond the human limitations which could prevent the biblical authors from understanding in all their extension the words which they used : 1 Pt 2, 9 echoes Ex 19, 5-6 by conferring to this definition of the people of God a depth which the author of the passage did not as yet fully understand, but which only reveals the true meaning of his text.

The criterion of this fuller meaning is obviously the revelation of the New Testament.   However, what the New Testament calls " fulfilment of the Scriptures " does not necessarily relate to it; one must take into account the flexibility with which Jewish exegesis, whose techniques are familiar to the authors of the apostolic age, used to adapt to new situations scriptural texts torn from their context.   In order for there to be a fuller meaning a certain homogeneity is required between the literal meaning consciously envisaged by the sacred author and the one which the New Testament allows us to attribute to his text; in other words, the same object, and the same mysterious reality must both be envisioned : this must be seen even if confusedly in the first case, and fully revealed in the second case.   When Christ on the cross recites Psalm 22, he defines its fuller meaning because there flows in it the prayer of the Just One suffering *par excellence*, already sketched in the text by a just one suffering in the Old Testament.

III. LITERAL MEANING, *SENSUS PLENIOR* AND TYPOLOGY [8]

As St. Thomas had already clearly seen, typology is not properly speaking an exegesis of biblical texts; it is a theological interpretation of the things of the Bible, an exposition of their religious significance understood in terms of a Christian perspective. It follows that it is never independent from the literal meaning of Scripture. It is revealed little by little, as revelation progresses. Thus, in the most ancient biblical traditions, the events of Exodus already signify the mercy of God with respect to his people as a *Salvation* granted in the past, as a manifestation (written in history) of divine intentions, of the dispositions of God towards His people. In the second part of Isaias, the Salvation of the past becomes the prophetic image of another *Salvation* expected now in the future, at the end of time, in an eschatological context : the meaning of the events of the Exodus has become enriched, a typology emerges. In the New Testament, the *Salvation* announced in the book of Isaias is henceforth achieved : the Christian participates in it sacramentally through baptism and the Eucharist; the events of Exodus are therefore justly regarded by St. Paul as the figures *(typoi)* of the Christian sacraments, while the Apocalypse of St. John sees in them equivalently the image and the anticipation of eternal Salvation won by the elect (Ap 15, 3). The revelation of the typology of Exodus is therefore linked to the development of a doctrinal theme enunciated in the *literal* meaning of Scripture. There is a homogeneity between the religious meaning found in them by the Christian faith.

On the other hand, the principle of typology is often linked to the clear manifestation of the *fuller* meaning deposited by God Himself in the ancient texts. The Canticle of Moses, which celebrates God as the author of Salvation and Liberation takes on all its meaning only in the framework of the heavenly liturgy (Ap 15, 3) and, thereby, in that of the paschal liturgy which anticipates it (that is why it is sung during the Easter Vigil). Such is its fuller meaning, its Christian interpretation, which is homogeneous to the obvious literal meaning but which surpasses the historical conditions whose borders cannot be crossed by biblical criticism. However, in the case at hand, the fuller meaning cannot be evaluated in the details of the text without a certain number of transpositions which recall Pauline allegory. The enemies of the people of God, in the Christian perspective, are no longer Egypt and the Philistines; they are the wordly powers who are the supporters of Satan by opposing

---

[8] W. EICHRODT, " Ist die typologische Exegese sachgemasse Exegese? " *Suppl. VI*, IV (Congress Volume), pp. 161-180.

the plan of Salvation, but they can be " symbolically called Sodom and Egypt " (Ap 11, 8). The Christian reading of Ex 15 therefore legitimately allegorizes the details relative to a revolved economy : typology allows this to be done.

There would remain for us to determine precisely the criteria of an authentic typology. In fact, the patristic tradition (prolonged until our own day by spiritual writers, orators and poets) sometimes used allegorization in a much freer manner, so that the biblical text served as a point of departure for expositions unrelated to its literal meaning. To see this question clearly, we must start from its principle. Typology has as its basis a relation of the two Covenants which implies at the same time continuity and change of perspective. The same divine Mystery is revealed in both; but in the second, the temporal horizons which were a condition of its expression in the first are surmounted. The same attitude of faith corresponds to the word of God in Jews and Christians; but in its latter stage, the object of faith is clearly manifested and is stripped of the provisory clothing by which it was veiled until then. It is therefore by carefully comparing the structures of the Old Testament and of the New, as well as the experience of Jewish faith and that of Christian faith, that authentic typology can be brought into the open. The things of the Bible are figurative when they occupied in the theology of the Old Testament a situation analogous to that occupied in the theology of the New Testament by the things of Christian Revelation, when they played in the Jewish faith a role analogous to the role played in the Christian faith by the things of the economy of Salvation revealed in Jesus Christ : it is for this reason that the king of Israel is the figure of Jesus Christ and Jerusalem is the figure of the Church. But we must be careful lest we found typology on purely material *rapprochements* between objects detached from their living context or on coincidences of words or of images without real theological relation. Thus the color red of the cloth worn by Rahab at the time of the capture of Jericho (Jos 2, 18) can evoke in the imagination of an interpreter the color of the blood of Christ; but this is not sufficient to base a typology. This is accommodation, about which something will be said later on.

IV. DIVISIONS OF TYPOLOGY

The Thomistic classification distinguishes three species of typology : *allegory*, *anagogy* and *tropology*. This distinction is not arbitrary (whatever one thinks of the vocabulary used to express it); but it is necessary to give it accurate content. Typology is related to eschatology. The matters of the Old Testament are figurative because they are modeled in advance on an archetype whose revelation occurred at the end of time (cf. Epistle to the Hebrews). Now this archetype, which is the Mystery of Christ, is realized in two parts : an inauguration in the framework of human history and a heavenly consummation. The first part includes the life of Christ on earth and the life of His Church here below; the second is already attained by Jesus Himself, but the members of His Body only enter it when they die, and still they will fully participate in it through resurrection only at the end of this world, when the Church as such will experience its final transformation. However, the eternal truths are already really present in time : present in the person of Jesus, whose historical acts have a meaning for the Church and for eternity; present in the life of the Church whose sacraments are signs of these very realities.

From this fact, the matters of the Old Testament are figures at the same time of the Mystery of Christ and of the Church in their earthly existence (this is what St. Thomas calls *allegory*) and the heavenly consummation of the Mystery (what he calls *anagogy*). Finally it is legitimate to look for the repercussions for the personal life of each Christian, of this economy of Salvation to which he participates right here on earth while waiting to accede to " the world to come. " They can be compared to the repercussions caused in the life of the Jewish people by the first sketch of this economy, defined by the Old Covenant : at its level they prefigured the Christian life (this is *tropology* : cf. 1 Cor 10, 6-10; Heb 3, 7 ff.). On their own part, the matters of the New Testament can also include in certain cases a symbolic meaning. The acts of Christ in history (miracles) are signs of His spiritual action (sacraments). The sacramental structures of the Church have an anagogical meaning. From the history of Christ and of His Church there can be drawn tropological applications. In short, a whole series of correspondences links between them the aspects and stages of the Plan of Salvation which is deployed here below to be consummated beyond history.

V. WHAT IS THE SPIRITUAL MEANING?

In the Thomistic classification, the *spiritual* meaning is the equivalent of typology. The idea is clear, but the terminology is somewhat ambiguous. Some would deem it preferable to understand by this what St. Paul called the *spirit* of Scripture, once it is understood that in the New Testament all is spirit. In this sense, there would be an equivalence between *sensus plenior* and *spiritual* meaning. But the encyclical *Divino afflante* (§ 29-30), starting from the Thomistic classification, gives a much more accurate notion of the *spiritual* meaning. It understands by this the applications of biblical texts which, while implying a certain transposition, find their justification in typology (whose name however is not used). We have seen that such applications can be called the *sensus plenior*, which they allow to become enlightened wherever the expression of the biblical doctrine is related to certain historical conditioning surpassed today. Such a notion of the spiritual meaning is perfectly acceptable; it offers as an advantage to show in it a real meaning of the biblical *texts*, to circumscribe it with sufficient accuracy, and to clearly distinguish it from accommodations not supported by any typology. If the encyclical distinguishes it from the literal meaning, it is because it sees the latter especially in terms of the sacred authors. [9] It seems to us that the *sensus plenior* establishes a bridge between the two.

VI.   CONSEQUENT MEANING AND ACCOMMODATION

For a long time, theologians have established a consequent meaning. A. Vaccari defines it as a theological conclusion from two premises, one of which is revealed, the other rational. J. Coppens holds that it is a true scriptural meaning, because it is virtually included in the literal meaning, of which it is the logical conclusion. R. de Vaux shows more restraint in this matter : he sees in it only " deductions, explanations and utilizations starting from Scripture. " [10] The more attention will be paid to the unity of revelation and to the profound relations between Scripture and the Church (which does not have as its mission to add to Scripture but rather to discern and to indicate its slightest resonances) the more will we be led to include the consequent meaning into the *sensus plenior*, which itself is only the flourishing of the literal meaning. This, however, does not justify all the consequences which private scholars would believe they could relate to Scripture with the help of logical reasoning. Between their teaching and Scripture there is not that vital link which exists between Scripture and the Church, the latter receiving from the Holy Spirit a special light to authentically interpret the sacred books.

It is, however, quite another matter concerning the *accommodated* sense. It is sometimes called the *allegorical* meaning, but this is an ambiguous term which can be used to describe quite different realities. When allegory, that is, the transfer of a text from one object to another, has for its basis a solid typology, its result is to hearken back to the spiritual meaning, such as it is defined by the encyclical (e.g. Ex 15).

---

[9] *EB*, p. 550, *in fine* and 552.
[10] *RB* (1950), p. 281.

When it does not have this basis (as in the red cloth of Rahab), its result is not a scriptural meaning. It is possible that a distant analogy authorizes certain accommodations of this type. In particular, it would be difficult to blame the liturgy for looking into Scripture to find a language or a play on symbols, capable of expressing Christian prayer : nourished in the Bible, its words come spontaneously to its lips in all circumstances. This was also an essential characteristic of the style of St. Bernard; this is also the way in which Origen's spirituality is expressed in his homilies on the Pentateuch or on the Canticle, with the help of a constant allegorization which greatly surpasses the bounds of typology. But his techniques corresponded to the habits of the day and to the forms of his culture. It is known also that it was not without danger.

This is why the encyclical *Divino afflante* is very careful in this respect : " It may indeed be useful, especially in preaching, to illustrate and present matters of faith and morals by a broader use of the Sacred Text in the figurative sense, provided this be done with moderation and restraint; it should, however, never be forgotten that this use of the Scriptures is, as it were, extrinsic to it and accidental.... The faithful, in particular those who are well-informed in the sciences sacred and profane, wish to know what God has told us in the Sacred Letters rather than what an ingenious orator or writer may suggest by a clever use of the words of Scripture. The word of God... does not need artificial devices and human adaptation to move and impress souls " (§ 27).

VII. A CLASSIFICATION OF SCRIPTURAL MEANINGS

Let us summarize in outline form the previous considerations. We can distinguish : 1) the symbolic meaning of matters of the Bible; 2) the meanings of Scripture.

1) *The symbolic meaning of matters of the Bible* (events, characters and institutions). This is a datum of *biblical theology*, included in the meaning of the texts but revealed therein in a more or less profound manner.

A. In the Old Testament it can deal with :

   a) the mystery of Christ and of His Church in its earthly realization (*allegory* in the Thomistic sense).

   b) the mystery of Christ in its final and heavenly consummation *(anagogy)*.

   c) the life of the Christian in the mystery of Christ *(tropology)*.

B. In the life of Christ, it can deal with :

a) the mystery of the Church in its earthly realization (miracles of Christ, signs of the sacraments in St. John).

b) the heavenly consummation of the mystery (transfiguration and parousia).

c) the life of the Christian in the mystery (the attitudes of the Jews around Christ, a type of the attitudes taken by all men at the announcing of the Gospel).

C. In the earthly realization of the mystery of the Church, it can deal with :

a) the heavenly consummation of the mystery (eucharistic presence and parousia).

b) the personal life of the Christian (situation of the Church in the world and situation of each faithful).

2) *The meanings of Scripture.*   Here we get into exegesis properly speaking.

A. The *literal* meaning.   It can be taken on two levels :

a) on the level of criticism : *obvious* (or *immediate*) meaning or whatever it is called.
   —It can adopt all the nuances of speech.
   —It always aims at a theological reality, perceived according to the horizon of each human author.

b) on the level of Christian theology : *sensus plenior* (which includes the *consequent* meaning; " *spirit* " in St. Paul's terms).
   —It aims at the same theological reality as the literal, immediate meaning, but perceived on the level of total revelation.

   1. It is sometimes used without allegorization, by the simple deepening of the meaning of words and propositions, without transferring them from one object to another.

   2. At other times, it is used with allegorization founded on typology (the *spiritual* meaning according to the encyclical *Divino afflante*).

B. Accommodation.   It is accomplished :

a) either by artifice of speech.

b) or by allegorization without typological foundation.

§ 4. The Catholic Meaning

What is the Catholic meaning of Scripture? Nothing more than the meaning of the objective revelation of the living God as assigned by Scripture; God makes Himself known through His action in the world, both creative and redemptive, and in the intimate mystery of His being. The Word of God fixed in Scripture is, in its totality, the *sign* of what God is and does, He who gives life and gives it in abundance (Jn 10, 10). It is therefore not merely a simple human testimony on this action of God; nor even, as could be inferred from certain Protestant works, a force hidden under the letter, which would act on the souls of readers by its existential dynamism. It is as a written testimony that it depends on divine inspiration, signifying to the intelligence of men the gift God made of Himself, of His light and of His life.

God has so loved the world that He gave His only Son (Jn 3, 16); but this Son will remain with His Church until the consummation of the world (Mt 28, 20), assuring it the gift of the Spirit who teaches the truth (Jn 16, 13). Since God has thus totally given Himself through Christ and the Spirit, He is sure that the authentic meaning of Scripture has never been able to be lost in the course of centuries in the Church. This is why, far from constituting a hindrance for critical research, the tradition of the Fathers and the doctrine of the Church are a providential help in refinding what the inspired authors thought and taught. [11] To loyally apply these scientific philological and historical methods which form the basis for modern criticism, a profound knowledge of this doctrine and this tradition is more than ever necessary.

---

[11] R. SCHNAKENBURG, " Der Weg katolischen Exegese*, " *BZ*, 2 (1958), pp. 171ff.

APPENDIX

The Dogmatic Constitution on Divine Revelation *(Dei Verbum)*
by W. HARRINGTON, O.P. and L. WALSH, O.P.

§ 1. Text

PAUL, BISHOP

SERVANT OF THE SERVANTS OF GOD
TOGETHER WITH THE FATHERS OF THE SACRED COUNCIL
FOR EVERLASTING MEMORY

DOGMATIC CONSTITUTION ON DIVINE REVELATION

PROLOGUE *

1. Hearing the Word of God with reverence, and proclaiming it with faith, the sacred Synod assents to the words of St. John, who says : " We proclaim to you the eternal life which was with the Father and was made manifest to us—that which we have seen and heard we proclaim also to you, so that you may have fellowship with us; and our fellowship is with the Father and with His Son Jesus Christ " (1 Jn 1, 2-3). Following, then, in the steps of the Councils of Trent and Vatican I, this Synod wishes to set forth the true doctrine on divine Revelation and its transmission. For, it wants the whole world to hear the summons to salvation, so that through hearing it may believe, through belief it may hope, through hope it may come to love. [1]

I. DIVINE REVELATION ITSELF *

2. It pleased God, in His goodness and wisdom, to reveal Himself and to make known the mystery of His will (cf. Eph 1, 9). His will was that men should have access to the Father, through Christ, the Word made flesh, in the Holy Spirit, and thus become sharers in the divine nature (cf. Eph 2, 18; 2 Pt 1, 4). By this revelation, then, the invisible God (cf. Col 1, 15; 1 Tm 1, 17), from the fulness of His love, addresses

---

* Translated from the Latin by Liam Walsh.
[1] St. Augustine, *De Catechizandis rudibus*, c. 4, 8 : *PL*, 40, 316.

men as friends (cf. Ex 33, 11; Jn 15, 14-15), and moves among them (cf. Bar 3, 38), in order to invite and receive them into His own company. This economy of revelation is realized by deeds and words, which are intrinsically bound up with each other. As a result, the works performed by God in the history of salvation show forth and bear out the doctrine and realities signified by the words; the words, for their part, proclaim the works, and bring to light the mystery they contain. The most intimate truth which this revelation gives us about God and the salvation of man shines forth in Christ, who is Himself both the mediator and the sum total of revelation. ²

3. God, who creates and conserves all things by His Word (cf. Jn 1, 3), provides men with constant evidence of Himself in created realities (cf. Rom 1, 19-20). And furthermore, wishing to open up the way to heavenly salvation, He manifested Himself to our first parents from the very beginning. After the fall, He buoyed them up with the hope of salvation, by promising redemption (cf. Gn 3, 15); and He has never ceased to take care of the human race. For He wishes to give eternal life to all those who seek salvation by patience in well-doing (cf. Rom 2, 6-7). In His own time God called Abraham, and made him into a great nation (cf. Gn 12, 2). After the era of the patriarchs, He taught this nation, by Moses and the prophets, to recognize Him as the only living and true God, as a provident Father and just judge. He taught them, too, to look for the promised Saviour. And so, throughout the ages, He prepared the way for the Gospel.

4. After God had spoken many times and in various ways through the prophets, " in these last days He has spoken to us by a Son " (Heb 1, 1-2), He sent His Son, the eternal Word who enlightens all men, to dwell among men and to tell them about the inner life of God. Hence, Jesus Christ, sent as " a man among men, " ³ " speaks the words of God " (Jn 3, 34), and accomplishes the saving work which the Father gave him to do (cf. Jn 5, 36; 17, 4). As a result, He Himself—to see whom is to see the Father (cf. Jn 14, 9)—completed and perfected revelation and confirmed it with divine guarantees. He did this by the total fact of His presence and self-manifestation—by words and works, signs and miracles, but above all by His death and glorious resurrection from the dead, and finally by sending the Spirit of truth. He revealed that God was with us, to deliver us from the darkness of sin and death, and to raise us up to eternal life.

---

² Cf. Mt 11, 27; Jn 1, 14 and 17; 14, 6; 17, 1-3; 2 Cor 3, 16 and 4, 6; Eph 1, 3-14.
³ *Epistle to Diognetus*, c. 7, 4 : Funk, *Patres Apostolici*, I, p. 403.

The Christian economy, therefore, since it is the new and definitive covenant, will never pass away; and no new public revelation is to be expected before the glorious manifestation of our Lord, Jesus Christ (cf. 1 Tm 6, 14 and Ti 2, 13).

5. " The obedience of faith " (Rom 16, 26; cf. Rom 1, 5; 2 Cor 10, 5-6) must be given to God as He reveals Himself. By faith man freely commits his entire self to God, making " the full submission of his intellect and will to God who reveals, " [4] and willingly assenting to the revelation given by Him. Before this faith can be exercised, man must have the grace of God to move and assist him; he must have the interior helps of the Holy Spirit, who moves the heart and converts it to God, who opens the eyes of the mind and " makes it easy for all to accept and believe the truth. " [5] The same Holy Spirit constantly perfects faith by His gifts, so that revelation may be more and more profoundly understood.

6. By divine revelation God wished to manifest and communicate both Himself and the eternal decrees of His will concerning the salvation of mankind. He wished, in other words, " to share with us divine benefits which entirely surpass the powers of the human mind to understand. " [6]

The sacred Synod professes that " God, the first principle and last end of all things, can be known with certainty from the created world, by the natural light of human reason " (cf. Rom 1, 20). It teaches that it is to His revelation that we must attribute the fact " that those things, which in themselves are not beyond the grasp of human reason, can, in the present condition of the human race, be known by all men with ease, with firm certainty, and without the contamination of error. " [7]

II. THE TRANSMISSION OF DIVINE REVELATION *

7. God graciously arranged that the things He had once revealed for the salvation of all peoples should remain in their entirety, throughout the ages, and be transmitted to all generations. Therefore, Christ the Lord, in whom the entire revelation of the most high God is summed up (cf. 2 Cor 1, 20; 3, 16—4, 6) commanded the apostles to preach the

---

[4] First Vatican Council, *Dogm. Const. on Cath. Faith*, c. 3 (on Faith) : *Denz.* 1789 (3008).

[5] Second Council of Orange, can. 7 : *Denz.* 180 (377). First Vatican Council, *loc. cit.* : *Denz.* 1791 (3010).

[6] First Vatican Council, *Dogm. Const. on Cath. Faith*, c. 2 (on Revelation) : *Denz.* 1786 (3005).

[7] *Ibid.* : *Denz.* 1785 and 1786 (3004 and 3005).

* Translated from the Latin by Liam Walsh.

Gospel, which had been promised beforehand by the prophets, and which He fulfilled in His own person and promulgated with His own lips. In preaching the Gospel they were to communicate the gifts of God to all men. This Gospel was to be the source of all saving truth and moral discipline. [8] This was faithfully done : it was done by the apostles who handed on, by the spoken word of their preaching, by the example they gave, by the institutions they established, what they themselves had received—whether from the lips of Christ, from His way of life and His works, or whether they had learned it at the prompting of the Holy Spirit; it was done by those apostles and other men associated with the apostles who, under the inspiration of the same Holy Spirit, committed the message of salvation to writing. [9]

In order that the full and living Gospel might always be preserved in the Church the apostles left bishops as their successors. They gave them " their own position of teaching authority. " [10] This sacred Tradition, then, and the sacred Scripture of both Testaments, are like a mirror, in which the Church, during her pilgrim journey here on earth, contemplates God, from whom she receives everything, until such time as she is brought to see Him face to face as He really is (cf. 1 Jn 3, 2).

8. Thus, the apostolic preaching, which is expressed in a special way in the inspired books, was to be preserved in a continuous line of succession until the end of time. Hence the apostles, in handing on what they themselves had received, warn the faithful to maintain the traditions which they had learned either by word of mouth or by letter (cf. 2 Thes 2, 15); and they warn them to fight hard for the faith that had been handed on to them once and for all (cf. Jude 3). [11] What was handed on by the apostles comprises everything that serves to make the People of God live their lives in holiness and increase their faith. In this way the Church, in her doctrine, life and worship, perpetuates and transmits to every generation all that she herself is, all that she believes.

The Tradition that comes from the apostles makes progress in the Church, with the help of the Holy Spirit. [12] There is a growth in insight

---

[8] Cf. Mt 28, 19-20 and Mk 16, 15. Council of Trent, sess. IV, Decree *On the Canonical Scriptures* : *Denz.* 783 (1501).

[9] Cf. Council of Trent, *loc. cit.*; First Vatican Council, sess. III, *Dogm. Const. on the Catholic Faith*, c. 2 (on Revelation) : *Denz.* 1787 (3006).

[10] St. Irenaeus, *Adv. Haer.*, III, 3, 1 : *PG*, 7, 848; Harvey, 2, p. 9.

[11] Cf. Council of Nicea II : *Denz.* 303 (602). Council of Constantinople IV, sess. X, can. 1 : *Denz.* 336 (650-652).

[12] Cf. First Vatican Council, *Dogm. Const. on the Catholic Faith*, c. 4 (on Faith and Reason) : *Denz.* 1800 (3020).

into the realities and words that are being passed on. This comes about in various ways. It comes through the contemplation and study of believers who ponder these things in their hearts (cf. Lk 2, 19 and 51). It comes from the intimate sense of spiritual realities which they experience. And it comes from the preaching of those who have received, along with their right of succession in the episcopate, the sure charism of truth. Thus, as the centuries go by, the Church is always advancing towards the plenitude of divine truth, until eventually the words of God are fulfilled in her.

The sayings of the Holy Fathers are a witness to the life-giving presence of this Tradition, showing how its riches are poured out in the practice and life of the Church, in her belief and her prayer. By means of the same Tradition the full canon of the sacred books is known to the Church, and the holy Scriptures themselves are more thoroughly understood and constantly actualized in the Church. Thus God, who spoke in the past, continues to converse with the spouse of His beloved Son. And the Holy Spirit, through whom the living voice of the Gospel rings out in the Church—and through her in the world—leads believers to the full truth, and makes the Word of Christ dwell in them in all its richness (cf. Col 3, 16).

9. Sacred Tradition and sacred Scripture, then, are bound closely together, and communicate one with the other. For both of them, flowing out from the same divine well-spring, come together in some fashion to form one thing, and move towards the same goal. Sacred Scripture is the speech of God as it is put down in writing under the breath of the Holy Spirit. And Tradition transmits in its entirety the Word of God which has been entrusted to the apostles by Christ the Lord and the Holy Spirit. It transmits it to the successors of the apostles so that, enlightened by the Spirit of truth, they may faithfully preserve, expound and spread it abroad by their preaching. Thus it comes about that the Church does not draw her certainty about all revealed truths from the holy Scriptures alone. Hence, both Scripture and Tradition must be accepted and honored with equal feelings of devotion and reverence. [13]

10. Sacred Tradition and sacred Scripture make up a single sacred deposit of the Word of God, which is entrusted to the Church. By adhering to it the entire holy people, united to its pastors, remains always faithful to the teaching of the apostles, to the brotherhood, to the breaking

---

[13] Cf. Council of Trent, sess. IV, *loc. cit.* : *Denz.* 783 (1501).

of bread and the prayers (cf. Acts 2, 42, Greek). So, in maintaining, practicing and professing the faith that has been handed on there should be a remarkable harmony between the bishops and the faithful. [14]

But the task of giving an authentic interpretation of the Word of God, whether in its written form or in the form of Tradition, [15] has been entrusted to the living teaching office of the Church alone. [16] Its authority in this matter is exercised in the name of Jesus Christ. Yet this Magisterium is not superior to the Word of God, but is its servant. It teaches only what has been handed on to it. At the divine command and with the help of the Holy Spirit, it listens to this devotedly, guards it with dedication and expounds it faithfully. All that it proposes for belief as being divinely revealed is drawn from this single deposit of faith.

It is clear, therefore, that, in the supremely wise arrangement of God, sacred Tradition, sacred Scripture and the Magisterium of the Church are so connected and associated that one of them cannot stand without the others. Working together, each in its own way under the action of the one Holy Spirit, they all contribute effectively to the salvation of souls.

III. SACRED SCRIPTURE : ITS DIVINE INSPIRATION AND ITS INTERPRETATION *

11. The divinely revealed realities, which are contained and presented in the text of sacred Scripture, have been written down under the inspiration of the Holy Spirit. For holy mother Church relying on the faith of the apostolic age, accepts as sacred and canonical the books of the Old and the New Testaments, whole and entire, with all their parts, on the grounds that, written under the inspiration of the Holy Spirit (cf. Jn 20, 31; 2 Tm 3, 16; 2 Pt 1, 19-21; 3, 15-16), they have God as their author, and have been handed on as such to the Church herself. [17]

---

[14] Cf. Pius XII, Apost. Const. *Munificentissimus Deus*, 1 Nov. 1950 : *AAS*, 42 (1950) 756, taken along with the words of St. Cyprian, *Epist.* 66, 8 : Hartel, III, B, p. 733 : " The Church is the people united to its Priest, the flock adhering to its shepherd. "

[15] Cf. First Vatican Council, *Dogm. Const. on the Catholic Faith*, c. 3 (on Faith) : *Denz.* 1792 (3011).

[16] Cf. Pius XII, Encycl. *Humani Generis*, 12 Aug. 1950 : *AAS*, 42 (1950), 568-569 : *Denz.* 2314 (3886).

* Translated from the Latin by Wilfrid Harrington.

[17] Cf. Vatican Council I, *Const. dogm. de fide catholica*, c. 2 (de revelatione) : *Denz.* 1787 (3006). *Bibl. Commission, Decr.* 18 June 1915 : *Denz.* 2180 (3629); *EB*, 420; Holy Office, *Letter*, 22 Dec. 1923 : *EB*, 499.

To compose the sacred books, God chose certain men who, all the while
He employed them in this task, made full use of their powers and
faculties; [18] so that, though He acted in them and by them, [19] it was as
true authors that they consigned to writing whatever He wanted written,
and no more. [20]

Since, therefore, all that the inspired authors, or sacred writers, affirm
should be regarded as affirmed by the Holy Spirit, we must consequently
acknowledge that the books of Scripture, firmly, faithfully and without
error, teach that truth which God, for the sake of our salvation, wished
to see confided to the sacred Scriptures. [21] Thus " all Scripture is inspired
by God, and profitable for teaching, for reproof, for correction and for
training in righteousness, so that the man of God may be complete,
equipped for every good work " (2 Tm 3, 16-17, Greek text).

12.   Seeing that, in sacred Scripture, God speaks through men in
human fashion, [22] it follows that the interpreter of sacred Scripture, if he is
to ascertain what God has wished to communicate to us, should carefully
search out the meaning which the sacred writers really had in mind, that
meaning which God had thought well to manifest through the medium
of their words.

In determining the intention of the sacred writers, attention must
be paid, *inter alia*, to " literary forms, " for the fact is that truth is
differently presented and expressed in the various types of historical
writing, in prophetical and poetical texts and in other forms of literary
expression.   Hence the exegete must for that meaning which the sacred
writer, in a determined situation and given the circumstances of his
time and culture, intended to express and did in fact express, through
the medium of a contemporary literary form. [23]   Rightly to understand
what the sacred author wanted to affirm in his work, due attention must

---

[18] Cf. Pius XII, Encycl. *Divino Afflante Spiritu*, 30 Sept. 1943 : *AAS*, 35 (1943),
p. 314; *EB*, 556.
    [19] *In* and *by* man : cf. Heb 1, 1; 4, 7 (*in*); 2 Sm 23, 2; Mt 1, 22 and *passim*
(by); Vatican Council I, *Schema de doctr. cath.*, note 9 : Coll. Lac., VII, 522.
    [20] Leo XIII, Encycl. *Providentissimus Deus*, 18 Nov. 1893 : *Denz.* 1952 (3293);
EB, 125.
    [21] Cf. St. Augustine, *Gen. ad Litt.*, 2, 9, 20 : *PL*, 34, 270-271; *Epist.* 82, 3 :
PL, 33, 277; *CSEL*, 34, 2, p. 354.—St. Thomas, *De Ver.* q. 12, a. 2, C.—Council
of Trent, sess. IV, *de canonicis Scripturis* : *Denz.* 783 (1501).—Leo XIII, Encycl.
Providentissimus : *EB*, 121, 124, 126-127.—Pius XII, Encycl. *Divino Afflante* :
EB, 539.
    [22] St. Augustine, *De Civ. Dei*, XVII, 6, 2 : *PL*, 41, 537 : *CSEL*, XL, 2, 228.
    [23] St. Augustine, *De Doctr. Christ.*, III, 18, 26; *PL*, 34, 75-76.

be paid both to the customary and characteristic patterns of perception, speech and narrative which prevailed at the age of the sacred writer, and to the conventions which the people of his time followed in their dealings with one another. [24]

But since sacred Scripture must be read and interpreted with its divine authorship in mind, [25] no less attention must be devoted to the content and unity of the whole of Scripture, taking into account the Tradition of the entire Church and the analogy of faith, if we are to derive their true meaning from the sacred texts. It is the task of exegetes to work, according to these rules, towards a better understanding and explanation of the meaning of sacred Scripture in order that their research may help the Church to form a firmer judgment. For, of course, all that has been said about the manner of interpreting Scripture is ultimately subject to the judgment of the Church which exercises the divinely conferred commission and ministry of watching over and interpreting the Word of God. [26]

13. Hence, in sacred Scripture, without prejudice to God's truth and holiness, the marvellous " condescension " of eternal wisdom is plain to be seen " that we may come to know the ineffable lovingkindness of God and see for ourselves how far He has gone in adapting His language with thoughtful concern for our nature. " [27] Indeed the words of God, expressed in the words of men, are in every way like human language, just as the Word of the eternal Father, when He took on Himself the flesh of human weakness, became like men.

IV. THE OLD TESTAMENT *

14. God, with loving concern contemplating, and making preparation for, the salvation of the whole human race, in a singular undertaking chose for Himself a people to whom He would entrust His promises. By His covenant with Abraham (cf. Gn 15, 18) and, through Moses, with the race of Israel (cf. Ex, 24, 8), He did acquire a people for Himself,

---

[24] Cf. Benedict XV, Encycl. *Spiritus Paraclitus*, 15 Sept. 1920 : *EB*, 469.—St. Jerome, *In Gal.* 5, 19-21 : *PL*, 26, 417 A.

[25] Pius XII, *loc. cit.* : *Denz.* 2294 (3829-2830); *EB*, 557-562.

[26] Cf. Vatican Council I, *Const. dogm. de fide catholica*, c. 2 (de revelatione) : *Denz.* 1788 (3007).

[27] St. John Chrysostom, *In Gn* 3, 8 (hom. 17, 1) : *PG*, 53, 134. *Attemperatio* corresponds to the Greek *synkatábasis*.

* Translated from the Latin by Wilfrid Harrington.

and to them He revealed Himself in words and deeds as the one, true, living God, so that Israel might experience the ways of God with men. Moreover, by listening to the voice of God speaking to them through the prophets, they had daily to understand His ways more fully and more clearly, and make them more widely known among the nations (cf. Ps 21, 28-29; 95, 1-3; Is 2, 1-4; Jer 3, 17). Now the economy of salvation, foretold, recounted and explained by the sacred authors, appears as the true Word of God in the books of the Old Testament; that is why these books, divinely inspired, preserve a lasting value : " For whatever was written in former days was written for our instruction, that by stead-fastness and the encouragement of the Scriptures we might have hope " (Rom 15, 4).

15. The economy of the Old Testament was deliberately so orientated that it should prepare for and declare in prophecy the coming of Christ, redeemer of all men, and of the Messianic kingdom (cf. Lk 24, 44; Jn 5, 39; 1 Pt 1, 10), and should indicate it by means of different types (cf. 1 Cor 10, 11). For in the context of the human situation before the era of salvation established by Christ, the books of the Old Testament provide an understanding of God and man and make clear to all men how a just and merciful God deals with mankind. These books, even though they contain matters imperfect and provisional, nevertheless show us authentic divine teaching. [28] Christians should accept with veneration these writings which give expression to a lively sense of God, which are a storehouse of sublime teaching on God and of sound wisdom on human life, as well as a wonderful treasury of prayers; in them, too, the mystery of our salvation is present in a hidden way.

16. God, the inspirer and author of the books of both Testaments, in His wisdom has so brought it about that the New should be hidden in the Old and that the Old should be made manifest in the New. [29] For, although Christ founded the New Covenant in His blood (cf. Lk 22, 20; 1 Cor 11, 25), still the books of the Old Testament, all of them caught up into the Gospel message, [30] attain and show forth their full meaning in the New Testament (cf. Mt 5, 17; Lk 24, 27; Rom 16, 25-26; 2 Cor 3, 14-16) and, in their turn, shed light on it and explain it.

---

[28] Pius XI, Encycl. *Mit brennender Sorge*, 14 March 1937 : *AAS*, 29 (1937), p. 151.

[29] St. Augustine, *Quaest. in Hept.* 2, 73 : *PL*, 34, 623.

[30] St. Irenaeus, *Adv. Haer*, III, 21, 3 : *PG*, 7, 950 (= 25, 1 : Harvey 2, p. 115). St. Cyril of Jerusalem, *Catech.* 4, 35 : *PG*, 33, 497. Theodore of Mopsuestia, *In Soph.* 1, 4-6 : *PG*, 66, 452D-453A.

V. THE NEW TESTAMENT *

17. The Word of God, which is the power of God for salvation to everyone who has faith (cf. Rom 1, 16), is set forth and displays its power in a most wonderful way in the writings of the New Testament. For when the time had fully come (cf. Gal 4, 4), the Word became flesh and dwelt among us full of grace and truth (cf. Jn 1, 14). Christ established on earth the kingdom of God, revealed His Father and Himself by deeds and words; and by His death, resurrection and glorious ascension, as well as by sending the Holy Spirit, completed His work. Lifted up from the earth He draws all men to Himself (cf. Jn 10, 32, Greek text), for He alone has the words of eternal life (cf. Jn 6, 68). This mystery was not made known to other generations as it has now been revealed to His holy apostles and prophets by the Holy Spirit (cf. Eph 3, 4-6, Greek text), that they might preach the Gospel, stir up faith in Jesus, Christ and Lord, and bring the Church together. The writings of the New Testament stand as a perpetual and divine witness to these realities.

18. It is common knowledge that among all the inspired writings, even among those of the New Testament, the Gospels have a special place, and rightly so, because they are our principal source for the life and teaching of the Incarnate Word, our Saviour.

The Church has always and everywhere maintained, and continues to maintain, the apostolic origin of the four Gospels. The apostles preached, as Christ had charged them to do, and then, under the inspiration of the Holy Spirit, they and others of the apostolic age handed on to us in writing the same message they had preached, the foundation of our faith : the fourfold Gospel, according to Matthew, Mark, Luke and John. [31]

19. Holy mother Church has firmly and with absolute constancy maintained and continues to maintain, that the four Gospels just named, whose historicity she unhesitatingly affirms, faithfully hand on what Jesus, the Son of God, while He lived among men, really did and taught for their eternal salvation, until the day when He was taken up (cf. Acts 1, 1-2). For, after the ascension of the Lord, the apostles handed on to their hearers what He had said and done, but with that fuller understanding which they, instructed by the glorious events of Christ and

---

* Translated from the Latin by Wilfrid Harrington.
[31] Cf. St. Irenaeus, *Adv. Haer.* III, 11, 8 : *PG*, 7, 885 ; ed. Sagnard, p. 194.

enlightened by the Spirit of truth, [32] now enjoyed. [33] The sacred authors, in writing the four Gospels, selected certain of the many elements which had been handed on, either orally or already in written form, others they synthesized or explained with an eye to the situation of the churches, the while sustaining the form of preaching, but always in such a fashion that they have told us the honest truth about Jesus. [34] Whether they relied on their own memory and recollections or on the testimony of those who " from the beginning were eyewitnesses and ministers of the Word, " their purpose in writing was that we might know the " truth " concerning the things of which we have been informed (cf. Lk 1, 2-4).

20. Besides the four Gospels, the New Testament also contains the Epistles of St. Paul and other apostolic writings composed under the inspiration of the Holy Spirit. In accordance with the wise design of God these writings firmly establish those matters which concern Christ the Lord, formulate more and more precisely his authentic teaching, preach the saving power of Christ's divine work and foretell its glorious consummation.

For the Lord Jesus was with His apostles as He had promised (cf. Mt 28, 20) and He had sent to them the Spirit, the Counselor, who would guide them into all the truth (cf. Jn 16, 13).

IV. SACRED SCRIPTURE IN THE LIFE OF THE CHURCH *

21. The Church has always venerated the divine Scriptures as she venerated the Body of the Lord, in so far as she never ceases, particularly in the sacred liturgy, to partake of the bread of life and to offer it to the faithful from the one table of the Word of God and the Body of Christ. She has always regarded, and continues to regard the Scriptures, taken together with sacred Tradition, as the supreme rule of her faith. For, since they are inspired by God and committed to writing once and for all time, they present God's own Word in an unalterable form, and they make the voice of the Holy Spirit sound again and again in the words of the prophets and apostles. It follows that all the preaching of the Church, as indeed the entire Christian religion, should be nourished and ruled by sacred Scripture. In the sacred books the Father who is in

---

[32] Cf. Jn 14, 26; 16, 13.

[33] Jn 2, 22; 12-16; cf. 14, 26; 16, 12-13; 7, 39.

[34] Cf. the Instruction *Sacra Mater Ecclesia* of the Pontifical Biblical Commission : *AAS*, 56 (1964), p. 715.

* Translated from the Latin by Liam Walsh.

heaven comes lovingly to meet His children, and talks with them. And such is the force and power of the Word of God that it can serve the Church as her support and vigor, and the children of the Church as strength for their faith, food for the soul, and a pure and lasting fount of spiritual life. Scripture verifies in the most perfect way the words : " The Word of God is living and active " (Heb 4, 12), and " is able to build you up and to give you the inheritance among all those who are sanctified " (Acts 20, 32; cf. 1 Thes 2, 13).

22. Access to sacred Scripture ought to be open wide to the Christian faithful. For this reason the Church, from the very beginning, made her own the ancient translation of the Old Testament called the Septuagint; she honors also the other Eastern translations, and the Latin translations, especially that which is called the Vulgate. But since the Word of God must be readily available at all times, the Church, with motherly concern, sees to it that suitable and correct translations are made into various languages, especially from the original texts of the sacred books. If it should happen that, when the opportunity presents itself and the authorities of the Church agree, these translations are made in a joint effort with the separated brethren, they can be used by all Christians.

23. The spouse of the incarnate Word, which is the Church, is taught by the Holy Spirit. She strives to reach day by day a more profound understanding of the sacred Scriptures, in order to provide her children with food from the divine words. For this reason also she duly fosters the study of the Fathers, both Eastern and Western, and of the sacred liturgies. Catholic exegetes and other workers in the field of sacred theology should zealously combine their efforts. Under the watchful eye of the sacred Magisterium, and using appropriate techniques they should together set about examining and explaining the sacred texts in such a way that as many as possible of those who are ministers of the divine Word may be able to distribute fruitfully the nourishment of the Scriptures to the People of God. This nourishment enlightens the mind, strengthens the will and fires the hearts of men with the love of God. [35] The sacred Synod encourages those sons of the Church who are engaged in biblical studies constantly to renew their efforts, in order to carry on the work they have so happily begun, with complete dedication and in accordance with the mind of the Church. [36]

---

[35] Cf. Pius XII, Encycl. *Divino Afflante* : *EB*, 551, 553, 567.—Biblical Commission, Instruction on the Teaching of S. Scripture in Seminaries of Clerics and Religious, 13 May 1950 : *AAS*, 42 (1950), pp. 495-505.

[36] Cf. Pius XII, *ibid.* : *EB*, 569.

24. Sacred theology relies on the written Word of God, taken together with sacred Tradition, as on a permanent foundation. By this Word it is most firmly strengthened and constantly rejuvenated, as it searches out, under the light of faith, the full truth stored up in the mystery of Christ. Therefore, the " study of the sacred page " should be the very soul of sacred theology. [37] The ministry of the Word, too—pastoral preaching, catechetics and all forms of Christian instruction, among which the liturgical homily should hold pride of place—is healthily nourished and thrives in holiness through the Word of Scripture.

25. Therefore, all clerics, particularly priests of Christ and others who, as deacons or catechists, are officially engaged in the ministry of the Word, should immerse themselves in the Scriptures by constant sacred reading and diligent study. For it must not happen that anyone becomes " an empty preacher of the Word of God to others, not being a hearer of the Word in his own hear, " [38] when he ought to be sharing the boundless riches of the divine Word with the faithful committed to his care, especially in the sacred liturgy. Likewise, the sacred Synod forcefully and specifically exhorts all the Christian faithful, especially those who live the religious life, to learn " the surpassing knowledge of Jesus Christ " (Phil 3, 8) by frequent reading of the divine Scriptures. " Ignorance of the Scriptures is ignorance of Christ. " [39] Therefore, let them go gladly to the sacred text itself, whether in the sacred liturgy, which is full of the divine words, or in devout reading, or in such suitable exercises and various other helps which, with the approval and guidance of the pastors of the Church, are happily spreading everywhere in our day. Let them remember, however, that prayer should accompany the reading of sacred Scripture, so that a dialogue takes place between God and man. For, " we speak to Him when we pray; we listen to Him when we read the divine oracle. " [40]

It is for the bishops, " with whom the apostolic doctrine resides " [41] suitably to instruct the faithful entrusted to them in the correct use of the divine books, especially of the New Testament, and in particular of the Gospels. They do this by giving them translations of the sacred texts which are equipped with necessary and really adequate explanations.

---

[37] Cf. Leo XIII, Encycl. *Providentissimus* : *EB*, 114; Benedict XV, Encycl. *Spiritus Paraclitus* : *EB*, 483.

[38] St. Augustine, *Serm.* 179 : *PL*, 38, 966.

[39] St. Jerome, *Comm. in Isaias*, Prol. : *PL*, 24, 17.—Cf. Benedict XV, Encycl. *Spiritus Paraclitus* : *EB*, 475-480; Pius XII, Encycl. *Divino Afflante* : *EB*, 544.

[40] St. Ambrose, *De Officiis ministrorum* I, 20, 88 : *PL*, 16, 50.

[41] St. Irenaeus, *Adv. Haer.* IV, 32, 1 : *PG*, 7, 1071; (= 49, 2) Harvey, 2, p. 255.

Thus the children of the Church can familiarize themselves safely and profitably with the sacred Scriptures, and become steeped in their spirit.

Moreover, editions of sacred Scripture, provided with suitable notes, should be prepared for the use of even non-Christians, and adapted to their circumstances. These should be prudently circulated, either by pastors of souls, or by Christians of any rank.

26. So may it come about that, by the reading and study of the sacred books " the Word of God may speed on and triumph " (2 Thes 3, 1) and the treasure of Revelation entrusted to the Church may more and more fill the hearts of men. Just as from constant attendance at the eucharistic mystery the life of the Church draws increase, so a new impulse of spiritual life may be expected from increased veneration of the Word of God, which " stands forever " (Is 40, 8; cf. 1 Pt 1, 23-25).

Everything which is stated in this Constitution satisfied the Fathers of the sacred Council. And we, by the apostolic power given to us from Christ, along with the venerable Fathers of the Council, approve it in the Holy Spirit, decree it and enact it, and we order what has been enacted in synod to be promulgated for the glory of God.

Given at Rome, in St. Peter's, November 18, 1965.

I, PAUL, Bishop of the Catholic Church.

Then follow the signatures of the other Fathers.

§ 2. Commentary

PROLOGUE

The opening words *Verbum Dei* (The Word of God) state the special emphasis to be developed in the Constitution. In modern biblical, liturgical and catechetical thinking the Word of God is understood to be more than a message or doctrine about God. It is God revealing Himself, as much by what He does as by what He says. It is history as much as metaphysics. Whether this history is written down under inspiration, or recorded in any other way, it is still the Word of God. And as such it is more than a record of history; it continues to make history through the community of believers. This manifestation of the Word of God through the Scriptures underlies all the Second Vatican Council's teaching on revelation.

The Prologue also states the attitude of the supreme Magisterium of the Church regarding the Word of God. The Fathers of the Council "hear... proclaim... assent." But they have to explain the Word as well, as previous councils did. The original contribution that Vatican II makes to the doctrine on divine revelation is suggested by the words "and its transmission." The Council takes a dynamic, descriptive, historical approach to the question of how revelation, once made, reaches us. In that way the Council escapes the dilemma created by the theological debate about whether Scripture and Tradition are two distinct and independent sources of revelation.

The final sentence of the Prologue states the pastoral purpose, not alone of this Constitution, but of all the documents of the Council.

I. Divine revelation itself

This chapter grew directly out of the conciliar debates. There was a need to get to the bottom of the dispute on the sources of revelation, which had led to a stalemate in the preparation of the Constitution, by having a fresh look at the nature of revelation itself. Revelation is presented as a personal disclosure of Himself by God, made through the happenings of sacred history, for the sake of man's salvation. It is this personalist and historical emphasis, rather than any new doctrine, that distinguishes this chapter from what Vatican I had to say on the nature of revelation.

Article 2 states the fact and meaning of revelation, explains how it is made, and points to its fulfilment in Christ. The revelation which God has given us is a gratuitous call to personal intimacy with the Blessed Trinity. It is described, in one of the most fundamental and characteristic sentences of the Constitution, as an "economy," that is, a divine providence directing men, as they make their history, towards salvation. The direction is given by an interplay of word and action in such a way that neither words alone nor actions alone provide revelation. The doctrine taught by God and the mysterious divine realities He communicates to men are made concrete, visible and credible by the things He does in the course of sacred history. The events, on the other hand, become significant, become revelation, when their meaning is expressed in words. This may be described as a " sacramental " view of revelation. And the supreme sacrament of God is Christ, who both reveals and realizes salvation.

God prepared the way for Christ by revealing Himself progressively to men from the beginning of time (art. 3). Apart from the evidence of Himself which He gives at all times in the created universe, He has given a historical manifestation of Himself from the beginning of our race, in view of our call to salvation. After the Fall, this revelation became a promise and a beginning of redemption. There followed, in time, the call of Abraham, the sending of Moses and the Prophets, by which God taught a historical people to know and serve Him, and to prepare for the coming of the Saviour.

Christ is the fulness of revelation. With the help of the opening words of Hebrews, article 4 situates Christ at the climax of prophetic history. Then it exploits the personal name of the Son of God to show that He is the fulness of revelation. The Son is the Word of God in person. God has nothing more to say or do for men when He has sent His Word in the flesh. Next there is a description of the complete range of Christ's revealing action. He revealed, not only by the words He spoke, but by everything He was and did. He used every feature of His human presence on earth to communicate with men. He Himself, and everything about Him is revelation, the fulness of divine self-disclosure, in human terms. Thus His signs and miracles are revelations. They are also, of course, motives of credibility but, since they enter into the sacramentality of revelation, they have more than an apologetical value.

After Christ nothing remains to be added to revelation. The only divine manifestation the world may look forward to is the Second Coming of Christ at the end of time.

In the following article faith is defined as the response which men are required to make to God when He reveals Himself. As revelation has been described in personalist terms already, so now faith is said to be a free, personal commitment of oneself to God. The more traditional description of faith in terms of intellect and will was added in order to make it clear that commitment includes an assent of the mind to the truth of what has been revealed. It is beyond the power of man to make this response to the Word of God. The fact that he does so is, in all stages of development, the gift of God's grace.

Article 6 deals with revelation as it is seen in creation. Underlying this statement is a distinction between what can be known about God by man's unaided reason, and what surpasses the range of human intelligence. Revelation bears on both areas of truth, but for different reasons. It throws light on fundamental truths about God and human destiny which, ideally speaking, could be discovered by unaided human reason. It does this because the majority of men would have neither the leisure nor the culture to discover these metaphysical truths for themselves. But the primary object of revelation is the intrinsically supernatural mystery. Revelation is absolutely necessary here, because no created mind has the right or the power to penetrate these secrets.

The Council considered this theoretical distinction necessary to maintain the supernatural quality of the Christian revelation. But it does not mean that there is, in fact, any such thing as a purely natural religion. All men, whether they know it or not, are caught up in the economy of salvation. At the same time, the Christian revelation is relevant to the natural problems and destiny of men.

II. THE TRANSMISSION OF DIVINE REVELATION

In Chapter Two the Constitution deals with the functions of Tradition, Scripture and Magisterium in the handling of revelation. Here the Council faced a crucial problem. Before Vatican II conventional Catholic theology held that Tradition and Scripture were two distinct and independent sources of revelation and that there were truths in Tradition which were not to be found in Scripture. Furthermore, it was claimed that this position had been defined by the Council of Trent, and was therefore unquestionable Catholic faith. The Fathers of Vatican II were sharply divided on this whole issue and at one point their discussions seemed to have reached an impasse.

They found a way around the impasse eventually by by-passing the problem of the Two-Source Theory and taking a fresh starting point. In Chapter One they described revelation as a saving historical event, which reaches its climax in Christ. The next question to be asked, then, was how this saving event is communicated to men down through the ages. This is the question answered in Chapter Two. Its title indicates that it will deal with Scripture, Tradition and also Magisterium as agents of live, historical transmission, rather than as static sources of ideas. This approach allows the Council to show, in a very positive fashion, the correlation and inter-dependence of Tradition, Scripture and Magisterium. It avoids, from a position of strength, rather than out of weakness, the controversy about the Two Sources.

By not pronouncing for or against the Two-Source Theory the Council implicitly admits that this is simply a theory and not the defined faith of the Church. If the matter had been defined by Trent, Vatican II could not have remained neutral about it. Theologians remain free to discuss it. But perhaps Vatican II should have taught them that such a discussion is not very profitable, and that they would throw far more light on the faith of the Church by following the Council's approach to Scripture, Tradition and Magisterium.

God wished His saving revelation, which is summed up in the historical person of Christ, to reach men of all ages and places (art. 7). This was the task which Christ Himself entrusted to His apostles. They communicated the gift of God by preaching the Gospel. The term " Gospel " does not mean only the four written Gospels, but the total message of Christ, the " good news " of salvation. This Gospel is described, in the language of the Council of Trent, as " the source of all saving truth and moral discipline. " This is the only time the word " source " appears in the present chapter of the Constitution. It is used in the singular, and occurs before any distinction has been made between Scripture and Tradition.

In transmitting the Gospel to others the Apostles used various media of communication. The list of media they used is given in two stages : mentioned first is transmission by word of mouth, by force of example and by the way they organized the community of believers; and then separate mention is given to transmission by writing. Among the ways of transmitting a message to posterity writing certainly stands apart. And when the Holy Spirit has inspired the writing, so that the product not alone records but is the word of God, this means of transmission becomes all the more sacred and remarkable. In making this distinction between unwritten and written means of communication the Council is saying nothing about *how much* of the Gospel can be found in each. It puts the basis of its distinction between Scripture and Tradition in terms of form.

When the authoritative, creative, live witness of the apostles ended, the Gospel was already constituted for all time. It had been left to the Church in a communicable form, written and unwritten. To ensure that the message of salvation would continue to be communicated in its unchanging fulness, the apostles appointed bishops to succeed them in the Church. They gave them a magisterial power, which would ensure the faithful transmission of the Gospel. And so, in its pilgrim path through history the Church remains in contact with God, who continues to reveal Himself in Scripture and Tradition, as it is maintained by the successors of the apostles.

Then in article 8 the Council describes the main features of the transmission of revelation within the Church. This process of passing on the Gospel is Tradition, in the active sense of the term. (Tradition in the passive sense is the content that is passed on.) However, the chapter is not discussing Tradition as something apart from Scripture. The very first sentence points out that the apostolic preaching which is being transmitted is " expressed in a special way in the inspired books. "

There is no suggestion that Tradition contains more of revelation than the Scriptures, but simply that it is a distinctive means of transmission, which is being specially examined in this chapter. This point is reinforced by the references to texts from Thessalonians and Jude. The next sentence describes briefly the content of the transmission—Tradition in the passive sense. What is handed on is not merely a doctrine but an entire way of life. What Tradition perpetuates is the Church herself.

If Tradition is to preserve the living Church that was constituted by the apostles, it must constantly develop in its expression. By contemplative reflection on the words and institutions in which the Gospel has been handed on to them, each new generation of Christians is led by the Holy Spirit, under the infallible direction of their bishops, to re-express the Gospel in new, contemporary terms. Under the influence of the Word of God the Church comes to know the fulness of divine truth, is transformed by it and thus makes progress in " all that she herself is, all that she believes. "

Next the text mentions some of the main manifestations of living Tradition within the Church. Tradition and its development are witnessed by the Church Fathers in their writings and embodied in the religious practices they created, especially in the forms they gave the liturgy. Tradition also expresses itself in relation to the Scriptures. It establishes the canon of the inspired books. And it also gives the Church a living, authentic understanding of the inspired word. When Tradition is brought to bear on the written word it makes it alive and relevant. Thus through the joint action of Scripture and Tradition, animated by the Holy Spirit, God speaks here and now to the Church and leads her to truth.

After the descriptive statements of article 8 the Constitution now passes to a more theoretical statement on the close connection and intercommunication between Tradition and Scripture. It traces their unity to a common origin in God and a common purpose, which is salvation. They both contain and faithfully transmit the Word of God, although each in its own way. Hence the Church hears the Word from both Scripture and Tradition. If God has chosen to speak to her in this complex way the Church can never confine its listening to Scripture alone. The Council did not intend the words " not... from the holy Scriptures alone " to be understood in the sense that Scripture contained only part of revelation and had therefore to be complemented by Tradition. The Council was not speaking of the quantity of truth that Scripture may or may not contain, but of its quality as a means of transmitting revelation. Its quality is such that, in the dispensation of God, it cannot stand as an all-sufficient, independent means of transmitting the living Word of God. God never meant it to; the Church cannot presume to make it so. She cannot claim certainty in her teaching if she has only read the Scriptures. She must simultaneously, and with equal reverence, listen to the witness of Tradition.

Having correlated Scripture and Tradition, the Constitution goes on to relate both of them to the Church. In the first paragraph of article 10 it takes the Church in the full sense of the term, as a community of faithful and clergy. The entire People of God, each in his own rank, has a community responsibility for maintaining, professing and expressing the Word of God that has been deposited with the Church in the double currency of Scripture and Tradition. Given the concern of Vatican II to revaluate the place of the laity in the Church, it is understandable that their function in the transmission of the Word of God (what is called the *sensus fidelium*) should be clearly recognized here. Of course the faithful do not exercise this function apart from, but in community with their bishops.

The second paragraph of article 10 explains the position of the Magisterium within the Church. When it comes to decisive judgments about the meaning of the Word of God that is being handed down those who exercise the Magisterium have sole authority. Their authority is part of the divine structure of the Church. But since it is a Christian authority it will take the form of a service to the Word rather than domination. The Magisterium can only teach what it has received from Scripture and Tradition. It must first listen to the Word and then preserve and expound what it hears, and nothing more. It can only bind the faithful to believe on divine faith what it has itself heard from the Word.

The final paragraph states that Scripture, Tradition and Magisterium are so interdependent that, in the present arrangement of things, they cannot be disassociated. The reason given is profoundly theological : they have been designed to work together by the wisdom of God; they are unified in their action by the Holy Spirit; and they are directed to a common purpose, which is the salvation of souls.

III.   SACRED SCRIPTURE : ITS DIVINE INSPIRATION AND ITS INTERPRETATION

Chapter three of the first draft of the Constitution was devoted to the inspiration, inerrancy and literary composition of sacred Scripture. It introduced the Scriptures as " another source " of revelation, apart

from the " living voice " of the prophets and apostles, a source in which
the Word of God was " more accurately conserved. " It gave a technical
definition of inspiration, seen only as a personal charism given to
individual sacred writers, and insisted on absolute inerrancy. Its approval
of certain methods of modern exegesis seemed to arise more from the
fact that they provided a way out of difficulties against the inerrancy of
Scripture than from their positive value in helping the understanding
of the Word of God. In the second draft, the chapters on Scripture were
shortened by the removal of much that was condemnatory and negative
in the previous draft—and afterwards remained substantially unchanged.

In the matter of the inspiration and interpretation of the Bible, the
Constitution (art. 11), on the whole, is content to draw attention to the
most important aspects of the relevant teaching set forth in earlier
documents. However, the work of recent theologians has not gone
unnoticed and its influence may be discerned more than once. And while
there is not a notable advance in doctrine, the entirely positive approach,
and the care taken not to harden any particular theological position,
encourage a free and fruitful study of the nature of the Bible and of
scriptural inspiration.

The text speaks of the " divinely inspired realities " which Scripture
contains. This is significant because it is clear that if we are to be true
to the data of the Bible we may not understand " revelation " only in
the sense of declarations of abstract, purely speculative truth; we must
take it to include the whole field of God's self-manifestation—it must
embrace action as well as words. And the mediator or interpreter of
this revelation is, first and foremost, a man who has had an encounter
with God, one who has come to recognize the Saviour and Creator, one
who has experienced the creative and salvific love of God.

The text also stresses the freedom enjoyed by the men chosen by
God as His instruments in writing these books. The sacred writer indeed
is, most often, not aware that he is being used by God and moved by him
and so he sets about his work in a perfectly natural way. While the
whole Bible is to be attributed to God (who moved the writers) and to
the human authors (as moved by God), yet the special characteristics
of the writers were not submerged but are clearly visible in each book.
Many of the writers chosen by God were highly talented and they exploited
their literary gifts to the full in presenting the divine message. Others
who served God's purpose were not so gifted and some parts of Scripture
are, from a literary standpoint, quite pedestrian! But, gifted or not,
it is through these human instruments that God speaks to us from one
nd of the Bible to the other.

One may, with reason, complain of a negative and defensive approach to Scripture due to a preoccupation with the " inerrancy " of the Bible; it would surely have been more rewarding to speak of the " truth " of Scripture. Now we find that *Verbum Dei* does just that. It does even more than that; it asserts that the divine authorship of Scripture guarantees that the truths taught and the realities described in the Bible provide the sure way of salvation without error. For, indeed, the message of the Bible is essentially religious and is altogether concerned with what is pertinent to salvation. Our text clearly echoes the views of some who, in recent years, have studied in a more rewarding manner the problem of biblical inerrancy and the nature of revelation.

When we turn to article 12 we find that a parallel drawn in the following paragraph is a helpful pointer to an understanding of the fact of God speaking to men, a parallel between the two incarnations of the Word of God : in human language and in human flesh. Just as Christ is not only *like* men but is truly man and truly God, so Scripture is not only *like* human language : it is human language in the fullest sense, while all the while it remains the Word of God. We may not ignore the human conditioning of God's Word under peril of misinterpreting God's message. This means, for one thing, that we should learn to identify and rightly evaluate the literary forms employed by the biblical writers, that is, the types or species distinguished from one another by distinct form or structure in which the Bible, like all literature, is cast. Yet, it is to be borne in mind that literary forms cannot be determined *a priori*; often we have to be well aware of the literary conventions of an age in which a writing took shape before we can establish its form. It also means that, as a more fundamental step, we should strive to understand and appreciate the Semitic origin and the Semitic cast and background of the Bible—for all this is an essential part of it. We may not measure the Scriptures by our Western standards, but we should, rather, seek to understand the mentality of its writers.

While the Catholic exegete must apply the methods of rational interpretation, he must take the Bible too for what it really is, the Word of God. It is necessary that the scholar should be guided not only by his scholarship, nor only by his belief in the divine origin of Scripture, but also by the teaching authority of a divinely founded Church. What is important is that the exegete should be guided, not hampered, by the Magisterium. The Constitution not only implies this, but goes much further when it declares that the labors of exegetes will help to speed the surer judgment of the Church in scriptural matters. For, it is not too much to expect that those who study the inspired Scriptures with dedication, humility and in the service of the Church, may confidently hope to receive a measure of enlightenment from the Spirit and so may contribute, in some degree, to the Church's ever-growing awareness and understanding of the Word of God.

IV. THE OLD TESTAMENT

The shortest chapter of the Constitution is that on the Old Testament. Article 14 presents the Old Testament as salvation history : Israel is a chosen and covenanted people with a special role in God's economy; the writings reflect different facets of God's revelation. Salvation history is the history of what God has done in the lives of men in order to fulfil in them His saving purpose; the history of the experiences and embodiments of salvation as they are ordered to the Christ-event—the midpoint of salvation history. The Old Testament, as a record of the time of preparation for the culminating event of Christ, is a distinct period of salvation history : the " time of Israel. " Israel's experience of election meant her awareness of a singular situation which was not due to a blind concurrence of circumstances nor to a series of human successes, but to a deliberate and sovereign initiative of Yahweh. She was chosen by God to be the recipient of His revelation and to give expression to that revelation in her life : for He had willed to join Himself to men by establishing a cultic community dedicated to His service, ruled by His law, the bearer of His promises. The covenant of Sinai made clear this aspect of the plan of salvation. However, the election of Israel is election for service. Hence the prophets, Second-Isaias in particular, cast Israel in the role of witness and mediator : it stands as a witness to monotheism and as a mediator because it is to be the means of the conversion of all nations. And though God's economy of salvation has moved on to its definitive phase, yet, in prose and poetry, throughout the great literary heritage that is Israel's gift to mankind, He still speaks to men of all centuries. Isaias declared : " The Word of our God will stand forever " (Is 40, 8). And Paul assures us that in the pages of the Old Testament we Christians will find instruction and encouragement and hope (Rom 15, 4).

The meaning of the Old Testament for Christians (art. 15) brings up the question of Messianism and the relevance of the Old Testament in the Messianic age. Thus, the first point made in this article is the Messianic sense and orientation of the Old Testament. A study of Messianism does confirm the implication of the article's short statement —the realization that Messianism is an essential feature of the Old Testament and pervades the whole of it. As the centuries and events brought clarification and refinement, that constant hope was accompanied by a steady growth in Israel's appreciation of her election and of her true destiny. The figure of the Messias emerged and began to assume an increasingly important place in the nation's hope.

Its opening sentence has established the Messianic hope of Israel; the rest of the article brings out the abiding worth of the Scriptures of Israel. In the era of preparation, before the coming of Christ, the inspired writers of the Old Testament brought to men a unique understanding of God and man. That is why the Constitution, while admitting the imperfect and the provisional, inseparable from a preparatory dispensation, yet stresses that the books contain " authentic divine teaching. " Of course that pedagogy can turn to advantage even the imperfect factors; but we should never underestimate the theological wealth of the Old Testament.

The unity of God's plan is illustrated by the harmony of the two Testaments and by the manner in which one sheds light on the other (art. 16). Though from the human standpoint the Bible is not a book, not even *the* book, but the literature of a people, yet, in a true sense, it may be considered as one great work—the work of a divine author. And because He is the author of the whole, God has not only imposed a real unity on the Bible but has maintained enriching relationships between the succeeding stages of His unfolding Word. If, when seen in the light of fulfilment, the Old Testament takes on a new dimension, it is very true that the New cannot be really understood unless one has a solid understanding of the Old. The reason for this is not only the preparatory role of the Old; it is also because the New Testament writers are, all of them, versed in the Old Testament. They have been nourished on it; they constantly refer to it, directly or indirectly; they are in sympathy with its spirit. Above all, they reverence it as the Word of God, a source of life and light. At the same time, they are followers of Him who is life and light, and in His light they read a deeper meaning into that former word.

V. THE NEW TESTAMENT

Though this chapter is concerned with the New Testament as a whole, in practice it concentrates on the Gospels : two of its four articles treat of the Gospels exclusively. It is evident that these two articles (18 and 19) presuppose, and lean heavily on, the instruction from the Pontifical Biblical Commission, *Sacra Mater Ecclesia.*

In his Epistle to the Romans, St. Paul shows that the Gospel (the revelation of God's salvation) is the very power of God, working for the salvation of all who receive it by faith. Though the Old Testament is indeed the Word of God, now there is a decisive step, a new dimension in God's self-manifestation (Heb 1, 1f.). In the fulness of time, the Son of God came forth, born of a woman (Gal 4, 4). The creative and revealing Word which issued from the mouth of God, the wisdom of God which the sages had personified, now, in very truth, appeared on earth (Jn 1, 14). The expectation of the Old Testament is fulfilled : the Messias has appeared, the kingdom has come. In the teaching of Jesus the kingdom is, first and foremost, an intervention of God in history, made manifest in the coming of the Son of God; for in Jesus, in His words and works, the kingdom was present. Christ, the Word of God, one with God, made known to men the Father and Himself. He did so not only by His teaching but also, and above all, by His deeds. Clearly, revelation is understood in its biblical sense; there is no place for the inadequate theoretical notion which had prevailed for so long. The supreme revelation of Jesus is the great saving event—His " elevation " in the Johannine sense : His death, resurrection and exaltation, all together. That is why, lifted up from the earth, He draws all men to Himself (Jn 10, 32). But His teaching, too, is efficacious, life-giving : He speaks the words of eternal life (Jn 6, 69). At best vaguely known to the prophets of the Old Testament, the mystery is revealed to Christian apostles and prophets and is now made known through the Church. The mystery is this : the Gentiles are fellow-heirs with Judeo-Christians, members of the same body (cf. Eph 3, 4-6); or, more simply, it is the salvation of all men by faith in Jesus Christ. Taking their stand on this basic truth, the Christian preachers must proclaim the Word of God and bring men to acknowledge the one mediator, the only saviour, to lead them to " believe that Jesus is the Christ, the Son of God " (Jn 20, 31). By preaching Jesus and the salvation to be found in Him, they bring the Church together.

The Church has always affirmed the historical value of the testimony of the evangelists. Yet, we need to be aware that the apostles, companions of Jesus during His public ministry, witnesses of His death and of His glorification had, after these events, understood more clearly what their Master had said and done. Now that He had entered into His glory and that they had been enlightened by the Spirit of God, they at last grasped who and what He was; it is their witness and their preaching which come to us through the written Gospels.

The evangelists drew from the rich treasury of oral teaching and written records whatever suited the purpose of each, in the process often synthesizing the facts or the discourses. The teaching may, in its expression, have been adapted to meet the conditions of the churches for which the writings were designed. But always this work was done in sincerity and truth. We find therefore in our Gospel texts the narrative of events as those who from the first were eyewitnesses and servants of the Word have transmitted them to us; or as those who, following them, have undertaken, after serious research, to draw up an account of the life of Christ. Thus we, in our turn, can recognize the objective value of our faith (cf. Lk 1, 1-3). We have three stages to consider : Jesus Christ, the apostolic Church, and the evangelists. It is only when we have taken all three into account that we can really hope to understand the Gospels. Full recognition has been given to the positive values of Form Criticism and Redaction Criticism.

It is not a little surprising, after a relatively long treatment of the Gospels, that the other New Testament writings get no more than a brief mention. It is simply stated that their role is to formulate more precisely the teaching of Christ and to make it better known. They describe the beginnings of the Church in which His saving power reaches to men, and they proclaim the ultimate victory of Christ. All of them bear witness to the activity of the Spirit whom the Lord had sent upon His apostles.

VI. SACRED SCRIPTURE IN THE LIFE OF THE CHURCH

It is in this final chapter that the pastoral aim of the Constitution is most apparent. In the light of its doctrine set out in the previous chapters the Council takes up the particular pastoral problem of the place of Scripture in the life of the Church. The concentration on Scripture here does not imply any disregard for Tradition. It simply means that the Bible, because it is the Word of God written in a book, presents pastoral problems that need specific treatment. Tradition does not lend itself to such precise pastoral directives. However, the text reminds us at a number of points that the Bible cannot be isolated from Tradition in the life of the Church.

The chapter begins by affirming the Church's reverence, at all times in her history, for the Scriptures. Her veneration for the Bible is likened to and linked with her veneration for the eucharistic body of our Lord. Christ Himself is the bread of life. He feeds those who believe in Him in two distinct, but closely related ways : by the bread of His Word and the bread which is His Flesh. There is one food, which is Himself, one life to be nourished, which is that of faith. But there are two forms in which the nourishment is given and received (cf. Jn 6). The unity of the two forms appears very clearly in the Liturgy of the Church.

The Church has also venerated Scripture by seeing in it, taken along with Tradition, the supreme rule of her faith. Inspired Scripture is the Word of God in unchangeable form. It is this permanence of the written word which makes Scripture such an appropriate rule of faith. Tradition, because it is so fluid and flexible, lacks the definition and practical availablility required in a rule, especially if it is to serve over a long period of history. However, it is not the dead " letter " of the Bible that moves the Church to faith, but the living voice of the Holy Spirit. Scripture has the power to convey this voice when it is read in the Church, within the apostolic Tradition and under the direction of the Magisterium. It is the living Word of the Scripture which is the supreme rule of faith. The remainder of the paragraph emphasizes that the Word of Scripture has a power to make the heavenly Father present, to sustain the Church and the spiritual life of its members. It is living, efficacious and sanctifying.

The end of the post-Tridentine reserve on the reading of Scripture by the faithful is marked in article 22. From now on they are to have free access to the Bible. The translations made by the Church into the vernaculars of the past (incidentally, the reference to the Vulgate here is more significant for what it does not say than for what it does) had this in view; new translations are to be made, preferably from the original texts, into the vernaculars of the present. The needs of ecumenism are to be taken into account, so that, where possible, the Christian Churches of a single language area should have a common Bible.

Although article 23 is primarily addressed to biblical scholars and theologians its ultimate interest is the breaking of the bread of the Word to the faithful. It calls for cooperation between biblical scholars and other theologians. And if, formerly, the efforts of Catholic scholars have often met with suspicion and criticism within the Church, the Council now gives them its official blessing.

Scripture is described as the *foundation* of theology (art. 24). This is a non-technical term, which theologians will want to define more precisely. The metaphor of the foundation will suggest to them that it is from Scripture that theology gets its contact with solid reality. Theology is the science of the reality that is God as He has been manifested in Christ. It is only in the mystery of Christ, which is the center and the climax of the Scriptures, that the full truth about God can be studied. Unless theology constantly returns to the Scriptures it will lose touch with its proper reality and remain lost in unfounded speculation. And what is true of theology is also true of any other human handling of the Word of God—preaching, catechetics and homiletics.

Article 25 sketches, in a way that needs little commentary, the obligations of every class of Christian people to know the Scriptures. Both prayer and study are required in reading the Scriptures. The article emphasizes the obligation of bishops and priests to promote and facilitate this prayerful study of the Scriptures.

The chapter ends, as it began, with the analogy between Scripture and Eucharist. Just as the liturgical movement has given the Church new life and nourishment, so the Council hopes for a similar renewal and growth from the Church's increased participation at the table of God's Word.

INDEX

Accommodated (sense), 208 ff.
Acts (of the Apostles), 145 ff.
Adiabene, 95
Ahiram (inscription of), 72
Akiba, 77
Aleppo (MS. of), 83
Alexandrinus (codex), 89, 103
Allegory, 182, 187, 206 ff.
Alphabet, 72
Antioch (MS.), 118
Apocalypse (canonicity), 41 f.
Apocalyptic genre, 152 f.
Apocrypha, 40 f., 44 f., 93
Apostles, — and canon, 51
Aramaic (targums), 92 ff.
Aramean (script), 73
Archeology (biblical), 157 ff.; (oriental), 160 ff.
Archetype, 112, 118
Aristeas (pseudo), 9, 28, 86
Armenian (versions), 97, 107
Artaxerxes I, 48
Assistance (of Holy Spirit), 14 f.
Assyrian (script), 73. *See :* Assyro-Babylonia
Assyro-Babylonia (literature), 110, 132
Athanasius, St. (and canon), 31 f., 38 f.
Augustine, St., 31, 39, 56, 60, 97
Authenticity, 33; — of Vulgate, 56 f.
Author, divine —, 11, 13 f., 18, 21, 60, 217; human —, 12 ff., 18, 23 f., 33, 52 f., 218, 232 f.; plurality of —, 24 f.

Baai, 133
Bar Kochba, (Bar Kosiba), 77, 79
Baruch (book of), 20, 38
Ben Asher, 82 ff.
Ben Chayyim (Jacob), 83 f.
Ben Nephthali, 80, 82
Bengal, 116
Benoit, P., 19, 23, 28, 50 f.
Ben Sira (Sirach), 75 f.
Benizen, A., 136 f.
Beth-Sham, Stelae of —, 158, 160
Beth-Shemesh, 158
Bezae (D) (codex), 103, 117
Biblical commission, 201 f.

Biblical criticism, 17, 23; limitations of —, 171 ff., 231
Bronze Age, 158 ff. *See :* Archeology.
Bultmann, R., 147 ff.

Caesarea, 92, 111
Calvin (on Canon), 45
Cano, M., 14
Canon and canonicity, 30 ff., 43 ff., 75, 216
Carthage, council of, 43
Cassiodorus, 99
Cassite Period, 110
Ceramics, 158 f.
Chanaan, 72
Chester Beatty (papyrus), 89, 102, 119
Chrisman, 15
Christian reading of Bible, 172 f.
Church, and Scripture, 14 ff., 28; — and Canon, 47 ff., 51
Claromontanus (codex), 103
Citations, explicit and implicit, 57
Codex, 82, 101, 104
Comma Johanneum, 201
Community and inspiration, 26 f.
Complutensian polyglot, 90
Concordances, 88
Confession, of La Rochelle, 46; — of Westminster, 46
Contamination, 112
Context, 57
Coptic (versions), 94, 105 f.
Copyists (faults of), 109 f.
Coste, J., 28 f.
Cullmann, O., 46

Decalogue, 85
Deissman, A., 101, 151
Deuterocanonical (books), 36 f., 44, 52
Devreesse, 91
Dhorme, E.P., 121, 132
Diacritical (points), 80
Dialogue, 137
Diaspora, 86
Diatessaron, 102, 105
Dictation (of epistles), 109
Dictation (inspiration) 10 f., 14
Diez-Macho, A., 81, 94

Index 243

Literal meaning, 203 f., 210. *See :*
Meaning of Bible.
Literary criticism, 68 f., 126-153
Literary genres, 62 ff., 69, 202; — in
the Old Testament, 135 ff.; — in
the New Testament, 145 ff.
Loisy, A., 56
Lucian of Antioch, 110
Lusseau, H., 17, 22
Luther, 44
Lyonnet, S., 107

Magisterium and Bible, 217, 228, 231
Manuscripts (families of), 111
Marchalianus (codex), 89 f.
Marcion, 40, 49 f., 117, 186
Massoretes, 80 f., 110
Mati'ilu, 133
Matres lectionis (mothers of the
reading), 74, 80, 85
Meanning of Bible, 165 ff., 188 ff.
Meaningfulness of Scriptures, 175 ff.
Meanings of Scripture, 202 ff., 218 f.
Megiddo, 158
Melito of Sardis, 38
Mercati, G., 92
Mesha, 73
Michigan (papyrus), 102
Midrash(im), 77 f., 174, 178
Montanus, 40
Moral (in Bible), 58 f., 215
Moses, 7 f., 24 f., 36, 73
Muratori (Canon of), 37
Music (Israelite), 145
Mythology, 132 f.

Narratives, 138 f.
Nash (papyrus), 76
Nehemias, 9, 92
Neirab (Stelae of), 161
Nequdôt, 80
Neutral (text), 117
Newman, H., 52
Nun, 80

Onkelos (Targum), 93 f.
Onomastica, 133
Origen, 187 f., 209; — and Canon,
38, 41; — and texts, 91 f., 111, 118
Original texts, 67 f.
Orlinsky, H., 87
Ostraca (potsherds), 72, 115
Oxyprhynchus (papyrus), 79, 89

Palimpsest, 72, 89, 92, 103
Pamphilus, 111
Papyrus, 74, 88 ff., 100 ff.

Parchment, 102 ff.
Parrot, A., 161
Pastoral epistles, 102
Paul, St., and exegesis, 181 f., — and
inspiration, 9; epistles of —, 101,
151 f.
Pedagogy, 59
Pentateuch, 24, 88; Samaritan —, 85;
texts of —, 74 f., 83
Pesher, 176
Peshitto, 96
Philistine (ceramic), 159
Phylacteries, 78
Pietro della Valle, 85
Peter of Ailly, 14
Poetic forms, 137, 143
Politics, 156
Porphyrianus, 103
Posener, G., 109
Priestly genre, 137 f.
Pritchard, J.B., 72, 161
Prophetic instinct, 20
Prophets, 34, 19 ff., 75 f. *See :*
Literary genres
Proto-Sinaitic, 71
Providentissimus (Encyclical), 16, 18,
21 f., 24, 27, 56, 60 ff.
Proverbs, 132
Psalms, 98 f., 137
Pseudepigraphy, 142, 153
Psychology of sacred authors, 22

Qînâ, 144
Quentin, H., 108, 119
Quinisext (council of), 39, 43
Qumran, 36, 74 f., 77 f., 84 f., 87 f.,
122

Rahlfs, A., 90
Ras-El-Ain, 159
Ras Shamra, 72, 120, 161
Recensions, 110 f.
Redactor, 25
Reuchlin, 82 f.
Revelation, 19, 26, 62, 172, 196, 212 ff.
Rossi, G.B. de, 84
Rufinus, 39
Rylands (papyrus), 88, 101

Sacred Scripture, 3, 7 ff.
Sakkara (papyrus), 73
Samaria, 158
Samaritan (Pentateuch), 84 f., 123
Samaritans, 73 f., 84 f.
Scheide, W.H., (papyrus), 89
Schürer, E., 161
Science and Bible, 59 f.

TABLE OF BIBLICAL REFERENCES

NY. 35bis. — Printed in Belgium by DESCLÉE & CO., ÉDITEURS, S. A. Tournai — 10.960

D — 1969 — 0002 — 9